NAPLES 13

NAPLES
1343

THE UNEXPECTED ORIGINS
OF THE MAFIA

AMEDEO FENIELLO

Translated from the Italian by Antony Shugaar

Other Press
New York

Originally published in Italian as *Napoli 1343: Le origini medievali di un sistema criminale* in 2015
by Mondadori Libri S.p.A., Milan, Italy.

Production editor: Yvonne E. Cárdenas
Text designer: Patrice Sheridan
This book was set in Arno Pro by Alpha Design & Composition of Pittsfield, NH.

1 3 5 7 9 10 8 6 4 2

Library of Congress Cataloging-in-Publication Data
Names: Feniello, Amedeo, author. | Shugaar, Antony, translator.
Title: Naples 1343 : the unexpected origins of the Mafia / Amedeo
Feniello ; translated from the Italian by Antony Shugaar
Other titles: Napoli 1343. English
Description: New York : Other Press, 2024. | Includes bibliographical references.
Identifiers: LCCN 2024002091 (print) | LCCN 2024002092 (ebook) |
ISBN 9781590511039 (hardcover) | ISBN 9781590511046 (ebook)
Subjects: LCSH: Crime—Italy—Naples (Kingdom—History—To 1500. |
Organized crime—Political aspects—Italy—Naples (Kingdom) |
Naples (Kingdom)—History—Joanna I, 1343-1382. | Naples (Kingdom)—
Social conditions. | Naples (Kingdom)—Politics and government.
Classification: LCC DG847.5 .F4613 2024 (print) | LCC DG847.5 (ebook) |
DDC 945/.7—dc23/eng/20240325
LC record available at https://lccn.loc.gov/2024002091
LC ebook record available at https://lccn.loc.gov/2024002092

to Silvana Abete, fierce warrior (1951–2014)

Nearly all our production was meant as polemic and struggle. But to say that our polemic in any way undermined the truth, that we falsified history, would be defamatory.

—BENEDETTO CROCE

CONTENTS

I

THE NIGHT OF 1343

My Night

The night, my personal night, began on January 31, 2005. It was on that night that three young men between the ages of twenty-five and thirty were murdered right in front of the school where I worked as a teacher in Casavatore, in the province of Naples. I can still summon up a number of pictures in my mind that concern both the murders themselves and my own direct involvement. Concerning the event, one need only review the newspaper accounts from that time to get a clear idea of three aspects that caught my attention immediately. First of all, of course, the savagery of the crime. Three young men: not crime bosses, not leaders, not criminals in charge of narcotics marketplaces. No, nothing more than simple foot soldiers. Perhaps not even that. Murdered in an especially brutal fashion: they'd been captured, each handcuffed to the other, led to the gate in front of the school, ordered to kneel, and then shot to death, each with a bullet to the head. Then there was another element: the level of organization. The death squad that carried out the massacre was ready for anything that might crop up. They enjoyed uncontested control of the territory, where they could move freely, practically undisturbed, whatever they might choose to do. Disciplined in their dispensation of violence. And cunning. Tactically clever. Professional killers who operated in disguise, dressed as carabinieri, meaning policemen...and in those uniforms, they'd had absolutely no difficulty detaining the three young men. Stopping them and handcuffing them. And then leading them off to the slaughter.

Last, the third point, perhaps the most horrifying of them all. The murderers had operated with virtually complete impunity. It was as if the dead men had been submerged in a bottomless pool of silence even before they were killed. In a pool of silence: apartment buildings, televisions playing—themselves a form of silence—bowls of pasta set out for the evening meal. Hush, everyone, those corpses seemed to whisper. A single order was issued...and everyone fell silent. Except for a young girl who—a few days later, or perhaps it was a few months—wrote a short essay, a *very* short, unassuming essay, that told the story—with just enough detail—of exactly what she and her family and her neighbors had glimpsed that evening from the windows of their homes overlooking the school. The cars coming to a halt, the men getting out, the handcuffed victims shouting, shoving, realizing it was all over, and begging for mercy. The gunshots. The cars driving away.

That is all that need be said about the three crucial acts that characterized the core elements of this slaughter. To that I must add my own personal involvement. Because two things happened that surface frequently in my mind and that I've told others about perhaps ten thousand times, in all sorts of different settings, places, locales, and contexts. First of all: the principal of the school, the educational director, decided that it would be important to send a clear signal immediately after the murders. She said so clearly, as was her wont: an institutional signal. A signal that would cause a loud noise in the midst of all that nothingness, all that silence. She started talking about town council sessions to be held right there, outside the gates of that school. That school, on the outskirts of the outskirts of Naples. A message about calling radio stations, newspapers, television news crews. Demonstrations that could serve to involve the city's civil society, trade unions, political alliances. And even—why not?—local intellectuals... She never tired of saying that those three deaths were a burden, something significant, even though the gang war now raging between the Di Lauro clan and the breakaway renegades had by then resulted in many, many deaths indeed. But after the initial uproar and the first excellent resolutions, that woman, who was powerfully committed to her civil engagement, began to see herself and her school as increasingly lonely and abandoned. No one seemed to care anymore about those three dead men. Dragged down into the riptide of the vast number of other dead men—dead bodies that meanwhile continued to drop to the pavement.

And so we did what we thought most needed doing: we went together, she and I, right to the office of the regional government's commissioner for social policy, to explain to her that however you looked at it, three dead men are nothing to overlook—they weren't just some overwhelming, inconvenient burden, pressing on the gates of a public school. It had been no easy matter to arrange for that meeting. We had to reach out to friends, rely on a network of personal contacts. That was our only hope for wangling an audience, even at such a tragic juncture, when you would normally have expected all doors to swing open to us, wide open. Already, this was an unsettling indicator... But in the fullness of time, the commissioner welcomed us into her office. For ten minutes. She spent more time glancing at her watch than listening to us, however. We didn't know exactly what to do, and my colleague, the principal, had no choice but to talk excruciatingly quickly. Like a machine-gun burst: five intense minutes in which she spewed out thousands of words. Each slamming into the next. Perfect those words were, though, in their specific content of anguished grief. Still, they counted for little if anything. At last, the meeting came to an end. We were entrusted to a secretary who promised us a future agenda abounding with initiatives, interventions, alliances, decisive actions, and official measures. But it was all smoke and mirrors. A soap bubble. We never heard another word from either the commissioner or her secretary.

The second thing I can't help but remember, even now, is something far more subtle, because it had nothing to do with the central focus of political initiative, but instead my everyday life. The surrounding territory, the school. I can't say now whether this happened a few days after our meeting with the commissioner or practically simultaneously with it, perhaps even the very same day—but I am quite sure, and I insist on pointing this out: there was absolutely no connection between the two things. It happened in the afternoon. At school. During my working day. At around six p.m. There were still people in the classrooms, lessons were still underway. There were other people outside, awaiting their turn. In all, roughly a hundred people, students, teachers, and support staff. Suddenly a carabinieri squad car arrived, pulling right in—through that same cursed gate. An officer got out. I couldn't say whether he was a marshal, a brigadier, or a captain. But I remember exactly what he proceeded to do: he immediately asked who was in charge of that school. I was there and I replied that it was me, that *I* was in charge of that school. So then he looked at me, and just like in a movie, he flashed his badge. And then he started talking. He was really a very nice man. And he carefully weighed his words, words that must have carried a certain burden for him, as well as for us. He told me not to worry. But that this was a critical moment. That what had happened was truly something out of the ordinary, and that extraordinary measures would therefore need to be taken. And therefore, since not even they, the authorities, were capable of maintaining control of the territory on their own—the surrounding buildings, the town as a whole—it was going to be necessary to shutter our school. I remember how, in my astonishment, I took off my glasses, something I do only when there's some great pressure inside my head. I told him that was out of the question. Not even if the mayor of Casavatore ordered it. Or the superintendent of schools. Or the president of the regional government...the carabiniere immediately dismissed my objections. And still just as courteous as ever, he carefully doled out the following words.

Verbatim: "Sir, you really don't get it. You and your school are not a normal thing. You constitute a soft target." So that's what we'd become, a soft target, a game piece in that exceedingly strange round of Monopoly where, on the playing board of gang interests, the presence of a living location, a shred of social existence, could actually do serious harm to their business, even just to their desire for control based on a foundation of silence. And so we shut the school. Not for good. But shut the school we did.

A few months later, I left that school and began another life, another profession. A very different one. A privileged one. A more fortunate path. A career as a historian. Still, that January 31—and the moments that immediately followed it—stayed with me. Powerfully. And they began to ferment and agitate within me. For years already, I had been deeply interested in the medieval history of Naples. And I found myself wondering, urgently: What is the source of all this savagery? Is the energy that people devote with such determination to violence solely the product of choices guided by economic factors? Is it merely the progeny of an urban fabric that crumbles and disintegrates, thereby creating stagnant pools of corruption and crime that gradually grow and expand, creeping like a weed up the trunk of a healthy tree? And is the clear separation between my world—a world of solid institutions, civil coexistence, social cooperation—and *their* world nothing more than a matter of sociology, bound up with immediate factors, *their* here and now, this diseased everyday existence of ours, where the urban outskirts become clogged, creating a social desert? Or is it something else? Something deeper, so deep-rooted that it has carved its way into the viscera of time, allowing the weed of corruption to grow and germinate?

That's what I wondered. Until, in the months that followed that night, I was reminded of an episode I had read about a few years previously. An age-old episode, perhaps *too* old, and which at first glance had nothing in common with that horrifying event of 2005. Something that had happened in 1343. A story of violence, hunger, and criminal clans. An entirely Neapolitan story. I know that trying to put together episodes so distant—in terms of era and setting—can be dangerous. That's not how history is measured out, and I'm fully aware of the fact. All the same, this event from 1343 struck me—and strikes me still—because to me it seems emblematic of something that can help us to progress a certain distance beyond the customary view of the phenomenon of Neapolitan criminality. It's a fragment that I'd like to think may allow us to extend that vision, enlarging it, expanding it, and in a certain sense completing it. With the working hypothesis (*contrived*, one may very justifiably say, but still, I think, absolutely legitimate from the historian's point of view) that there is, perhaps, something linking the two episodes—a nexus—the episode from 1343, which we shall explore, and the episode from 2005 I have just recounted. A bond that links them together. A thread that we may call—to use the terminology proper to those whose profession is historiography—a *struttura di lungo periodo*, a long-period structure, or to hearken back to the *Annales* school, a structure of the *longue durée*. A structure that can be sliced thinner and thinner until it becomes as minuscule and imperceptible as a filament, or else takes on ever-larger dimensions and physiognomies until it resembles a six-lane highway, but which preserves one overriding characteristic: that it is a *constant*. A constant that abides in its substantial features even when its impact wanes, because those features persist. Something that is not limited to the realm of the economy or the sociological or the anthropological, but which is instead deeply rooted in the memory, impressed there faithfully, like a groove in a vinyl record, in the fundamentals of life in a city like Naples. An indestructible seed, made up of time, duration, stability, codes, traditions, prejudices, and norms that has taken root deeply—over the course of the past seven centuries—and with little if any variation.

Chronicles of 1343

But now, let me tell you this story of 1343. Before I begin, though, I must say a few words about the sources that made it possible for me to reconstruct it. Setting out, once again, from another personal point of reference. There are experiences in life that are useful. Extremely useful. To those who practice my profession I would offer the recommendation of participating, at least once, in a criminal trial as a juror. I have enjoyed that privilege. It's an experience unlike any other, because you enter the courtroom completely unaware of what's going on around you. You don't know what's being discussed. You don't know what the trial's going to be about. Whom you're going to be confronted with. You're a blank slate. Then a first witness is seated. And they begin to speak. Followed by another witness. Then another. In a game of hide-and-seek, between prosecution and defense. And little by little, thanks to the questions and the words that flow, a story takes shape, a story that is *not* the event, but an interpretation of it that each witness on their own part offers of the event—with their memories, their caveats, their details and observations, their hesitations and defenses. And from this interpretation, with a maieutic effort (intellectual midwifery), the judge and jurors must work their way back to a truth that is anything but certain. Where the sum of all the interpretations ought to lead to a final judgment of the defendant's guilt—or innocence. In other words, what they call, in legal jargon, "courtroom truth."

Like a body on an autopsy table, but instead of limbs, body parts, and guts, it was a steady flow of snippets, faint voices, episodes, contexts, and settings, from which we were expected to derive, in the end, an impression. An impression that was anything but innocuous, because it was going to determine a human being's fate—their very life. A person who'd be leaving that courtroom bearing an assortment of stigmata. Signs of guilt or innocence. A powerful experience, and it taught me a great deal. Above all, it taught me that courtroom truth is sometimes very different from factual truth: it's no accident that in this situation we found our-selves at a crossroads, because all the evidence pointed toward conviction, but the body of evidence was not sufficient for a find-ing of guilt, even if you stacked up all the evidence, item by item, one piece after another. So the only positive thing I could take home with me was the awareness of a working method based on evidence, to be assembled with scrupulous patience, until you could reach a truth—if not a factual truth—but at least an inter-pretation of truth. In other words, a verdict.[1]

This digression should help to explain what a historian's job consists of. A job I try to do in the simplest possible fashion. There is evidence, which we historians call sources. This is, as we all know well, the salt, the essence, the bread and butter of every work of history. It is the foundation, the structure, the basis upon which the essence of historical narrative rests. In some cases, those sources are numerous and clear. Definitive. Immense and massive. When that happens, historians count themselves lucky and raise prayers of thanksgiving to their chosen deities. There are other oc-casions when the sources are fragments. Bits and pieces of colored glass. Tattered shreds of pages. In Naples, for a medievalist, it's as likely as not that you'll find yourself in the latter situation, rather than the former. After all, countless sources have been lost. I don't want to burden you, dear reader, with the usual jeremiad that we Neapolitan historians constantly repeat. The story of how most of our invaluable documentation was lost with the destruction of the Angevin and Aragon archive in San Paolo Bel Sito during the Sec-ond World War. A problem that certainly weighed like a boulder on anyone who ever expressed interest in southern Italian medi-eval history from the 1950s on. And yet, to a certain extent, and as often as not with great difficulty, it has been possible to make some repairs, dam up the flood of destruction, both by attempting to reconstruct the lost historical treasure, with the painstaking re-creation of the long series of the Registri Angioini e Aragonesi (Angevin and Aragonese Registries), the undertaking of an entire generation, and also by going in search of replacement sources.

Sources that were sought in the vast reservoirs of documentation that Naples still possesses, such as the Archivio di Stato (State Archives), or documents held by other private entities, such as the Società Napoletana di Storia Patria (Neapolitan Association of Fatherland History), or archives like that of the Annunziata. Or by setting out to find other sources that survive outside the city. Buried, for instance, in the papers of some great historian, such as Léon Cadier, who transcribed hundreds and hundreds of Angevin documents before the immense destruction of September 1943. Or else by pursuing a different strategy: facing up to the daunting challenge of perusing the archives of Florence or Genoa or Rome in search of information that can cast a reflected light to illuminate Neapolitan history. Something that I have done myself in my own career as a historian. This gap in the record of documentation, which might very well have fatally sapped the energy of the small band of historians who study medieval Naples, actually only made us a little stronger. After all, it taught us one fundamental truth: it is necessary to make the best of things as they are, as they have to be. We have to do our best to extract the greatest possible quantity of information from what few sources survive. By turning over and over, a thousand times if necessary, a scrap of surviving parchment. A well-worn page. An epigraph long since chipped and worn by the ages, the elements, and the mistreatment afforded by human beings. By turning the available information—the scanty fragments of information—inside out like a sock. With the intention of blending, as one of my teachers used to say, the greatest possible admixture of philology and interpretation. Because sources, whether great or small, should be read and above all interpreted. As Paco Ignacio Taibo once put it, documents are a shared heritage, but interpretation and interpretation alone is the property of whoever tells the tale. That's why there are so many different books about any given single historical topic. Because even on the basis of single, identical handfuls of accounts, a writer's point of view can change, the field of view can be distorted, words can be modified according to the questions that one asks of a witness, as is likewise true for an investigating magistrate. And that witness, to a historian asking questions, would be the source documents.

This introduction is necessary. Especially when it comes to talking about the night of 1343. Because there are a number of things to say. And many different interpretations to offer. Starting with the evidence. Do you think that there is a long series of snippets, accounts, and testimony about that night? You could not be more wrong. There are, as far as I know, three versions. Just three... and they are truly minimal in length and scope, dating from wildly different eras. This is not a story that anyone shouts into your face, as if using an enormous megaphone. It isn't reiterated incessantly in books upon books that carry it echoing down the halls of history due to the importance that this event has taken on for the world at large. No: it's a story you run into only if you happen to stumble across it. Three eyewitness accounts, then. Short ones. In some cases, extremely brief. With perspectives that change every time. As we are told much more or much less. Allowing those of us who are alive in the present day to gain an idea (but no more than an idea) of what happened. All right, then, let's step into this piece of history. Stepping cautiously. A slowly creaking door that leads us into another time and another place. Venturing into this Naples of 1343.

The first documentation is as old as the time in which it occurred. We find it in the *Annales Genuenses*, by Giorgio and Giovanni Stella: a book, we should add, that was begun around 1396 and which recounts the history of Genoa in the years from 1298 until 1405. Pay close attention to this first aspect. The gaze and the horizon: not Neapolitan, but Genoese. So what does one of the two chroniclers, Giorgio, write at the time? Let me translate:

> In that same year [1343] a galley from Savona, bound from Sicily, transporting meat and other goods, was captured with great violence by four armed Neapolitan galleys, led by the lieutenant of the late King Robert. And that galley was taken to

Naples with its entire crew still alive, save for the ship's owner
and commander, who was beheaded. For that cause, the Genoese ambassadors to Naples presented a complaint.[2]

Just a few lines. It's all here. Just a first piece of the puzzle,
dry and minimal. But if you read between the lines, it does tell
us a few things. Starting with a route that was fundamental to sea
trade in the Mediterranean, connecting Sicily to Liguria. A route
along which provisions and foodstuffs were conveyed, in accordance with the habitual forms of trade between the southern
end of the Italian peninsula and the North and its coastline—
foodstuffs (meat and other goods) in exchange for manufactured
and finished products. Let us move on then to the nature of the
attack. It all seems quite abstract. The galleys that attack the
cargo ship seem to emerge out of nowhere, children of the fog.
It's not clear where the raid takes place. In the waters off the city?
Not far from its coastline? Who knows…there are four ships.
And they would seem to be part of the Kingdom's fleet. Commanded not by some generic captain, but directly by the former
lieutenant to King Robert of Anjou, a recently deceased monarch, with no mention whatsoever of Queen Joanna, who had
succeeded him roughly a year before this. There is no mention
of the names of the protagonists. There are no other indications.
All we know is that the attack was violent. And that it seems to
have been ordered by specific superiors who belonged, we might
say, to institutions of the state. With a victim: the captain of the
galley, about whose identity we know nothing. What's more, this
captain is also the ship's *patrono*, or owner. His head, then, is
barbarously chopped off. An episode that results in diplomatic
complications, seeing that the Genoese ambassadors in Naples
present their complaints. End of story.

We've learned something, that's true. But if we carefully observe the pages of the chronicle, the episode is not given any particular emphasis. If anything, it appears practically concealed,
buried amid a slew of details of other information from that same

year. Other more alluring and fascinating information. This piece of news, on the other hand, vanishes immediately. It disappears. Erased. Subsumed into other items. By the report, for example, of extraordinary importance for all Christendom, that the church has ordered that the Jubilee, instead of being held every hundred years, will now be held every fifty. That on June 8 Giacomo da Santa Vittoria entered Genoa, where he was received by the archbishop, to the sound of pealing bells and solemn celebrations. Or that in Tana, on the Black Sea, in the course of a brawl, a Genoese killed a Tartar (a murder that triggered a war with Jani Beg, the khan of the Golden Horde, resulting in the destruction of the Genoese and Venetian warehouses. This war was the so-called Rotta della Tana, or Rout of Tana, which is also mentioned by Giovanni Villani). That in Genoa and in the castles of Cervo and Noli on the Riviera di Ponente and in Tassarolo, in Piedmont, the township was betrayed and thereafter certain of the traitors were crucified or else subjected to execution by drawing and quartering. That Luciano Grimaldi, traitor and pirate, plundered the galley of Daniele Cibo, bound from Flanders, loaded with cloth and many other valuable goods. And so on and so forth…

In the midst of all these accounts, it is clear how our chosen story becomes diluted. Transformed into an insignificant nugget from the chronicles. With the occasional minor aftermath and not much larger meaning. No different from hundreds of companion pieces, accounts of similar episodes, tales of crime and piracy. A story that was included in that chronicle, though we cannot say either how or why. With no particular interest, save for the simple impulse of recording an event.

On that basis, I would surely have just read past it. If, that is, I hadn't found another crumb along my path, just like Hop-o'-My-Thumb. This same event was noted at the turn of the twentieth century by the historian Michelangelo Schipa, but in this case it's sourced from an eighteenth-century manuscript by Luca Giovanni d'Alitto, and it reads as follows:

Having learned of the landing at Baiae of a galley of Savona, bound from Sicily, with a cargo of meats, grains, and other provisions at a time of great hunger in Naples, the Neapolitans decided to take possession of it. In great numbers, armed, from every walk of life, proving themselves well accustomed to factions of this sort, they boarded a royal galley and, with three other ships besides, they attacked the unfortunates, killing the commander and owner, taking their captured galley to Naples, with all its cargo and crew. The masterminds of this anything but admirable exploit were the nobles of Capuana and Nido, the militia of other towns, as well as commoners and artisans.[3]

Unmistakably, the picture changes and gains in scope and breadth. What emerges first and foremost is that there's something specific that drove the Neapolitans to carry out the raid, that it wasn't the result of mere chance. It's not as if nothing notable is happening in Naples. There's a famine raging, a very severe famine. So the attack was practically an act dictated by necessity. The content of the ship's cargo becomes clearer: aside from the meat, the freight primarily consists of wheat. Next the king's lieutenant vanishes from the picture, as do any indications of the involvement, however indirect, of officials of the state (that makes it clear to us that the report offered by Giorgio Stella of the presence of members of the court was surely contrived, an attempt to entangle the highest authorities of the land in this event). Instead, the focus is shifted to Neapolitan townsfolk, alone, without any other involvement. There's a king's galley, but it's the king's solely in name, because truth be told, that vessel was hijacked by various Neapolitans, who made use of it along with three other ships. These were people who did not simply constitute a chaotic and riotous crowd on the city beach which then proceeded to simply up and set sail in pursuit of the Savonese ship, recklessly and on the spur of the moment, in a burst of collective hysteria. Instead, their actions seem quite intentional and organized because, and let me emphasize the point, they did so *proving themselves well accustomed to factions of this sort.*

And that's not all: the expedition was organized in a manner anything but random: indeed, it was guided in a clearly hierarchical fashion. Guided by several leading figures of Neapolitan society, aristocrats of the two *seggi*—a word that will become much more familiar over the course of this book—of Capuana and Nido (though their specific names are not mentioned) who possessed clear leadership and laid out specific instructions: they readied the expedition; they seemed to choose the best men, including several knights (*milites*) who belonged to other city quarters, and joining them were members of other social classes (artisans, common folk); they took possession of the royal galley and the other vessels with the utmost impunity and, to all appearances, with absolutely no fear of criminal prosecution. What's more, the Savonese vessel was not, as we had previously assumed, in the waters off Naples. Instead, we are given a fairly precise location. Neither terribly distant from nor all that terribly close to the city. Along the Phlegraean coast. At Baiae. For someone intending to row there, it's hardly a walk in the park. Certainly a matter of considerable importance. Because it points to a level of planning, bound up with the issue of distance—and we can't say how long it would have taken them to cover that distance. The crossing took place at night: that's not specifically stated, but the surprise attack certainly suggests it. Concerning the details of the attack, both accounts match up, however: the concluding murder of the captain (though leaving out the brutal decapitation), and the conveyance of the vessel, with its complete cargo and crew, to the port of Naples.

Now we come to the last fragment. It dates from 1889 and was recorded by Matteo Camera. The reconstruction here is clearer and more complete, and it includes a brief transcription of an original document:

Despite the appropriate measures having been taken, the famine worsened at a steady gallop in Naples. It was during that terrible calamity that a Genoese ship laden with grains and bound from ports in Sicily, braving the fortunes of the sea, landed during the month of November, twelfth indiction, in the port of Baiae. As soon as word of the ship's arrival spread through the starving capital, a great many nobles of the *seggi* of Nido, Capuana, and other towns, followed by a numerous and ravenous throng, promptly readied to launch a royal galley with other boats, and—well armed—hastened to the port of Baiae, where they wasted no time taking possession of the Genoese vessel, quickly sailing it to Naples. The owners of both the ship and the cargo of wheat, Bartolomeo Squarciafico and Bonifacio Cattaneo, both Genoese, lodged a complaint regarding the losses suffered at the hands of the Neapolitan government, which turned a deaf ear. Frustrated in their quest for justice, they sought out their doge Simon Boccanegra and their city government. On learning of this high-handed behavior, both doge and government grew indignant and demanded restitution for the damage from Queen Joanna. She entrusted the judicial examination of the same to the regent of the Curia of Vicaria Roberto de Poncy and also Judge Berardo de San Flaviano. A great deal of time passed without these magistrates reaching any conclusion whatsoever, whereupon the cardinal legate Almerico arrived in Naples, and took for himself the judgment of that case, conveying documentation and a decision to the queen herself, who then sent it to the magistrates Roberto and Berardo. Given that back-and-forth and legacy of indecisions, in part due to the uprisings that were then underway in the capital, the bereft Genoese merchants, weary of the lengthy delay, decided they would reach an understanding at some later day, through a pecuniary transaction with the government of Naples.

There then follows a passage taken from the original document concerning the lawsuit that summarizes in detail the entire episode. That document repeats the things we already know, but in summary form: that the ship, by now no longer described as being from Savona but instead as Genoese, had docked in the port of Baiae. That it had been attacked by Neapolitan citizens, "both noblemen from Capuana and Nido, and also *milites* from other towns, as well as common folk and artisans." That they had been motivated "by the impending famine" (*propter imminentem caristiam*). There is no mention of the ship's captain being killed, but considerable space is devoted to the lawsuit over reparations for the damage suffered. That the lawsuit had been entrusted first to Roberto de Poncy, the regent of the Curia of Vicaria, and Berardo de San Flaviano, a knight and a member of the queen's family, and thereafter to Cardinal Almerico. And it had been impossible to reach an acceptable resolution since "the clashes that arose between the Neapolitan citizens themselves kept them from arriving at a conclusion or taking money from the gabelle of the *quartuccio* and the *buon danaro* to satisfy the claims of the Genoese merchants." At last, however, the solution, albeit a clear compromise, after the fact. It was achieved nearly two years later, in September 1345, with an understanding with Luigi di Ventimiglia, Giorgio di Arduino, and Guidelio Torrello, all from Genoa, representatives of the plaintiffs, namely the aggrieved shipowners Bartolomeo Squarciafico and Bonifacio Cattaneo, who surface here for the very first time. They received a sum in compensation, unfortunately not stated in this document, which was deposited with the Neapolitan merchant Leone Carnegrassa.[4]

Now let us connect the three accounts and see what happens. And let's try to recount the whole story in a single thread. On an unspecified date in the month of November 1343, and certainly prior to the notorious November 25 tsunami of that year, when Joanna I, successor to King Robert, had only been seated on the throne for less than a year, a Genoese ship, bound from Sicily, laden with wheat and other foodstuffs, had made port at Baiae, probably on account of a sudden storm. By channels unknown, in a Naples gripped by famine, word reached the city of a ship bearing a rich cargo of provisions, which could have been a godsend for the citizenry. Perhaps it was pure word of mouth, the grapevine, the way this sort of thing used to work in the old days. Rumors that wrap their tendrils around other rumors, clinging and sliding, projecting out doors and windows and making their way to where they're bound to arrive eventually: into the right pair of ears. The ears of the person who knows exactly what needs to be done. To the highest-ranking members of the most powerful family-led clans of the two *seggi* of Nido and Capuana. Where matters are quickly taken in hand. The word goes out to fetch other armed men from other city clans, knights, artisans, longshoremen, commoners. And they all make the decision together: they'll go attack the ship and bring the load of provisions back to the eagerly awaiting city. It's short work. At sunset, vessels are readied, a galley is hijacked from the royal fleet, perhaps with the tacit approval of guards and soldiers. They make best use of the night and of stealthy silence. They board the Genoese ship. The clash is quickly over. The ship's captain is killed, brutally, while the rest of the crew is allowed to live. The cargo is transferred. They sail back to Naples.

Those who had organized the raid, those who had materially carried it out, returned to the city with their plunder amid, if you'll allow me to let my imagination roam freely, the rejoicing of the populace, and particularly the latitudinarian, laissez-faire approval of the authorities, who did nothing to intervene, both because they turned a blind eye and because, as we shall later see in greater detail, they lacked the energy to react, at this moment of great deterioration of political life and the monarchy's grip on power. Indeed: when the Genoese demanded an accounting of what happened, the first response they received amounts to, at first, the statement that the men aboard the Genoese vessel were simply the wrong people in the wrong place. They were, all things considered, a *soft target* as well.

But the Genoese wouldn't stand for it. They demanded reparations for damages. Suddenly we hear from the ship's owners, who are prominent citizens: Bartolomeo Squarciafico and Bonifacio Cattaneo. And they reach out to the ambassadors in Naples. Pleas and objections ensue. The case is entrusted by the queen to two of her trusted men. To Roberto de Poncy, the regent of the Curia of Vicaria, and Berardo di San Flaviano, a knight and a member of the royal family. But delays ensue, procrastination gums up the works. The Neapolitans resist. No one seems interested in paying. They do their best to weary their counterparts. Now the case is handed over to Cardinal Almerico, also known as Almericus. But in the meantime, disorders break out in the city, for other reasons unrelated to our story. Tensions are sky-high. It's hard to keep the peace. There are greater priorities, and the case of Squarciafico and Cattaneo's ship is relegated to the back burner. And so two years come and go. The Genoese ambassadors, Luigi di Ventimiglia, Giorgio di Arduino, and Guidelio Torrello, are at their wits' end. It seems to have been impossible to reach a solution. At this point, they opt for a compromise. Which is reached, true, even though we'll never know—unless a fourth or a fifth account is found…some umpteenth account—exactly what sum it amounted to.

This is what happened on that night of November 1343. A reconstruction that, however, remains incomplete. In fact, there is more to be learned about this episode, which took place in a Naples that, in order to remain intact, to stave off utter destruction, entrusted itself to its men, its people, its citizens, the families of its nobility. Without relying at all on the assistance of the state or the institutions. A story that unfolds from here on, turning into a labyrinth. Because there's a great deal left to explore. Concerning the motive. Who ordered it and who carried out those instructions. About the victims. And what role the royal family played in all this.

All this to understand one thing: whether that night in 1343 really was just another in a long succession of moments of routine violence, like a thousand others in the long Middle Ages, with no linkage, no connection to past or future. Or, instead, as I believe: a specific tile in the larger mosaic that begins to take shape a century after the year 1000, developing into a skein that still extends over the streets of present-day Naples, along with an accompanying wake of popular beliefs, mindsets, and horrors.

II

THE MOTIVE

The Great Famine

The motive, as you've surely understood, is clear. To explain it, we need only six letters: famine. By this point, in 1343, famine is endemic and threatening. But it's not a problem limited to Naples, to the capital. The entire Kingdom is suffering from famine. And the rest of western Europe is suffering along with the Kingdom, though that's cold comfort indeed. We are obliged, at this point, to offer some thoughts about famine and to make it clear that it's not merely a phenomenon afflicting bygone eras, such as this distant fourteenth century. Hunger is not only a problem afflicting preindustrial societies. No, it's also something that strikes deeply at our everyday life in the modern world. Suffice it to note what has been happening since 2008, in the regions of North Africa, where the initial impetus driving the so-called Spring Revolutions came, in fact, from famine, from the tremendous drought plaguing vast expanses such as the Sahel, due not merely to inevitable constraints of climate, but also glaring misjudgments of agricultural planning. Famines that are also the main factors—along with a lack of security—driving so many refugees to brave the Mediterranean Sea in our times . . . and how can we fail to take into consideration, however briefly, the current hike in grain prices, price hikes on the order of as much as 150 percent? Price hikes due not so much to a decline in amount of supply available but rather a sudden increase in demand—correlated, let it be clear, with the deplorable enrichment of certain speculators![1]

Doubts. Which drive us to reflect on the past. To ask numerous new questions about this universe in our past. With one glimmer of awareness: there can be no question that in a world like that of the Middle Ages, punctuated so much more frequently than our modern world by the sheer constraints of *need* and the constant pressure of their surroundings, the urgent demands of nourishment were certainly the problem of all problems.

For ages, in order to explain this, historians turned to a very simple little formula: as long as the population remained constant and food production kept pace, there would be no difficulties. But in cases where the population begins to grow and food production fails to keep pace, trouble ensues. And along with that trouble, prompt as you please, arrives famine. In every self-respecting textbook you will find this same explanation. Here is what you'll read: When Europe's population levels, after the year 1000, began to rise, things went just fine for more than a century, because food production kept pace quite well, thank you. Then, starting in the mid-thirteenth century, that balance collapsed. Production fell below subsistence level. The production curve dropped. Hence the systemic crisis and the beginning of a cycle of underproduction and famine. Which in turn unleashed the fourteenth century's Great Famine. And that was the exact motive driving our Neapolitans to attack the Genoese ship.

So that's the idea. And I'm not saying it's wrong, okay? But it simply fails to explain everything. Because, as always, matters are more complicated than that. This approach, which we can rather generically describe as Malthusian (in fact, Malthus's thinking was far more profound, with implications that are frequently brilliant), fails to take a multiplicity of factors into account. These factors come to the surface nowadays in part due to the input of great theorists of present-day economic thought, such as Amartya Sen and Douglass North. For instance, let's take as an example the definition that the Indian economist, Sen, writing with Jean Drèze, offers of famine. A truly balanced definition, which opens various interesting points of view:

> Famine is, by its very nature, a social phenomenon (it involves the inability of large groups of people to establish command over food in the society in which they live), but the forces influencing such occurrences may well include, inter alia, developments in physical nature (such as climate and weather) in addition to social processes.[2]

If we talk about famines not as bolts from the blue but as social phenomena, bound up with the capacity for control of the resources of a given environment, then it is easy to understand that matters—and their basic nature—change greatly. In other words, keeping in mind the argumentation of an economic historian who is keenly attentive to these matters, Luciano Palermo, we should question whether the consumption of foodstuffs in the Middle Ages wasn't regulated purely by mechanisms of a structural nature, over which the control that could be exerted by human beings was minimal at best—but instead by something quite different. Let us, then, suggest that the conditioning factor was the "possibility of access" that people had to nutritional resources. As you can clearly guess, a determining factor: that possibility of access created, in fact, a yawning gap between those who found themselves in situations of outright famine and those who, instead, managed to ensure for themselves a steady and adequate supply of foodstuffs, albeit with some considerable difficulty. Because the problem was not gauged and determined solely by what economists call a food availability decline (FAD). Often there are other factors at play: the marketplace and its bottlenecks, the drifts and undertows of the market, its hidden objectives, its channels of distribution and geographic routes—the notorious failure of exchange entitlements (FEE, again a term of art in the theory of famines)—which as often as not have more to do with the needs of profit than the needs of the population at large.

Which brings us to an interesting point. Historians of famines have in fact noticed one thing, and we can take Michael Curschmann as a good example:[3] namely that famines, from the reign of Charlemagne until the twelfth century, in terms of frequency, gravity, and impact, had been, all things considered, a relatively minor factor. After the twelfth century, on the other hand, matters are reversed. And that change is found precisely in the transformations that sweep the marketplace. A market that becomes bigger and bigger, expanding until it takes on a European dimension. But like the toad in the fable, the larger it grows, the thinner and more fragile it stretches, devoid, as it then was (and still can be at times…), of the useful articulations that give it elasticity and resilience. That is to say, responsive to the impulses of supply and demand. A limitation that is not limited merely to the market's productive structures but also those of exchange. And why is that? What was happening? Why, in some situations, did terrible famines even afflict areas where production was functioning perfectly? That indeed happened, and with a vengeance. Because the owners of foodstuffs, instead of leaving them there to rot, with only the scantiest of profits to be enjoyed, would often choose instead to export them elsewhere, where prices were higher and conditions more agreeable, such as on the major marketplaces and trading floors. And then what remained on the local markets? Nothing but crumbs…And the struggle to lay hands on what little did remain quickly turned violent. With an explosion of prices, which rose incessantly higher, shooting skyward. In a condition that marginalized those who lacked hard cash to buy wheat. That, in fact, is the original meaning of *famine*: which doesn't so much mean "a lack of food to eat" but rather "how *expensive* this wheat has become!"[4] Therefore, famine was no longer a phenomenon that struck one and all: instead it struck some but spared others, according to the economic resources and wherewithal of each. We can see this unfold, right here in Naples. But the opposite situation could be found as well. Namely that in another region, hunger was unknown, even though agricultural production had collapsed, and this happened as a result of mechanisms of political intervention, rationing strategies, and the timely conveyance of foodstuffs from bordering regions or even distant ones through market operations. With transfers of stocks, or reserves, from one part of Europe to another, favoring locations that offered higher profits, but other advantages as well, and not merely to the sellers . . .

To put it briefly, what we rather simplistically call famine is actually, as I have tried to explain, a much more complex problem, which blends different processes: as much production as distribution and consumption. In a Western world that in this period, between the thirteenth and fourteenth centuries, is beginning to realize for the first time how pervasive a role the market plays— and increasingly so. A marketplace in which the circulation of cash increases day by day as self-consumption steadily shrinks. And food, the most appetizing and tempting means of exchange, finds itself exposed to a brand-new current in the larger stream of trade: what we can call price swings. A context in which varied and deeply contrasting interests face off, such as for instance those that variously pit producer and consumer against each other or else bring them together in a united front. With inequality in terms of forms of distribution, revenues, and wealth, creating gatekeepers that do not allow one and all equal access. A paradise based on discrimination. Discrimination between those who can afford to eat—and those who cannot. And not until the gatekeeper has waved you through can you say: Today I was lucky. And today I survived to see tomorrow, thanks to my ration of bread. I've lived another day. A condition in which it is important to understand that famine does not spring solely from a lack of food. More often, rather, from one's simple inability to gain access to the food that is there, in plenty.

Europe on Its Knees

Now let's take a closer look at what's happening in the rest of Europe. And then we can tighten the field of view, closer and closer in. All the way down to the eyes and the mouths of those who, in the city of Naples, no longer have a bite to eat. The early years of the fourteenth century were the worst ones: a turning point. After years of growth, as early as the second half of the thirteenth century, there was already plenty of ominous creaking and groaning to be heard. Now, however, matters truly seem to take a dire turn. In England, for instance, deaths from starvation in these years reach levels of 10 or possibly even 15 percent of the population. In Flanders, the outlook is no better. In the city of Ypres, for instance, the statistics are unmistakable: they describe a situation so stark and tragic that over the course of just seven months 2,600 people died, representing 10 percent of the population. In Spain, the famines keep rolling in like waves to the shore: in 1310–14 and 1324–28, until the famine of 1333, when our sources state that "there was famine of all foodstuffs, and we called this year *mal any primer*," that is, the first (worst) bad year, par excellence.[5] And the same thing happened elsewhere: in Portugal, in Germany, in France…

Things were bad, so bad that they undermined the foundations of an entire society. Because, even if it doesn't kill you, a famine will devastate, unnerve, and weaken you. The indirect consequences were enormous. There were ancillary effects that created a world of "dead men walking," easy pickings for epidemics of disease, and even non-epidemic outbreaks, especially in the major cities. People were suffering. And that was true both for farmers and for city folk, wage earners, small manufacturers. The countryside around the cities struggled to meet urban demand for crops. But what actually arrived in the city was, by and large, not foodstuffs but starving families in search of charity, assistance, and benefactors ready to lend a hand.

And the market for grain was becoming harder and harder to manage with every passing day, until it spun right out of control entirely, with price gouging, skyrocketing prices, and profiteering. In fact, there was an ongoing state of panic, where information, then as now, played its role—and not a secondary role. Simple information could unleash a series of complementary and unpredictable events, entailing chain reactions in which "the mere spread of a rumor of possible poor or insufficient harvests in a city or a region could often trigger chain reactions, resulting in the closure of markets, even in distant places, and repercussions in the form of profiteering and speculation, prompting sharp rises in wheat prices."[6]

This was a marketplace where absolutely divergent sensibilities clashed. There were small-scale buyers purchasing strictly for personal use and family consumption, with small resources, often insufficient to maintain even basic sustenance. These buyers were often swept rudely aside by the frequent spikes in prices. There were occasional sellers, who might become buyers at the drop of a hat, once their stores of foodstuffs dwindled, and often at the worst times imaginable. And then there were the large-scale merchants, accustomed to shaping the markets to suit their interests: capable of stockpiling their own reserves, setting them aside until the timing was perfect and then selling them off when the odds of making a killing seemed ripe. People turned to them for supplies, and if they lacked cash, they'd buy on credit. Sure enough, usury became increasingly common. If a starving buyer had no other options and owned a bit of land or some seed set aside, they might make a drastic decision: sell the wheat they had not yet harvested, while still underripe, as long as it got them through the critical moment, as long as they could put something in their bellies. This meant creating a spiral effect, where the rich just got richer. And the poor had no option but to hope. Or die.

We don't need to think of extremely lengthy periods of famine. This wasn't like the plague years of the 1340s, when the Black Death spread like the wind and in just a few years carried off nearly half of Europe's population. When it comes to famine, it might be a brief event. It might be cyclical. It might be seasonal. There might be bad months when it just became more difficult to find anything to eat. In a given year, one or perhaps more than one meteorological mishap might trigger a rise in prices, though nothing overarching, nothing structural. But if instances of famine began to line up, one after another, then matters certainly became explosive, with a negative result much greater than the sum of all the constituent parts. And the relentless rhythm of the famine made it impossible for a populace to catch its collective breath in the face of this constant state of desperation.

The crisis became cyclical. And the price hikes became constant. Hunger "without frontiers," to use the persuasive formulation employed by Pere Benito i Monclús, in which a climatic factor also played a powerful role, at this outset of the Little Ice Age. Historians of meteorology claim that the sun itself was a little sickly. But there are others who point to an increase in volcanic activity. In any case, the effect was disastrous. Waves of cold spells and advancing glaciers, with the onset of global cooling at the start of the fourteenth century, but which had already begun decades previously in the far north. In any case, as we can see nowadays, when the climate changes, those modifications aren't uniform in nature, but uneven in various zones across the planet. And so, while people's teeth might have been chattering in one region due to the bitter cold, elsewhere, such as the Mediterranean basin, for instance, the threat might be from unreliable rainfall, and the main problem might become drought and extreme heat.

The fact remains that at the beginning of the modern era, the climatic strip where farming was possible gradually began to shrink, while desertification advanced. As Wolfgang Behringer writes in his recent *A Cultural History of Climate*, "For, as at the beginning of the Iron Age, quality cereals proved susceptible to wet conditions and winter cold. In some regions of northern Europe—Iceland, for example—the cultivation of cereals had to be abandoned altogether; in others wheat was given up and people made do with oats and rye. From harvest observations we know that fruit blossom time, the haymaking season or the grape ripening period was delayed as a result of bad weather conditions. In some years, summer north of the Alps was too short for the grapes to ripen, or only sour wine was produced."[7] Crops, just like people, migrated. And grapes and wheat shifted southward. Nowadays the border of productive farming lies roughly five hundred kilometers (three hundred miles) farther south than it was around the year 1000.

Of course, a rainstorm wasn't enough to trigger a continent-wide famine. Still, in frequently fragile productive conditions, an excessively chilly or rainy winter or a succession of autumns with heavy levels of precipitation, verging on or reaching the level of torrential downpours, could profoundly affect the harvests. For that matter, an ongoing condition of excessive aridity, with resulting overheating of the soil, could bring about roughly the same set of problems, and here, too, solutions could only be achieved with great effort; these conditions could also unleash a stalemate in production spanning one or several regions, with a devastating domino effect. What's more, in a traditional agrarian economy like that of the fourteenth century, farmers seem all the more helpless in the face of bad weather. They had not yet reached advanced standards of development in the extended preservation of cereals, at least not at levels sufficient to withstand these various critical situations. Meanwhile, agricultural techniques struggled to prevent the deterioration of soils, unable to protect the most fragile farming territories, with ever-greater expanses of land abandoned to neglect and desuetude. At the same time, rivers overflowed their banks, mountain streams flooded, and there was a general condition of vulnerability that sharpened the danger of damage and disaster, both for humans and their crops.

For the first time in the West, state institutions took action instead of merely waiting. For once, they reacted in the face of the crisis. As early as the thirteenth century, nearly everywhere, in the small cities, the regions, and the territories of the centralized monarchies, laws began to be passed allowing public control over the supply of wheat, with inspections and monitoring entrusted to magistrates and specially established offices that had never before existed. A phenomenon, in the final analysis, of functional adaptation, developed in order to respond to the new challenge posed by the growing crisis of an environment burdened by the scarcity of nutritional resources. And were these policies effective? As often as not, yes, they were. But we can say one thing for sure: they marked "the fine-grained spread of a new culture, one of a fear of crisis."[8] The rationing policies therefore proliferated in the wake of a civic response, meant to limit the emergence of social tensions and to prevent the general state of public order from being significantly altered.

In fact, by this point the nutritional crises recurred one after another, at increasingly closer intervals. Regular as a clock. At growing frequency. What was to be done? What steps should be taken? The choice was to rely upon a culture of disagreement, based on serious individuals, shared norms, an acknowledged organization. In Europe, the cities were the first to take action, starting in the thirteenth century. Cities are freer, they're more enterprising. They tend to understand before everyone else exactly what is going on, in part due to the efforts of their merchants, who have information to offer, who know how to sniff the air and understand the changes and shifts in production, merchandise, trade, and commerce. And they have strategic outlooks that they can transform into shared culture. In Italy, and basically in all the cities and townships of the north-central area, they were ahead of the rest of Europe. Verona was the first city to equip itself with a statute to deal with crises, and that was as early as the twelfth century. In rapid succession, all the other cities followed suit, reforming their own statutes in the first half of the thirteenth century. In Germany the process began in 1218 with Hannover. And then it continued with Cologne, Szczecin, and Lübeck in the 1250s. Then Munich, Berlin, Freiburg, Hamburg, and Augsburg in the 1270s. The Flemish cities arrived later, in the final years of the century and in the earliest years of the fourteenth century. The monarchies reacted as well. In France, things began to move beginning in 1254, but many cities got organized independently. Strasbourg undertook the establishment of the new ordinances in 1256, and Metz followed suit in 1279. Paris and Lyon began the same process at century's end. In England, the new developments began in 1266. In Castile, matters moved forward by 1268 at the latest. In Catalonia, the process began in 1274. There was a spread of ordinances, statutes, and rules designed to regulate the bread market—that is, the ratio between foreseeable prices of wheat and those of other cereals. Tariffs were established on bread and on the prices of flours. Assizes of bread were established, for instance, by Henry III of England. These policies began to spring up, as I've said, more or less everywhere, but not always in the same manner. Everyone seemed to do things differently. They set up structures as they each thought best. Everyone did things for themselves. They created for themselves. They adapted rules to their own standards and needs. But they all felt the need to respond to these challenges, each as best they could. And they did so with a powerful and shared desire: "Provide organized and regulated stability for the market system."[9] Would they be successful? Well, as I said, not always. But given the fact that nowadays there is so much talk about Europe and its unity, this was really one of the first times that, aside from any political or administrative differences, dictated by the specific conditions of each individual entity, there seemed to spring up in all directions a shared stance toward something that is truly frightening. Something called "hunger." Famine.

Fear of Famine

Now let's take a look at the larger Italian context. Giuliano Pinto, along with Massimo Montanari, was one of the first to explain with his research the forms of famine in Italy. With one very important proviso: that we are going to try to explain first and foremost that this is a very peculiar situation, with a basic underlying distinction—one separating major areas of consumption (Venice,

Genoa, Florence, and Lombardy) and the centers of production, by and large located in southern Italy (Apulia, Sicily, Campania, and so forth). The distance separating these two major categories creates logistical and transportation problems. And it results in a state of affairs that we absolutely should not underestimate: there was a steady drain on the resources of the South in order to feed the North. This resulted in a substantial imbalance, with effects on the people of southern Italy that should not be overlooked: they were thus deprived of goods and resources that provided those in charge of this trade, those running the business, the opportunity to get spectacularly rich in the process. A market substantially dominated by operators who had little to do with the south of Italy and who were all too willing to exploit it. A dichotomy between North and South? One of the first and most substantial of those divisions? We'll come back to this point.

That said, I'd like to focus a little longer on the north-central region. Because that area offers explanations of a great many things, about the natural and societal climate as well as the policies of intervention. The first case we'll examine is that of Lombardy. The nutritional crisis seemed to strike here earlier than elsewhere. We have records of it in 1276–77 and again in 1286, with a return in 1311–12, and a surge in price hikes in 1329–30. The interesting thing, as we read the city chronicles, is that as the chroniclers describe the reasons for the crisis, they never discuss topics even vaguely economic in nature. They never mention prices or price variations. The thing they point to most often as the triggering cause is the bad weather. A cruel climate is the cause of everything, in their view. Pietro da Ripalta writes, in 1276: "In this year, there have been great rains [*magne pluvie*] in Lombardy and Rome and, due to those, there has been great famine, infirmity, and mortality among the people"; while, in the following year, we read in the *Annales Placentini*: "In the summer, there was heavy rain in Lombardy [*multas aquas*] [followed by] a great shortage of things and foodstuffs."[10]

The crisis arrives in any case. And it kills. The examples are numerous and are evocative of the dire consequences that famine brings with it. In 1311, the city of Parma came to life. But it was not a festive or joyous crowd. No: it was a maelstrom of starving beggars, shouting in desperation in the city's streets, in search of food or dying of hardship and hunger, their existence a living hell. All this had a series of deeply damaging effects on the city's artisanal and industrial activities, to such an extent that even craftsmen and laborers no longer had enough to eat and were forced to eat nothing but *pane de melica* (melic grass):

> there were vast numbers of poor beggars in Parma and weeping and moaning could be heard in the squares, the villages, and the churches, and countless numbers perished of starvation in both the city and the bishopric, and in both Parma and other cities the guilds and the tradesmen had great losses because no business could be transacted, and many artisans had to live on nothing but bread made of melic grass.

This snapshot should suffice, alone, to recount the disaster of a starving world. Everything halted in its tracks. Everything seemed to be enveloped in a surrealistic void, where physical weakness was so overwhelming that not even craftsmen had any remaining desire to work. A deafening silence. Punctuated by only a single sound, the screams of the starving. A horrible description, followed by another description of the following year. Which featured even worse weather. In which it seems as if a single rumor was flying from house to house, the rumor of a chilling human misery, which drove human beings to sell off the only thing remaining: roof tiles, which they peddled in exchange for that tiny handful of coins with which to purchase a fistful of grain seed to live on. Those who could no longer get by had only one option. They needed to take to their heels. Run away. Seek their fortune elsewhere:

On account of which famine many citizens threw open their homes, sold their household belongings and their own homes for a pittance, either in grain or in cash, and many starved to death, while others left Parma entirely; and there were many beggars crying out in the streets and the churches and squares.[11]

So what was the political response? The political intervention of the townships, as we see in the case of Parma, often proved decisive, even in emergency situations. The city acted accordingly. In the absence of wheat, they bought more on the marketplace of some other city. After which, the township established a fixed price, in an authoritarian manner. This type of intervention was successful, because cities had sufficient power to enforce their decrees. And what's even more important, because Parma had enough money in its coffers to be able to say, "Yes, we can invest that money to feed the city and its neighboring areas." But matters could easily go otherwise. It might happen that, despite the fact that these two conditions happened to coincide, fortuitously, there still might not have been even a speck of wheat to be had. In that case, things were really serious...But, in Parma's case, the city's institutions encountered no difficulties. And the public administration was able at least to put a patch on things.

In spite of all their efforts, the hoped-for results were not forthcoming: they were unable to dampen the collective sense of terror, the "fear of famine." Anxiety and fear proved overwhelming here, as throughout the rest of the Western world. The city was swept by *magnae processiones*. And in these processions, weeping, praying, and litanies were heard, demanding an end to the famine. People wanted to see an end put, as well, to the *fragility of existence*. This is a key element to any understanding of the mindset of the medieval populace.

The second case was that of Tuscany. And the situation was described by an exceptional source: the work of Domenico Lenzi, the author of a singular text titled *Specchio umano* (The human mirror), known to the broader public as the *Libro del Biadaiolo*

(The Biadaiolo codex): a diary, written by Lenzi himself, with a detailed account of the prominent Florentine cereal market of Orsanmichele in a series of crucial years, between 1320 and 1336.[12] What emerges from that account? Well, that famines "occurred continuously" in those years in Florence. Unlucky times. Before this, who wrote about famines? No one, because they were at best passing, episodic events. Of no particular importance. But starting in the third decade of the fourteenth century, Florence and its agricultural production were hit, and very hard hit indeed. The explanations offered by the Florentines were theological and moralistic in nature: God was sending famines to punish sinners. But here, too, we see the climatic aspect surfacing again. In fact, to say that there were bad seasons in this period is to radically understate matters. Because the climatic events that came crashing down were stunning in their intensity.

Chroniclers knew that climate played a fundamental role. That it is weather that determines harvests. And if the weather turns strange, then the harvests are bound to fail. And the weather seems to have gone completely crazy between the thirteenth and fourteenth centuries. With drought, rain, and intense cold. There are numerous accounts of all sorts of episodes. And, as Charles de La Roncière points out in a book that by now has become a classic, in at least twenty of those situations, "those famines were foretold as early as the previous year by a major outburst of bad weather, or several, such as to modify local or regional conditions."[13] Modifications that, in one way or another, undermined farming production, with an immediate impact on prices. But what is especially striking is the frequency, with a frightful cumulative effect: 1282–83, 1283–84, 1284–85, 1288–89, 1301–02, 1304–05, 1306–07, 1307–08, 1310–11, 1333–34, 1334–35, and 1338–39, culminating in the awful weather of 1346–47, which proved truly catastrophic.

In Tuscany, the winters were chilly, long, and harsh. The rivers froze over in 1303 and 1327. It snowed for weeks on end. The rains were heavy and extended. Especially the rains in spring and

autumn: those were the cause of the greatest damage, and they destroyed everything in their path. Villani repeats it, time and again:
"overwhelming rain...ruins the harvest," "not much that was
planted wasn't ruined," "the rains never seemed to stop...where-
fore...the harvest of the minor cereal crops." To say nothing of the
downpours, brutal and without warning, that devastated the sown
fields in 1333 and 1345, sweeping away the granaries with all of
their contents and destroying the mills. Those downpours were
followed by flooding: the Arno overflowed its banks in December
1282, in April 1284, again in December 1288, in November 1333,
and in that same month in 1345. The river Elsa flooded in January
1309 and September–November 1318. And in 1333 the flooding
"destroyed all plantings, overturning and uprooting trees as well."
Conditions that made work very difficult in the fields, with "flooding that destroyed a great deal of wheat and cereal." With violent
hailstorms and murderous gusts of wind, which "left little more
than the withered remains in the ears of wheat" and fruit falling
still-unripe from the branches of the trees.[14] On the other hand,
the summers were scorching. Blistering hot. Dry, with powerful
sirocco winds. What did all this mean, then? First of all, irregular-
ity in production. Which staggered along, limited by precipitation and bad weather, reducing the size of the harvest. And the
market contraction had profound effects on the economy of an
entire region, which based its strength on the driving engine of
agriculture.

   A meteorological tyranny...in the face of which humans had
very few resources. The Florentine government tried to pass administrative measures that, at times of especially severe drops in
production and pressure on prices, might be able to limit issues
with supply. And it responded with the creation of a sophisticated
institutional structure. By and large, in command of that structure was the captain of the people (*capitano del popolo*), who, with
his colleagues, his *boni homines* and his *sapientes*, was the judge
and master of the situation: together they oversaw the regulation
of sales; they worked to ensure the safety of roads and markets;

they guaranteed the free conduct of transactions; they ensured the quality of bread and cereals; they controlled prices. After the captain of the people, on the front lines, was the *officium bladi*, or Office of Forage, with the *officiales bladi*, or officials of forage, or rather, *sei del biado*, or the Six of Forage, who were in charge of a great many things. Supplies and reserves. Large-scale imports. The battle against smuggling, with confiscations and searches. In other words, great powers and police duties, with the very close monitoring of the wheat and grain trade, in part through border checks. What is more, with the option of sitting in judgment, both on cases of civil and criminal justice. This organization had a wide-ranging and varied array of tasks, considering the sheer size of Florence, with a population of well over a hundred thousand inhabitants, and the scale of its surrounding countryside, which was growing in population and production day by day: to such a degree that the Six were given command over another office, the Office of Abundance, which gradually drifted apart until finally splitting free of it entirely, becoming an independent structure.

Given the growing degree of complexity, there was no reason to assume that everything would flow smoothly. For instance, the closing of borders to prevent the passage of wheat, wine, and oil failed to be applied systematically. Hoarders, profiteers, smugglers all continued to buy and sell on the black market, even in the face of extremely harsh penalties. And it was very difficult to limit sales outside of the official marketplace, though that didn't stop the authorities from trying. Then there was the populace. Which blamed the Six of Forage for any food shortages. That was the case, for instance, in spring 1329, when wheat reached extremely high prices on the Florentine market and only small quantities were available, even at those prices. The Six of Forage soon became the favorite target for mass fury: "People walked weeping and wailing and cursing themselves as well as the heavenly powers in no uncertain terms. And they cried: these thieves [that is, the Six of Forage] are determined to starve us to death"; "and these people could not see how the Six of Forage in question were doing anything other than harm." And the rage spread and grew. It swelled in volume and depth. Until the people were railing against the entire city government, accusing their leaders of sheltering the profiteers: "Behold how poorly the city is run, as we can't even get wheat to eat! And they wanted to go to the homes of these thieves and burn them down with the officials inside, because they were forcing them to live in this famine."[15]

An outright uprising was right around the corner, and the scenario called for the revolution of the populace as a whole, in the throes as they were of starvation and a shortage of wheat. But the government, in contrast with the way things would later go in Naples, managed to put down any efforts at an uprising with a very firm hand. That story is told by Lenzi himself, when he talks about the awful times of spring 1329.[16] Events began on Friday, June 2. That day the city's Six of Forage ordered that seventy-two *moggi* of common wheat of less than remarkable quality, valued at a price of fifty-two *soldi* per *staio* (roughly a bushel), be conveyed to the Orsanmichele market. When the wheat reached the market, the crowd of buyers erupted in all directions. A mob made up of city folk and farmers, a throng more numerous than had ever been seen before (let God in His goodness, Lenzi says, preserve us and keep us from such an infamous time of misery and famine ever again) was there, waiting, even before the wheat was made available for sale. So many people that it was truly astonishing, in a general surging crush. Everyone pressed against their neighbor as they pushed to get to the counter and get their hands on a bit of wheat. That brawl was so furious that two men and two women were trampled and only extracted after they were already dead.

The men of the city militia arrived (the *familia*), just in time to prevent more deaths and injuries. They tried to calm down the mob, with blandishments and blows. In the end, the authorities decided to forget about persuasion. They reinforced the militia presence and set out the headsman's block and axe, and beside them, two executioners, ready and willing to do swift and summary justice if anyone tried to put up opposition. Two town criers began to declaim loudly an edict from the *podestà* that ordered all men older than age fifteen to disperse from the market square, Piazza del Mercato, on penalty of twenty-five lire. At that point, seeing no reaction on the part of the crowd, the *podestà* himself, Ser Villano di Gubbio, and his men began clearing the market square of people with blows from clubs and spears. More than a thousand men, young and old, who had all gathered in search of wheat, were forced to leave with rough clubbings. Then the militia blocked all entrances to the market with iron gates, stationing sentinels before them. The guards had orders to drive away anyone who might try to get in. And so it was: no one was allowed through. No matter their age, and no matter their excuse. Only after that did it become possible to begin selling with a certain peace of mind. The wheat was distributed only to women, in rations of half a *staio* apiece. With this strange situation: inside the market, it seemed that calm reigned supreme, while outside the gates, sheer bedlam ensued.

In the days that followed, the headsman's block and axe were left there for all to see. The message was that the government was always watching, ready to punish anyone who dared to get out of line. Finally, a clear decision was made: "Everyone out." Even women and children were expelled from the market. Just as Ser Villano had shown himself to be merciless with anyone who wanted to purchase wheat, he likewise showed himself relentless when it came to profiteers, and on September 18, with a view to discouraging anyone who might be tempted, he had thirty-nine profiteers arrested and tortured, each in the presence of another: just to make it clear to one and all that there was only one government, only one entity in charge, and a single market that established a single price. The same for everyone, without any differences, all fair and reasonable. The absolute witness to this event, Lenzi, did not disapprove of this violence—far from it. And he congratulated Florentine authorities, as Mathieu Arnoux points out, for having chosen, with discerning political pragmatism, "the obligatory path of market regulation, stern but fair":

Your succor is necessary, o Lord, and above all Your succor for
the poor. In truth, I do declare, if there had not been good men
in the Office of the Six over the course of this year, many poor
and less well-to-do people would surely have starved to death,
especially in the countryside. [17]

A Desperate Kingdom

What about in the Kingdom of Naples? Here, the numbers of
the crisis were truly implacable. Between the beginning of the
fourteenth century and the year 1505, something close to 876
inhabited towns disappeared.[18] There was an accompanying
phenomenon of the desertification of the territory that attained
apocalyptic proportions: likewise in Calabria, where 147 inhabited towns vanished. Or else in Abruzzo, both Abruzzo Citra and
Abruzzo Ultra, where the losses of towns rose to a total of 369. A
debacle that was bound up with many different causes, such as the
persistent series of dynastic wars that bloodied the entire Kingdom from the middle of the fourteenth century until the creation
of the monarchy of Aragon in the 1440s. That said, the overriding
cause was famine. And that hunger began in the capital, in Naples.

The city had grown, and dramatically so, since the middle of
the twelfth century, when it became part of the new Norman kingdom. A city that was anything but lacking in resources. Land was
Naples's true gold, the city's fortune. The countryside that emerges
from the accounts of the period is studded with an endless series
of observations about crops, farmland, vegetable gardens, vineyards, fruit orchards, and arable land, extending over the territory
practically without a single break. The product of a transformation dating back to the High Middle Ages, the result of practically
uninterrupted effort that carved away at woodlands, forests, oak
groves, pine stands, swamps, and marshes. That reclamation effort
created watercourses, landfills, vineyards planted high, all sorts
of infrastructure, cisterns, *palmenti* (structures for pressing wine
grapes), mills, and dovecotes.

A revolution propelled by a considerable surge in demographic growth and a growing hunger for land to clear and reclaim. A progression that had an exceptional profile, if you consider the serious environmental problems facing the region. Marshes and forests made a great deal of the countryside near the city completely inaccessible, especially along the coastal area west of the city. Then, to the north, the Clanio river, now enclosed by the immense public works project of the Regio Lagno that Charles III ordered to be constructed, constituted a disease-ridden barrier, with a completely unwholesome habitat, that separated Neapolitan territory from the so-called Terra di Lavoro. To the east, on the other hand, the great marshes around the Sebeto river hindered any settlements of the interior; while on the slopes of Vesuvius, especially along the southern slopes, the villages seemed to be devoured by the great forest that would later take the name of Selva Mala. And so the arable lands tended to cluster around small settlements— later known as the *casali*, meaning farming hamlets, of Naples— some of which had sprung up in the early Byzantine era and were considered, even then, an integral part of the city's urban system.

And it's by no means excessive to speak of an urban system for the Naples of this period. We certainly can't be talking about a mature system, like some new town of the twenty-first century. Still, in embryonic form, all the necessary features were already there. In fact, this was one of the salient features of the landscape. An integrated model consisting of land, whether being cultivated or not, productive structures and supply structures, road networks small and large, castles and other defensive structures, villages and towns, satellite settlements with their own ports, such as, for instance, Pozzuoli, which all had Naples as their prime point of reference: at once the region's administrative center, institutional headquarters, and the social and economic lung, so to speak. In short, the Neapolitan environment was made up of a myriad of interrelated segments that followed logical patterns whose meanings were frequently difficult to decipher. With uncomfortable and conflicting coexistences, with dispersive centrifugal forces at play and tides of resistance, both violent and recidivistic over time. But, taken as a whole, all these dynamics behaved like a single living entity, made up of an array of connective tissues that drew their strength from the cohesive and complex organization of all its component parts.

In this growing territory, there were unmistakable signs of a shift in direction as early as the second half of the thirteenth century. I wouldn't want to bring in the name of David Ricardo and his law of diminishing returns, but what was happening in Naples—and let me add in many other areas in southern Italy—was a textbook case: as long as colonization was expanding and the search for new land to cultivate had plenty of manpower and resources to draw on, plenty of farmland was extracted from forest and marsh. But the farther the reclamation of neglected land advanced, the harder it became to determine that these spaces could be managed profitably. And so the profitability of the new lands diminished: it was no longer a bargain to purchase new rural parcels, nor was it worthwhile to work new farmland on reclamation contracts. The whole process ground to a halt: there was a halt to investment in new land and the interest of investors in the agricultural market necessarily focused on those patches of land that either required no particular effort to bring under cultivation or else were already cleared and prepared for sowing and harvesting. In short, a process began of abandonment and neglect that affected broader and larger swaths of the territory surrounding the city. And that city therefore saw its rural base shrink, until it was smaller in the fourteenth century than it had been two or even three centuries previous. Literally sucked under by fields left fallow: a process that had effects both on the rural environment and on the rates of demographic growth.[19]

This is what was happening around the capital, Naples, where prices for the best farmland had already begun to skyrocket around the turn of the thirteenth century, with a dizzying increase of more than 300 percent over the starting numbers of the twenty-year period 1040–60. At the same time, the less-suitable land was rapidly neglected, with declining levels of agricultural productivity, resulting in a widespread deterioration in the landscape around the city, overrun in the fourteenth century by forests and marshes that were soon intruding on the territory around the city walls. Some instances of this are the *Paludes Casenovelle*, which began to the east of the city, from the outlying *borgo* (village) of Casanova, where King Charles II of Anjou had built one of his homes, soon abandoned due to the generally poor conditions of the air. These were marshes that made up just a small part of an extensive network of swamps, quagmires, and ponds that took the name of *paludes magnae*: an enormous area covering some 30,000 hectares (75,000 acres, or 115 square miles) and which spread all the way to the forested slopes of Mount Vesuvius. These vast wetlands had formed over the course of roughly a century and had swallowed up the reclamation work undertaken by Neapolitan farmers since the tenth century.

The marsh also met the forest in another point in the hinterland, in the northern outskirts of the city, that is, the Phlegraean Fields, with an impression of total desolation and a deterioration that can be seen over the long term. In fact, as late as the eighteenth century, the historian Gennaro Maria Galanti was depicting a somber image, pointing out that Cumae, Baiae, and the entire area were dominated by "poor air, and to sleep here even once in summer or autumn meant certain death."

The environment decayed, and as it did, it took with it arable soil, flourishing vineyards, and an entire agriculture patrimony that had been extracted with hard work and toil over the centuries. We need cite only a single example to illustrate what was happening. A small one, but a highly significant one. It has to do with a monastery on the city's outskirts, San Pietro ad Aram. Just a short distance outside the city walls, the monastery had played a fairly important role in the reclamation of the eastern portion of the Neapolitan countryside over the course of the thirteenth century. After a long period of growth, the monastery was on the verge of collapse. Between 1313 and 1325, the structures that made up that compound, the church, the food storage warehouses, and the surrounding houses all went to rack and ruin and were promptly abandoned. The reasons? Famine and malaria had combined into a murderous medley. Farmers grew weak and dropped like flies, mowed down by disease. And dropping alongside them were the clerical staff, who dwindled from twelve in number to just three. A general situation of deterioration that clearly affected the revenue as well. When the papal commissioners arrived in 1336, they had high hopes. They knew that this monastery wasn't exactly rich, but that it did have some capital. The commissioners expected substantial numbers. Practically dizzyingly high numbers. They estimated that the monastery could provide revenue of 650 *oncias*, which corresponded to 3,900 ducats. But they had calculated wrong. When the clerical staff presented their ledger books, the commissioners' eyes popped open. Did you say 650 *oncias*? You're dreaming. At the very most, revenue might reach 120 *oncias*, barely 720 ducats, as had been the case in 1322. And now, in 1336, the clerical staff would have fallen to their knees, rejoicing in a miracle if they had earned 100 *oncias*. In fact, even with rents and sales of agricultural products, they were bringing in practically nothing, not a penny. Just 70 *oncias*, or 420 ducats.[20]

So if those were the environmental settings outside of the city, with the so-called *casali*, or farming hamlets, its sources of foodstuffs, reduced at this point to small productive oases scattered across an uninhabited wilderness made up of forests and swamps, what can we say about the rest of the Kingdom? The situation was certainly no better. In much of it, from Teano to Capua, Aversa, Sora, Scafati, Eboli, Lagopesole, San Gervasio, Ugento, Bitonto, Bovino, Lucera, Salpi, Ortonova, Ortona, and Andria, as well as a large part of Calabria and Abruzzo, there was nothing but a vast expanse of forest.[21] Along with those forests, there were marshes and swamps, with their endemic venom of disease: very true of Abruzzo, in Celano, or the small town of Penne, near the Lake of Fucino.

Nevertheless, it was the basic nature of the land that prevented sufficient production. It appeared sterile, impoverished, partially abandoned in many areas in southern Italy. And so we read that the Terra d'Otranto is *poor and only very sparsely inhabited,* "its towns and villages scattered so far apart, the solitude of the region so vast and solemn that the general inquisitions of the *giustizieri,* or justiciars, in the individual towns cannot be conducted regularly." The territory of Gaeta "is sterile, and this is true on such a continual and organic basis that without the constant supply of victuals from more fortunate regions, the city *in loco sterile situata* could hardly help but rapidly empty of people and vanish." Calabria was by and large "a rocky heap of debris where only the narrow coastal areas of the Tyrrhenian and Ionian Seas, separated by harsh mountain ranges, can offer any stirrings of greenery." Basilicata "with its mountainous tangles, its forests, its poor patches of farmland perched high atop the hillsides, offers only the scantiest of nourishment to its children, and likewise Molise and part of Abruzzo."[22]

And climatic changes struck here as they did elsewhere. With phenomena that entailed arid soils alongside rare but powerful downpours. For nearly every year we find reports coming from the Kingdom's most vital areas and describing water shortages, lost harvests, lands abandoned because they'd become virtual deserts. In Apulia, the genuine breadbasket of southern Italy, terrible things happened, such as in this account from May 1315 concerning the royal farms in what is now the greater Foggia area, when "at planting time, there was no rain in all of Apulia," a phenomenon accompanied by a violent and unusual intensification of the sun's rays (*superveniente calore solis*) so powerful that it prostrated the inhabitants *immoderate et intollerabiliter.* A similar event took place seven years later, when Villani observed:

> In the year in question, MCCCXXII, and the months of November, December, and January, there was in Italy the greatest coldest winter and more snow than there had been in past years;

and in Apulia there was so severe a drought that for more than eight months running there was no rain, as a result of which there was great suffering and a famine of all foodstuffs in the land; and so it went nearly everywhere in Italy.[23]

Long and unexpected periods of drought, interspersed with sudden and catastrophic downpours. Like the one in the summer of 1345 that devastated Terra di Lavoro in less than an hour's time: houses were flooded and the Volturno violently overflowed, sweeping away many of the residents of the town of Caiazzo. The devastation that emerged in the aftermath of that flood was appalling. Fruit orchards, farmland, vineyards: all destroyed. Such desolation that many of the nearby villages' residents abandoned their homes and moved into the sheltering safety of the Naples city walls.[24]

The nutritional crisis in the Kingdom began in the second half of the thirteenth century. And among the triggering causes, one was entirely manmade: the War of the Vespers, the conflict that shattered the Mediterranean ambitions of the Angevin dynasty. The insurrection that broke out on Easter Monday of 1282 lasted for many years, twenty, to be precise. And it drained the resources and vital energies of the region, largely shunting them aside to supply the army in its martial pursuits, or else simply burning or otherwise destroying them in battle and plunder. Let us take into consideration the mainland section of the Kingdom: entire areas, like that to the south of Salerno (the Vallo di Diano, the Cilento, the Piana del Sele), were swept by fast-moving, violent guerrilla warfare, resulting in the wholesale flight of populations and the abandonment of quite a few villages, with truly devastating damage to local agriculture. As Giovanni Vitolo wrote: "That these were not temporary gaps, easy to fill once a peace treaty was signed (1302), is shown by the fact that in 1305–1309 the fireplaces, which is to say the family units, of the *casali*, or farming hamlets, of Castellabate in the Cilento, which had amounted to 1,000 prior to the war, had dwindled to just 206. Policastro, as well, along with one of its farming hamlets, burned to the ground over the course of the war, saw a sharp reduction in the number of their inhabitants, which dropped from 150 to 15 families."[25] Likewise hard hit was the Amalfi coast, where part of the populace was taken prisoner, only to be released following payment of a ransom. But the worst statistics were economic: the market froze solid. The Sicilian routes and those of mainland southern Italy were now practically impossible to travel. The gears of the economy, long spinning freely, were now rusted in place. And food, which had once shipped easily, became difficult to obtain.

When all these things wormed their way into a social fabric that was already troubled and struggling, there was nothing left to do. And to extreme ills, extreme solutions were sought. Such as, for instance, the destruction of the Muslim community of Lucera in August 1300, which had a single overriding goal, to raise money by auctioning off the population itself and all their possessions in order to finance the supplies needed for the troops that were off at war.[26]

The year was 1301. The new century began, and it started with a famine. Poverty was overwhelming and completely disproportionate to the resources that could be brought to bear. Luckily, this seemed to be an isolated episode, at least at first. Then another famine arrived, in 1310. Famine hit again, and hard, in 1327 in Abruzzo, at Sulmona. A year or two passed: 1328–1329. The surge of famine that we've already seen in Tuscany and other parts of Italy reached the South. The harvest was scanty at best. Profiteering was out of control. From this moment forward, the intervals between one famine and the next continued to shrink: 1333, 1338, 1339, 1343, 1347, and so on. From the hinterland, an army of hungry people poured into Naples. The number of mouths to feed grew and grew. There was rage and indignation.

And what was the government doing? Let us carefully observe what was going on. Because it is possible to understand a great deal from the government's actions in response to the Neapolitan reaction on that November night in 1343. In 1301, what leaps to the eye is the fact that beyond a shadow of a doubt, the monarchy was completely helpless. The government tried to impose measures designed specifically against the worrisome phenomenon of the hoarding of nutritional reserves, with resulting profiteering on the skyrocketing prices that ensued. The royal chancellery examined the problems that arose and, in contrast with other Italian regions, did so with a startling degree of clarity (which would have met with even Amartya Sen's approval). For the functionaries, it was clear that the reasons underlying the crisis in the food supply were not to be sought in the bad weather. No, the real problem was the *malitia hominum* ("the malice of men"), the thirst for profit. Smuggling. Profiteering.[27] Searches were among the measures undertaken, both in the city and in the hinterland, in pursuit of hidden *frumenta et victualia* ("wheat and victuals"). The government feared the black market. There was an attempt to limit the tariffs levied on imports to the Kingdom's capital. The main arteries were policed to ensure the safety of merchants bringing foodstuffs into the city, lest they be robbed. An array of measures that give us a sense of political will, but one that remained strictly provisional and episodic in nature.

And what was the response in 1329? Approaches remained unvaried. The same policy was followed as had been standard at the turn of the century, and it had little or no effect. Meanwhile, there was a steady increase in profiteering and corruption. In the face of that failure, on June 20 the king decided to order an absolute prohibition on any further export of wheat or food grains from the Kingdom. He ordered the house-to-house search of the entire territory of Aversa, to the north of the capital, in the belief that the residents of the area were hiding grain to sell on the black market. Officers entered every hut, every cabin, even semi-abandoned farmhouses. And from the outskirts, they moved into the city. They canvassed and poked into the *occulta repagula*, in derelict farmhouses. And in particular they burst into the homes of merchants, the prime suspects. No matter how sternly they proceeded, the results were nothing much to speak of. The stashes of grain that were thought to be hidden away only emerged in very small quantities. Whenever something was uncovered, forcible confiscations ensued, allowing the owners to hold on to only the smallest quantity to survive on. And sometimes not even that. That "smallest quantity" would be conveyed to Naples and sold at a stabilized price.

It wasn't enough, though, and the hunger only worsened. In February 1329, given the fact that the problem was disproportionately more complex than had been expected, and taking into consideration that searches had proven to be of little or no real use, King Robert made a radical decision. He opted for what we'd now call a tax holiday, ordering the suspension of all import tariffs in Naples for a month on any volume of wheat or food grains in transit. Anyone could take advantage of that benefit, however they thought best. It was a measure that seemed to be saying: Let's leave matters to the free market and hope for the best. It was a call of "olly olly oxen free," and it unleashed the greed of many. It didn't really improve matters, but it changed them. Because once all hopes for a good harvest in the spring of 1329 had failed miserably, prices shot upward to an unexpected extent. Whereupon it became necessary to apply the brakes again and shift direction. There was no more thought of deregulation, but instead, starting on June 20, the most rigorous form of protectionism took hold, with tight government control of exports and imports.

This burst of chaotic decision-making came at the worst-possible time—just when the crisis was at its direst and Apulia was on its knees, so badly hit there wasn't even enough wheat to satisfy the court's needs. Southern Italy was screaming with hunger. The king knew where the problem lay. He sounded the same notes as previously, placing the blame on the criminal behavior of the profiteers, the *abscondentium victualium*. And he was right. What was there to be done, however, if the king himself was not a victim of this situation, but actually one of the malefactors? Because we should not forget: the crisis in the Kingdom was also prompted by the fact that much of its agricultural production didn't even remain in its borders, but was instead exported, sent elsewhere, largely to north-central Italy. Hidden away in Florence, Genoa, and in other zones of north-central Italy. And the exportation of wheat was no small matter: it was the main profit center in the Kingdom's economy, through which the state channeled off the largest revenue by means of the system of the payment orders, that is, the tariff markets involved in the shipping of wheat. Or else by negotiating major loans from the major Florentine banking houses (in particular, the Bardi-Peruzzi-Acciaiuoli joint venture), ensuring lucrative deductions on exports to those bankers. Whereas blocking that flow of exports, international in nature, meant putting a halt to the river of cash flowing into the coffers of the court.

So what was to be done? It was surely preferable to deny resources to the local community rather than in any way hinder this flow of wealth into the hands of the monarchy. Therefore the residents of the towns of Apulia, namely Manfredonia, Barletta, Bari, and Taranto, beheld a strange spectacle. They might very well be starving. In spite of that fact, they were forced to stand by and watch while their future sailed away aboard ships owned and operated by powerful Tuscan merchants. Nearly all their wheat, nearly all their cereals of any kind. To be clear, in 1309 the Bardi, the Peruzzi, and the Acciaiuoli imported from the Kingdom 118,700 *salme* of wheat. In 1311, when the famine was raging, that number rose to 220,000 *salme*. In 1320, it was 140,000 *salme*. And in 1322, 144,000 *salme*. But the revenues received by the court bordered on the fabulous, even if you only looked at the arbitrage on variations in tariffs. For instance, in the year of 1333, on September 3, the fee was 12 *oncias* per 100 *salme*; two months later, those tariffs had practically doubled to 20 *oncias*! That means that for the export of 140,000 *salme* of wheat, the court enjoyed more than 17,000 *oncias* of profit, all captured by the top of the market with little if any trickle-down benefit for the less well-to-do. And who would willingly have given up that windfall? Certainly not a monarch well known for his proverbial greed...

Ironic though it might be, the royal court of Naples, whose osmotic interactions with Florentine high finance were one of its strongest buttresses, was absolutely incapable of giving up this relationship. And so, tragic though it may also be, we are forced to say that the king turned his back on his own people, sacrificing them by choosing options that brought greater personal benefit to him and his court. Paths that were more advantageous to the state. Whenever the problem of famines arose, every possibility was considered in terms of policies to limit the spread of hunger, be they police raids, house-to-house searches, or price controls. But the monarchy never took into consideration the possibility of interrupting the flow of grains and cereals to the large and ravenous international marketplace. And this was perhaps the largest and most burdensome ballast that worsened the social tensions arising from popular hunger.

And disasters occurred. It started in Barletta, in 1323. The Bardi, the Peruzzi, and the Acciaiuoli managed to obtain from the Curia Regia (the royal office) the usual right to import from the city 15,000 *salme* of wheat. The king issued the order, but the citizenry voiced its opposition. They said: If this wheat, which is ours, is taken away, then what are we supposed to do? Don't you know that "the threat looms of a very harsh shortage of victuals in the city?"[28] The agitation grew. The opposing forces squared off. But the Duke of Calabria weighed in and decided not to meet violence with violence. Instead he used tools of persuasion. He persuaded the people of Barletta to stand down. This time, it turned out for the best... but in the years to come, they were far less likely to stand by and watch impassively.

Seven years later, in Troia, in the Apulian hinterland, the populace was at the end of its rope. Everyone was complaining that there was nothing left to eat. That the only kind of cereal available to make bread was barley. People were looking around desperately for help. They wanted royal officers to make things better. But those same royal officers, confident that the city was full of hidden wheat, instead showed up and confiscated what little grain there was. They'd already taken 200 *salme* of wheat and 200 more of barley; now they confiscated another 270 *salme* of wheat and 235 *salme* of barley. In all the city, there was nothing left to eat. Not even what little had been set aside for hard times. Starvation and barley went arm in arm. And so it would remain for a long, long time.

Now we come to the year 1339. From the capital to the villages in the countryside, poverty and misery reached even less sustainable levels. The king admitted it: We're thinking about Naples first, which has greater needs given "its larger number of residents." The rest of the Kingdom could wait. The king stated once again that the main problem was presented by the *indebitatores*: unscrupulous merchants who were adopting the highly remunerative practice of storing up as much wheat as was available in order to steal a march on the harvest season, to buy grains when they were still in the field, and to sell everything, even at criminally high prices, and take advantage of the weakened position of the lowest and humblest. The king had spotted the culprits. A clarity of vision, however, that once again failed to hit the main target, which is to say the large Tuscan exporting operations, doubly bound to the finances of the state. And political action was still found wanting. The usual approaches were taken. Searches and confiscations. Public sales. Established grocery-basket prices. But most of the wheat, like a sieve with ever-growing holes, managed to elude all attempts to preserve it, spilling out in all directions.

The cities were suffering. Letters came from Giulianova to the court: there's nothing left to eat. Similar missives arrived from Vieste sul Gargano, not far from the wheat stores of Manfredonia, a town that suddenly discovered that it was poor as a church mouse and that there was nothing left to eat but what had been stored up in the royal warehouses, which were of course promptly plundered. Sinister reports came pouring in from all directions, from one end of the Kingdom to another, from L'Aquila to Reggio Calabria. And it wasn't really all that comforting to the people of the Kingdom to know that meanwhile, in Rome, people were going every bit as hungry, and that the Romans had a dream: to be able to feed themselves from the legendary granaries of Apulia ... and indeed in October of 1339 the gonfalonier of justice and the tribunes of the people of Rome demanded of King Robert the right to import from Apulia five thousand *salme* of wheat in order to be able to supply the Eternal City, confident that the Kingdom still had resources and wheat to sell. But Apulia didn't have so much as an ounce of wheat to put on the market. Robert, who had promised the Romans what they demanded, now found himself in an uncomfortable situation: Should he favor the city of the pope or his own subjects? For the moment, he ordered an investigation to understand the source of the shortfall. An investigation without any real solution, because the truth was right there for all to see. And he rejected the demands of the Roman populace.

Until the pot finally boiled over, after all that bubbling and seething. In December the patriarch of Aquileia tried to procure a thousand *salme* of wheat and export it from the Kingdom. He asked the king directly, who sent his officials to secure it at Barletta. But the people were having none of it. The mob shouted: Why are you depriving us of this wheat and sending it away up north? We've always given when asked. But must we go on giving? Is this justice? Taking from those who are already poor and have no other recourse? In the blink of an eye the crowd overran the wagons that stood ready to carry away the wheat. They kept the supplies from being loaded. The people began to loot and plunder, carrying off a thousand *salme* of barley. The funny thing is that the captain of the city, with all his family members, rather than weighing in to defend the Florentines, who were required to take care of warehousing and shipping the wheat, instead threatened them, attacked them, and went so far as to assault and wound several of them. They had nothing to do with what was going on, any more than did Lapuccio Bonaccorsi and Pietro di Stagio, who worked for Acciaiolo Acciaiuoli.

In Barletta, the situation was pure anarchy. Governmental control went completely off the tracks. The revolt spread. Robert didn't act the way the Duke of Calabria did. Words were not in order here. This situation called for brute force. So he unleashed full-fledged repression. And he ordered the justiciars of Capitanata and Terra di Bari to proceed, thus condemning the people of Barletta to bleak famine. In spite of these steps, the chaos grew. Hordes of brigands spilled out onto the roads of the Kingdom. Villages, towns, and cities all begged for aid, but none was forthcoming. In the capital, the ravages were appalling.

If that was the situation, who then to turn to? What saints could the common folk invoke for protection in order to get a crust of bread if the court and the king seemed miles and miles away, or just generally indifferent to the fate of their populace? Indeed, their rulers were actually ready to cut deals with the same people who were busy carrying off the wheat for their own ends. What's more, if anyone dared to raise their voice, the king's henchmen stood ready to mete out justice; they were unhesitatingly willing to resort to violence. In fact, they were the first to steal and make side deals with smugglers and fences. So, then, who could they turn to? Only themselves and their own God-given abilities. Making judicious use of violence, where necessary. Violence that now became commonplace and widespread. Uncontrollable. A violence that was the spawn of poverty and starvation, and that was a highly visible denizen of the Neapolitan hinterland: there thefts were commonplace, as were assaults and expropriations for the possession of arable farmland, or a working well, a vineyard, a wagonload of wheat or grapes. The tendency was to attack isolated land and farmhouses, places poorly endowed with methods of self-defense, but nonetheless rich, prevalently the possessions of churches and monasteries. More or less everyone went after them: ordinary farmers, village communities, and especially the *milites*, the leading figures in the aristocracy of the capital, members of the various noble factions. They were the most prominent families, and they became the leaders in the process of plunder, in defiance of both tradition and any sense of religion or law: families such as the Piscicelli, the Orilia, the Seripando, the Caracciolo, the Brancaccio, the Capece, the Zurlo, and so on. They left Naples and struck hard. They raped nuns. They stole what little livestock there was. They destroyed well-tended farmland and vineyards, thus setting back the harvest for years on end...

So there was hunger in Naples. Likewise throughout the West. And everything possible was being done to ward it off. Seriously, *everything* possible. There were those who prayed. There were those who looked to the heavens for an answer. There were those who marched in processions. Those who shouted curses at the rain and hail and took fright at the chill. There were those who folded over, heaving their last breaths, on the street corner, to die in convulsions. There were those who put their faith in their city and its administration to obtain a price for wheat, a price that might be, as much as possible, fair and equitable. There were those who sold the terra-cotta tiles off the roofs of their homes. Those who tried to push their way through a sprawling, unruly mob in the market square and faced off against the swinging clubs of Florence's Six of Forage. Those who decided that, in all this hunger, why not make even more money than they already had? Those who watched, in cold despair, as the ships of the Bardi and the Peruzzi set sail from their own home port, carrying off the wheat. *Their* wheat. There were those who took to the hills and became brigands...

...and others who reasoned differently.

Entrusting their woes to the only people who, traditionally, for centuries, long before the king, had actually looked out for their interests, safeguarding their lives and their families. The only ones who were ready to roll up their sleeves and take action. To help them emerge from the harrowing tunnel of hunger. Organizing their moves in advance. Helping them onto a boat. Putting weapons in the starving men's hands. Helping them to solve their own problems. Their hunger. At the very root...on this night in 1343.

III

MASTERMINDS AND PERPETRATORS

Ground Zero

I wouldn't want to give the reader the wrong impression. I wouldn't want to persuade them of something different from my intention. That I'm laying out some idea of a subversive banditry or brigandage where common crime is portrayed as some sort of "political" choice. A romantic parable set in a naïve utopia that turns to robbery as an ideological tool. A way of redistributing resources. A kind of emancipation from need, from hunger. In the absence of any responsible higher authority to watch over the interests of the weaker members of society. No, there's nothing of the sort in my book. And you won't find any *social bandits*. However, if a writer wants to tell the story properly, once that writer has clarified the motive for the November 1343 raid, we need to understand just who the masterminds were, how they acted, how they were attired. And exactly who their accomplices were, who the physical perpetrators. Thus explaining the larger context, with even the slightest detail. For that matter, is history not a narrative of details, allowing us to understand, in the final analysis, the larger and more general scenario?

The masterminds and the perpetrators in our story are face-less, nameless individuals. All we know is that the leaders were aristocrats, which meant they belonged to the urban elite. Individuals, we can safely presume, accustomed to issuing orders. Who came from one of two *seggi*, Nido or Capuana: names that, for anyone not an expert in the history of Naples, remain obscure, difficult to interpret. What about the names of the perpetrators? Do we have any way of knowing the names of those who took part in the assault on the ship? If we dig deep enough, yes, we can find the names. Indeed, we need only peruse a few books, especially books from the seventeenth and eighteenth centuries, packed with reports that are frequently surprising.

All the same, for now, I'm going to refrain from naming names. Not because I'm trying to build suspense. This isn't a detective novel. Rather, it's because I consider it a pointless exercise. What good does it do us, nowadays, to know whether this character or that individual was responsible for putting weapons in the hands of whoever brutally murdered the captain of the Ligurian ship? It does us no good at all. We're not holding a trial. And certainly not in a case dating back more than 650 years...In any case, at the end of this chapter I'll name a few names...

And they were some *big* names...

What I think, though, is that it's much more intriguing to understand another aspect of the case. We've established what objective the Neapolitans had in mind when they took action. But we should explain, point by point, exactly why they acted in the way that they did. Because what is so striking about the actions of 1343 is, admittedly, their unexpected rapidity, but we can confidently state that it was anything but the product of chaos. There were no mobs, no crowds, no scenes of people massing in disorganized fashion. No, there really weren't. The action was very tightly controlled. It was organized. *It was rational.* There were leaders and there were people obeying. There were clearly assigned roles. Roles that were clearly understood by all the participants. Participants who knew that there was a hierarchy, and that it needed to be observed. And the question I ask here is: Was the method employed simply the result of random chance? Or was the ability to organize *that way*, to assemble *that way*, to establish carefully assigned roles *that way* something inborn in the medieval Neapolitan world? Something bound up with an ancient, structural underpinning that belongs to the setting of city social life, as well as its mentality?

In this chapter, I will try to answer those questions. And I will do so by digging down into a well that will take us much further and much deeper than the year 1343. Back to the years that may constitute the genuine core of the city's history, when a universe made up of a thousand different social, economic, psychological, and attitudinal impulses all exploded into fragments, giving rise to an entirely new subject with a distinct identity all its own, the "Neapolitan nation." A birth that will allow us to discover not so much the names of whoever put weapons into the hands of the common folk in that now long-ago November, but instead to draw up a suspect sketch, a police Identi-Kit. A virtual archetype: a category that encompassed both masterminds and perpetrators. An Identi-Kit of the aggressive, hungry new Neapolitan, a man of both clan and family, a man quick to draw his sword, both solitary and violent. The progeny of a lengthy, *very* extended period of development that has a ground zero all its own, an unusual and tragic moment of inception. An instant amid which decisions were made that set the course for a deeper and more enduring fate that shaped the city's future life.

That ground zero, the catastrophic moment of inception when the city's embryonic form broke free and began its gestation, lasted for just three years. From 1137 to 1140. In 1137 one era ended and another began. That year was marked by a battle, the Battle of Rignano. As well as with the death of the last heir to the ancient dynasty of Byzantine origin that had ruled Naples for centuries: Sergius VII. He was the protagonist of an era that now belonged to the past, and he died in a paradoxical fashion. After withstanding Norman pressure for decades, much as other predecessors had

done, in the end he capitulated. But the sheer duration of his resistance stood out from the run-of-the-mill. That resistance held out
long after anybody else even believed in it, when all of southern
Italy, including Sicily, was already under Norman control (indeed,
the Normans used Sicily as the springboard for an incredible and
fast-paced conquest). A saga deserving a film of its own, epic but
pointless. And, inasmuch as it was the story of some of history's
losers, it's little known.

That it was already too late for the duke had become eminently
clear by early June 1135. The Normans were just a short distance
away, but there were still those willing to put up a fight. Sergius
still held a firm grip on power. And his *milites*, that is, his knights,
were still willing to follow his lead, as was the city's nobility. Naples knew how to defend itself. The Normans had previously, and
more than once, paid a stiff price for besieging the city, learning
at their own harsh cost what a losing strategy it could be to attack
Naples directly. The only way to take Naples was to starve it out.
Summer drew on. The Norman knights were suffering from the
heat, the lack of water, and the harsh conditions of the terrain.
King Roger II of Hauteville (Altavilla) wasn't willing to wait. He
lifted the siege and guessed, rightly, that if he wanted to annihilate
Naples, he'd need to go back to striking at its umbilical cord: its
roads, its supply lines. The Normans, from the surrounding castles
of Cuculum[1] and Aversa, spread out and ravaged the countryside.
They destroyed grapevines and burned crops. The effects of this
embargo began to make themselves felt. Famine began to break
out in the city, and it was a very different beast than the ones that
we have described before it.

Hour by hour, conditions simply worsened. The mercenar-
ies who were garrisoning Naples guessed that things were about
to turn ugly. And they took to their heels, leaving the duke even
more undefended than before. August arrived. Some reinforcements came from the sea. They arrived aboard Pisan ships. Those
vessels brought confidence, alliances, men, and resources. Roger
attempted another attack, this time from the sea. It failed. He tried

yet again, but this time a sudden gale scattered and damaged the fleet, which sought refuge in the bay of Pozzuoli. The historian Falcone Beneventano tells us that the king, realizing he could neither take Naples from the sea nor from the land, ordered the fleet to withdraw. He went back to a strategy of blocking all access, starving the city out. The city's hinterland was once again put to torch and sword by Norman knights. These knights numbered only roughly a thousand, but they were rapid and ruthless. The fear was enormous. Desperation was mounting. Groups of refugees fled the countryside. They arrived from the entire surrounding area and beyond, pouring right into the city. They came from as far afield as Benevento: roughly a thousand people, whole families in groups, with caravans and the pathetic belongings that refugees always carry with them. Other poured in from Aversa, Pozzuoli, Ischia, and the various fortresses that had fallen into Norman hands.

Such an embargo, a roadblock that relied on the means of that era, could hardly hold out for long. The number of Normans was reduced. From a thousand or so, it dropped to a squadron of no more than a few hundred. Knights who, alone, could hardly have faced off against open combat with the bloodthirsty Neapolitans. Still, those knights knew how to take advantage of darkness. They knew how to wreak havoc, set fires, and slaughter victims. To sow terror. The daunting wait only spread the virus of anguish. The city was on its last legs. The situation grew increasingly stark and dramatic from one moment to the next.

Sergius VII decided to break out of this stalemate. He went to sea and traveled to Pisa to join his allies. And at first they promised to help him, and then pulled back. Sergius had no time to spare. He went back to Naples. When he got there, he was tired, discouraged, demoralized, and upset. The embargo dragged on for months and months. It subsided, then strengthened, then subsided again. In waves. The Norman fist connected here and there, smashing constantly. More and more victims, damage, and fear. But the game was expanding. Naples became a pawn on a much larger chessboard. Not only was the city's defense at stake, so were a great many larger interests. The interests of other cities and potentates who were reluctant to see Roger's power expand. Among them, Pope Innocent II, the Pisans, the princes of Capua, even the emperor Lothar II, who was drawn into the fray.

The year was 1136. The emperor, at the earnest behest of the pope, decided to march down into southern Italy. He declared that, God willing, on St. James's Day, July 25, the invasion would begin.

Meanwhile Naples was dying. Old men and children fell where they stood. There was no more food to be had. Everything was running short. But the duke tried to rouse his populace. He urged his people to resist, to make a show of their ferocity. To think back to their history as a nation. The pride and dignity of those who'd come before them. The memory of the *milites*, determined to fight just as their fathers would have fought in their place. Better to starve to death than surrender, he told them. With a phrase that chroniclers record and which I find magnificent, because it's more than just a piece of well-tested rhetoric. In fact, it's a spirit of stalwart resistance that deserves to be remembered: *Mori prius fame malebant quam sub nefandi regis potest colla submittere* (Better to die of hunger than to bow our heads to an evil king).

Fortunately the emperor was drawing near: he sent letters from Spoleto and Pescara. He was about to enter Apulia. Sergius sent ambassadors. They approached the emperor. Together they established an alliance, the ambassadors spoke to him and regained a sense of confidence that, little by little, day by day, the siege was being shattered. Good news came to Naples. The city awaited the emperor. And so, even though Lothar was far from the city, the expedition still brought a beneficial sense of relief. The embargo was weakened. Still, it wasn't broken. Meanwhile, Lothar descended the Adriatic coast, passing through the towns of Troia and Siponto and arriving in Bari, where he slaughtered the entire Saracen garrison holed up in the castle. Meanwhile the other wing of his army, under the command of Duke Henry of

Bavaria, moved with the pope toward Naples. They freed Capua and entered the city. In July 1137, when the emperor issued the order to the Pisans, the prince of Capua, and Sergius VII to move against Norman-occupied Salerno, it was safe to say that the embargo of Naples had finally come to an end. The siege had lasted two years, from June 1135 until July 1137. With how many dead men, what with the generic tide of war, destruction, and famine? I believe a great many dead men.

And so everyone headed for Salerno. But now the horizon had shifted. The duchy, by this date, had already ceased to exist. By now, it consisted of Naples and nothing more, with no hinterland to speak of. All surrounding territory was now under Norman control. And Roger was a wounded lion. A critically wounded lion. But not a dead one…in fact, if anything, his strength was perfectly intact. Intact and protected by the vast basin of resources and energy that he could command from his dominions. While it might be possible to strike Apulia, who possibly had a long-enough reach to harm Sicily? Too far away! And it was from Sicily that the greatest aid and reinforcements might perhaps arrive. As if that wasn't enough, soon afterward, the emperor Lothar died. And with his death, the operation of stitching together a political alliance to put up a muscular resistance against Roger rapidly collapsed. It had proved useless. A castle built of sand that simply crumbled, and all at once.

Now Roger could go back on the offensive. One after another, all the outstanding outposts of resistance fell. Roger's fury knew no bounds. Alife, Telese, Capua, and then Pozzuoli surrendered. The noose was tightening. In Naples, too, it became clear that hope was no longer a strategy. All alliances proved short-lived. What few friends they'd been depending on were either too far away or had been scattered to the winds. Resistance was done for. The only possible solution was capitulation. The duke knew it. And, as Falcone Beneventano writes, he converted to loyalty. Loyalty to his one-time enemy, to Roger. And he prostrated himself at Roger's feet. Assuring him of his friendship and loyalty.

Not even two months had gone by since the end of the block-
ade. And the panorama of alliances was transformed on a wholesale basis. With a waltz in which the most clamorous developments
had to do with Duke Sergius, who now surrendered after having
fought against the Normans for years and years. Sergius went over
to the side of his former archnemesis, the Norman king, Roger.
He even went so far as to follow Roger into battle against his old
friend, Ranulf of Alife. They fought at Rignano: the date was October 30, 1137. Roger was beaten. It is said that thousands of men
were killed or taken prisoner. But the Middle Ages was never a
time of impressive precision on such matters, and the chroniclers
of southern Italy in particular were undistinguished. The one
thing we can be sure of, however, is that the king took to his heels.
He rode all night, finding safe haven in Salerno. Whereas Sergius
VII was killed in battle. What mockery fate brought to him: to be
killed by the swords of his own former friends and ex-allies.

   Thus ended five hundred years of history. The history of the
independent duchy.[2]

Now What?

The day after the battle, the people of Naples had only one question: Now what? Because what had just happened was truly
unprecedented. For the Neapolitans, accustomed to virtually im-
mutable social structures, unchanging, anchored to centuries and
centuries of habit, what was happening now amounted to a radical revolution. Up till now, there had been a single and overarching power to govern them: their rightful rulers, the dukes. With
a municipal dynasty that had embodied political legitimacy for
centuries. Political and institutional legitimacy. Based on a single
point of reference, one that drew its legitimacy in a straight and
unwavering line from the emperor in Constantinople. And that
was the highest authority that any Neapolitan could easily imagine, safely perched as they were on the farthest-flung outpost of
the Byzantine commonwealth.

On the other hand, the Neapolitans still thought of themselves as half-Greek: by the laws they lived by; by the way they reckoned dates (counting from the year of succession to the throne of the latest Eastern emperor); by the way they drew up documents and by the special class of municipal notaries, the so-called *curiali*; by the organization of their monasteries, the overwhelming majority of which were bound up with the rule of Saint Basil, not the rule of Saint Benedict... What's more, the guarantor of the entire system, as well as of the delicate balances both internal and external, was the duke. The element of connection (though increasingly distant) with that entire universe, glittering with history, power, and charisma, the new Rome, Byzantium.

There was one thing, then, that everyone was well aware of: the traditional world was not merely sunsetting, it had *already* sunset a while ago. People were going to have to start thinking in alternative terms. And they would have to come up with some new way of coexisting with the Norman Kingdom, which is to say, with a typology of powers that presented themselves as terribly unfamiliar from the Neapolitan point of view. Under these new masters, there would no longer be any talk of the city. Of the principality. Of any aggregation of a potentate, governing over a regional scale. No, now the conversation concerned a territorial context that for the first time assembled under a single denomination peoples of differing cultures and origins: the Muslims of Sicily, the Greeks of Calabria and Sicily, the peoples of the cities along the Adriatic coasts, the Langobards of the Apennines. People of the Tyrrhenian Sea, with one foot in the vineyard and the other in the boat, like the people of Gaeta and, above all, the people of Amalfi. The Normans: new masters who—even as they accepted as their working model many fine elements deriving from the Muslim and Byzantine civilizations, especially where the practices of government were concerned—nevertheless offered a subversive idea when it came to how they conceptualized their form of government. They no longer wanted to divide. They wanted to unite. They wanted to create a monarchy. And, indeed, they had already created one. The only structure that remained outside of it was Naples. And they were determined to impose a new, alien model of government, alien not only to this spot on the map but also to the rest of southern Italy. Both alien and utterly unknown. But one that constituted the standard model throughout much of Europe. Feudalism.

For the Neapolitans of the post-Rignano era, however, there was another question that must have kept people awake at night: Once this new order had been established, what role do we Neapolitans play in this structure? What margin of autonomy will we enjoy? These were necessarily the issues at the core of any discussion, once the power vacuum began to make itself felt (and make itself felt it did...), given the fact that the duke was gone and the Normans had not yet taken possession of the city.

Then something happened. In this challenging condition, Naples transformed itself into a sort of political laboratory. On the basis of a twofold body of experience: founded first and foremost upon a legacy of traditions and customs that had become consolidated over the centuries and that therefore demanded to be recovered and, where necessary, redeveloped and newly imposed; second of all, it was based upon the specific characteristics of the city's resistance to the Normans, where much of the effort, in terms of resources, energies, privations, and sorrows, had been supported by the nobility. The aristocracy, necessarily, demanded a leading role in the decision-making that ensued.

In the two years and eleven months that passed between October 30, 1137, and the end of September 1140, when King Roger made his ceremonial entrance, with full pomp and circumstance, into Naples, arguments raged throughout the city. Words flowed in rivers on the subject. Myriads of opinions that, sadly, we can only guess at. For anyone who writes about history, this is the hardest thing: trying to get the gaps in the record to speak from the past. And there are a great many gaps. Still, let us try to evoke them in some manner, these words, which basically follow two paths, each path functional and roughly equivalent to the other.

The first path attempts to create a bridge with a very long span, on the following premise: since the reign of the dukes had come to an end, and some understanding of that transformation demanded to be elaborated, it became necessary to find a form of municipal power to take its place, something equally effective and something that could ensure a transition while making it possible to consolidate a structure that could endure over time.

The second path, on the other hand, was contingent and immediate in nature and was bound up with the relationship with the Norman king. This was the nature of the reasoning: Naples still has a lot of things going for it. It's still a powerful city. A wealthy city, thanks to its surrounding territory and its port, one of the largest in all of southern Italy. The Normans were unable to take the city by brute force. We Neapolitans talked terms, we didn't merely collapse in surrender. If we want to, we can make an issue of this great vitality we possess. And while we may not be able to express it in terms of outright conflict, we can make our weight felt in terms of our contribution. And Naples, with all its economic and military energies, can guarantee an ongoing contribution, indeed a great many contributions. No doubt about it. It can be a useful factor in the consolidation of the new Kingdom.

So when the Neapolitans were preparing to present themselves with the Norman king, they were determined they would refuse to do so with heads bowed, prostrate and willing to swear unconditional obeisance. Instead they were eager to find shared territory for an understanding in which, though they might be the losers, they could make it clear that they'd lost honorably, maintaining a condition of equilibrium between Naples and the crown. How was that to be managed? The solution was political: the Neapolitans should negotiate an agreement with the king.

What I'm summarizing here should be imagined as applying to a sequence of diplomatic initiatives, decisions, advances and reversals, and discussions among the leading proponents, which must also have affected the other components of society. Reflections that blended fears and tensions, certainties and failures of comprehension. With an ultimate solution that was attained, first and foremost, on the matter of the form of urban government. A form that was in line with the evolution that had already begun at the end of the duchy, established by the agreement signed by Sergius VII with the families of the urban aristocracy. (The *pactum*, as this agreement was known, probably dated back to 1129.)

The expedient they came up with called for a very simple thing—namely, that they would seize power: the hegemonic families of the city. With this determination: that they would exercise "sovereign power in the context of their quarters and regions, articulating the function of sovereignty in domestic matters and almost certainly on a territorial basis, but perhaps deciding in a *council* of all the noblemen or of the representatives of the nobility of the individual regions into which the city had been divided, concerning the general problems of peace, war, and truce, as well as the introduction of new rules and customs, the administration of criminal justice, and so on."[3]

This was the turning point, and it imposed on the city an unprecedented appearance. There was no more centralized power. After this the decision was made that government should be exercised by family-based clans, closely linked one to another on the basis of relations between heads of families, regulated either through bonds of kinship or of personal friendship or else by hierarchies of clientelism and identity. Each of these groups controlled their own zone of jurisdiction, where each clan enjoyed sovereign control and settled their own issues and disagreements. Then, if they wished to make common decisions that affected the collective as a whole, the *nobiliores* of each zone, the noblest of the nobility, would assemble in council. And deliberate for one and all.

It was a clever move, no two ways about it, and it reinforced an ancient structural feature of the city that dated from the early Middle Ages. It set at the center of the new situation not a municipal government, with its deliberative assemblies and its popular gatherings, but rather a structure parceled out into areas of jurisdiction controlled by clans, which is to say family-based consortia that penetrate with their influence into every ganglion of city life. That penetration unfolds through an articulation in which the relations between topographic dimension and social and family control prove to be extremely powerful. And the city's existence is guaranteed by all these organisms that on a more or less cellular level bond each to the other, constituting a single organism when necessity demands, especially at moments of self-defense against threats that could easily compromise the safety and security of one and all. In the run-of-the-mill course of daily life, on the other hand, when there are no emergencies imposing demands of unity, these individual organisms can live unbound, in complete independence of one from another.

This was a decisive turning of the page in a city where, with this subdivision among and between areas and quarters, there was also a heightened reinforcement of the differences between one zone and the next. With a continuous assembly, disassembly, and reassembly of the various alliances on the basis of geometric arrays that vary from one episode to another. A process characterized by rivalries and tensions, of course, but also by alliances and clear alignments and affiliations that regain force at points of danger. That was the keystone of this highly original and renewed urban universe, which possessed—in the many quarters and clans that made up its controlling fabric—the foundation of a governing apparatus that was so deeply rooted that it endured for centuries. Until it became the city's own consciousness.

Late September, 1140. In Naples, the weather was fine. It may seem like a cliché, but the sun really was shining. Sunshine and only a few clouds. People were thronging the streets. In the windows, there were women of all descriptions, both young and old. All of them curious. Hanging beautiful fabrics from the balconies. Brightly colored, even garish. They were waiting for the king to go by. Roger the Norman. The king of this new Kingdom to which Naples now belonged, from this day forward. The *nobiliores* and the *milites* sallied forth through the Capua Gate, Porta Capuana, to welcome him. They stopped a short distance outside the gate, at the *campo de Napoli*. It was a scene of celebration and triumph. Those who were present reported that they could scarcely believe their eyes. The king was welcomed by a frolicking, festive crowd. What did you expect? Neapolitans making noise, on their worst behavior? Well, you would have been wrong. It all unfolded in the most orderly fashion imaginable. Guided by well-coordinated direction. Everything that happened was planned out and choreographed. With previously established rituals. Are we or are we not talking about a city that was heir to more than five centuries of obeisance to the manners of Byzantium? And so there was a determination to give the king an impression of a city fully conscious of itself. An image of dignity in the presence of that city's longtime enemy and rival. In fact, no one had entirely forgotten the grievous events of the siege that had taken place only a few years previous.

Now Roger was king. And the king demanded and expected respect.

The welcoming ceremony had a powerfully symbolic significance. The procession set out. It unfolded past all the city's elders, abbots, and clergy. They sang hymns of praise and thanksgiving. And they accompanied the king to the city gates. There a sort of handover of status took place: the clerics withdrew, making way for four noblemen. As if to say, with great clarity: from now on, the sacred power stands aside for the profane, worldly power. Which in this city was the real power. The noblemen took the reins of the king's horse. They walked ahead of king and horse, ushering Roger into the city and heading for the bishopric. Now the entire populace could see King Roger. The king rode down streets and lanes, followed by a long and winding procession. At last he arrived at the bishopric, where he was met by Archbishop Marino, who led him into the suite in the archiepiscopal palace, where he was offered accommodations.

All right, let's stop right here. Focusing on this freeze-frame. With Roger, back turned to the crowd, striding through the front portal of the archiepiscopal palace. Now let's take a quick step backward. We've seen this whole process of the entrance into the city once before, with lovely women leaning over balconies, the splendor and the ceremony that—let's be clear—are more than merely window dressing. More than mere obsequious kowtowing. This is the official seal set upon a lengthy negotiation that between July and August of 1139 unfolded between the king and several delegates of this new and very particular group of Neapolitan leaders. Among whom there was also the archbishop himself as a representative.

How were these Neapolitans chosen? Surely on the basis of prestige and personal authority. But also on the shared mandate of their fellow citizens. They were nothing less and nothing more than ambassadors, without any other particular power over their peers. What were they offering? They were offering their city and their loyalty to their new king. What were they demanding in exchange? There was a definitive discussion of that matter at the Castello del Salvatore, the castle later renamed the Castel dell'Ovo. The representatives of the families met to negotiate with Roger over the price of surrender.[4] The *nobiliores* formed a compact and homogeneous group. They had considerations they wished to offer in terms of decision-making, among them the profitable state of the city's economic balance sheet, the municipal wealth built on their land. And of course, unfailingly, there was the matter of the city's great military strength. They came to an understanding that the correct price that the king was expected to distribute to each of the *nobiliores* was five *moggi* of land and five *villani*, or serfs. How many such noblemen were to receive these benefits from Roger remained a dilemma. But we know where Roger obtained this land that he proceeded to distribute: from the properties that had once belonged to the dukes, taken by force during the latest episodes of warfare. They constituted what was traditionally called the Publicum, the public landholding, distributed over the city's hinterland and long the possession of the ducal family. In this case as well the fragmentation of a vast rural possession, made up of dozens and dozens of parcels of farmland that extended all around the city, was heading in the right direction: which is to say the direction of gifting each of the representatives of the new urban power with a slice of rural landed property to add to what they already possessed, in what amounted to an increase in their power. And we need to emphasize that the *nobiliores* managed to obtain another concession from the king: that the hinterland, in administrative terms, should remain under the city's control. That way what had once been Naples's area of socioeconomic influence over the territory remained unchanged and in fact was consolidated. Therefore, from the point of view of both property and administration, they reached a strategic result of extraordinary importance for Naples: the agricultural area around the city, which guaranteed subsistence and wealth and which had been taken by force by the Normans, was now once again property of the city. And it would remain such.

One last thing, in parentheses: it is clear that the strength and efficacy of Roger's donations surely lay in the prestige that issued from them. Still, though, they had another intrinsic value, namely that of establishing, within the city as well as outside it, a clear hierarchy, because there were those who reaped benefits and others who didn't. We don't know what criteria the king used to make those choices. What we do know, though, is that those choices became an important factor in differentiating within a given class. A term of discrimination. As well as a springboard, for certain clans, toward great new fortunes, as was the case for certain members of the prominent Capece family.

At the end of these three years, what was the upshot? Well, it seems that Naples, in this phase, experienced birth pangs that were certainly painful, but when viewed in perspective, beneficial. After centuries, there was finally a change. And for once, not a change that simply assured that nothing really *did* change. No, an elite was getting organized. It adapted to new circumstances and invented new institutions that were cellular—franchised, so to speak. Each zone of the city fielded a group of *nobiliores*, a primitive nucleus of what subsequently became the nobility of the *seggi*. They claimed for themselves some of the powers that had previously belonged to the duke. Among them, the most powerful—or the luckiest—incorporated into their family estates what was offered them by the new Norman sovereign. A solution that served to dismember and modify one of the principal and most venerable city institutions, that of the Publicum, which returned from the ducal family, as we have seen, only now badly fragmented, to the Neapolitan people, subdivided among various groups. The Publicum was no longer under a single organic authority, however. And this new development hinted at something more objective and substantial: what amounted to the formation, over the course of the twelfth century and the century that followed, of autonomous spheres of power led by coteries and family clans. These gradually, over time, increased their prestige and their ability to intervene, through the splitting up of the urban fabric and the appropriation of much of the system of urban defense.

The Transition

Defending themselves and their city had always been one of the prime concerns of the Neapolitans. They had long been masters at transforming their city into an impregnable fortress. The city's particular nature played a role: it stood atop three hills that were, at certain points, very steep. An appearance that is nowadays all too easy to overlook, given the way that the city has been smoothed out and leveled over the past thousand years. Everything was once far steeper. Vertical. Difficult to scale. Getting from the beach to the city entailed quite a climb, with staircases large and small, alleys that were steep and twisting, and narrow *pendini*. It was a place where you had to attack spaces on a continual basis.

The most imposing defensive structures were erected along the seacoast, built atop the ancient Roman walls as early as the seventh century. With continuous modification, as the coastline pushed farther and farther out and the beach made way for new settlements, huts, docks, piers, mooring structures, sewer and drainage systems, kilns for baking mortar and blowing and molding glass, bundles of wood to dry linen, which was set out to soak right there, in the principal curve of the port. With huge edifices to mark its boundaries. To the west, an especially large structure that would become the place where the Pisan colony would settle, also known as the *castellione novo*. Which had nothing to do with the Angevin Castel Nuovo, but was much older, possibly dating back to the turn of the tenth century, and equipped, in any case, with ten towers. Overlooking the entire port, however, was a large tower, the Torre Mastra, separate from the walls. And then, heading westward, a great many other towers, higher or lower above the sea, or else practically at beach level: a Cinta tower, a Romeno tower, a Ferule tower—it, too, unconnected to the enclosure wall but set farther forward. And a series of gates, like the Calcara gate, the Plaia or de Appaia gate, the Portanova gate, the Monaci gate, also known as the Cannabari gate, which is to say the hemp workers' gate. Some of those gates had a singular and unexpected cross section. With a structure that, moving from the line of the enclosure wall, opened out like a sort of powerful quadrilateral, as was the case of the Calcara gate, equipped not only with a main entrance but also with a *pusterula*, a side entrance or secondary gate. A space of considerable size, standing more than a story tall, and enclosing within it a succession of small courtyards, wells, a few workshops, colonnades of arches, kilns, ovens, and basins in which to steep linen fabrics. Even larger dimensions were to be found in the *barbacane de mare*, the sea barbican, where we find the "new gate," or Portanova, which was far more elongated than the other city gates and led directly out onto the beach, and in front of which the Norman customhouse had been built.[5]

A landscape rendered even more intricate if we add to it the series of breastworks and *moricini* (smaller partition walls) that enclosed the areas that had sprung up along the coastline and connected the areas less fortified to the enclosure walls, properly speaking. An agglomeration that was already densely populated and that could certainly be chaotic at times: with shops, warehouses, mercantile outposts, and *cellari* dug into the terracing of the slope. Sudden drops in the ground level where you might turn a corner and find yourself in a public bath or a synagogue. Wells and springs, which sharply increased the levels of humidity. Ruins of ancient Roman arches that had been reutilized in a wide array of manners, ranging from homes to shops and even public baths. It was a coacervate: the most visible essence of a city on the hunt for a brand-new identity.

This distinctly military character can also be seen in other sections of the walls. For instance, the vast number of towers. Or the massive strength of the eastern fortress of Porta Capuana, through which Roger entered in 1140: a full-fledged castle all its own that had long constituted the principal bulwark against the Langobard incursions from the east and which, in its physical composition, resembled the structure of the sea gates. Even inside the city, though, the houses with their particular structure— enclosed around a courtyard that you could only access through a narrow portal—must not have presented an especially inviting silhouette to anyone aspiring to enter by force... self-sufficient structures in case of attack, with their well, their enclosure for barnyard animals, warehouses on the second floor, or even higher up, in the attic. There are still traces of these configurations in the older parts of the city. Buildings that boast myriad numbers of staircases, walkways, windows, and loopholes that solved problems of lighting, space, elevation, all of this, including elevated passageways leading across from one building to another, a further defensive support structure available if needed.

The description of a military apparatus of this scale is seductive, but it doesn't delve deep enough. The reason is that we're missing a fundamental ingredient to any understanding of the city's spirit. The militarization, in fact, hardly ceased once you passed through the city gates. In fact, it also extended to the immediate hinterland, the crucial lungs of the Neapolitan economy. Suffice it to remember just what the situation was in the Phlegraean Fields, where both the stretch of coastline and the roads that ran along it had always represented a source of danger

Angevin
Naples

N

0   250   500 m

1. Cathedral
2. San Lorenzo Maggiore
3. Santa Maria
   Donnaregina
4. San Domenico Maggiore
5. San Pietro a Maiella
6. Santa Chiara
7. Santa Maria la Nova
8. San Pietro Martire

9. Castel Nuovo
10. Sant'Eligio
11. San Giovanni a Mare
12. Santa Maria dei
    Carmini, also called
    Santa Maria del
    Carmelo
13. Sant'Agostino
14. Santa Maria Egiziaca

15. Annunziata
16. Castel Capuano
17. The Malpertugio Area
A. Via San Biagio dei Librai
B. Decumano Maggiore (Via
   dei Tribunali)
C. Largo delle Pigne (Piazza
   Cavour)
D. Piazza del Mercato

to the west of the city. They had been routes taken by both Saracens and Langobards, fortunately for the Neapolitans without any irreparable consequences. Therefore, it had proved necessary to protect the area. The first ones to devote attention and effort to that project had been the Byzantine generals in the seventh century. The Neapolitans continued work on it. There sprang up a network of castles, the largest among them the Castrum de Serra, next to the pass of the same name, on the volcanic hill that rises next to the plain of Quarto. That castle served the vital function of guarding the Campanian Way (Via Campania). Next to the Lake of Averno, on the other hand, stood the *castra* of Sant'Arcangelo and Tripergole. To safeguard the short stretch of the Via Domitia or Domitian Way, there was Cumae, the site of an especially brutal battle of the Gothic War, reinforced around the year 730 by Duke John to ward off the Langobard threat. To garrison the Cape Miseno promontory, a *castrum* was built, only to be destroyed by the Saracens in 845, after which it was replaced by the Castrum Sancti Martini, which stood on the western side of Monte di Procida. Finally, on the far side of the Gulf of Puteoli (or Pozzuoli), probably on the island of Nisida, stood the Castrum Gipei. Even more interesting, Pozzuoli, too, as we know, lost its role as a trading center and metropolitan settlement in the transition from late antiquity to the Middle Ages, took on a closed aspect, and turned military in focus. The summit of its acropolis was in fact surrounded by walls and towers, many of which were built with recycled building material stripped from buildings of the ancient city. Frequently in contemporary accounts the word *urbs*, which had been used to describe it, now began to disappear. Instead, a different word began to crop up, one that was better suited to a castle-fortress: *castrum*.

In the new Norman order, who would be assigned control of the Neapolitan defensive structure? Who would take on the burden and underwrite the cost of strengthening the walls, protecting them, and finding funds to see to their maintenance? This was, as the reader will surely understand, a further issue, and one that was truly vital in nature. After all, keeping the walls strong and functional was hardly a luxury. It was, in fact, fundamental to any situation in which warfare, and specifically siege warfare, was the order of the day. And precisely because of a painstaking devotion to the maintenance of its walls, a continuous process of modernizing and adapting them to increasingly sophisticated requirements, Naples had managed to hold out for years. Resisting the assaults of all comers. Even the Normans. Never once succumbing.

As long as there had been a duke to rule the city, he'd taken care of things. Or perhaps we should say: his government had taken care of things. Either directly, through an early, embryonic administrative structure, or else by proxy, through the good offices of his *clientes*. There were various ways of raising money. One might be managing the revenues said to be *pro partem publicam*, such as the tariffs that had to be paid to import or export goods through the city gates. There was a clear interest in urban safety that, we should point out, remained a constant policy, even of the very last dukes. It became manifest at the times of worst crisis, both in terms of investing money and energies to encourage the recovery of construction in the zones of the city hit hardest by Norman aggression, and in terms of encouraging repopulation by luring groups of immigrants, right up to the end, in the third decade of the twelfth century.

But now, in the course of transition from one power to another, matters became complicated. With one decisive tile added to the mosaic: everything that had been assigned a public connotation due to its intrinsic strategic importance and the city's fundamental necessities when it came to defense—things like gates, towers, and enclosure walls but also wharfs, mooring sites, landing spots, et cetera—now no longer possessed that qualification. And that was due to the developments in political and social conditions. So now who was responsible for exercising this option of protection? The new Norman government assumed no obligations: it seemed to stand above the fray, refusing to weigh in, declining to issue orders, leaving the initiative to the Neapolitans.

Instead, it was the city's noble families that took on the burden of ensuring the maintenance of the city's defenses. And they did so through a method that was rapidly becoming common: namely, by apportionment. By fragmenting control of the defensive apparatus among ten, a hundred, or even a thousand different actors. With a single question: If we have to do it, what money are we going to use to do it? In order to solve this problem, they chose the most practical approach: the money that once came to the duke *pro partem publicam* in order to ensure the city's defenses now passed to them. And they deducted the *sexagesima*—or sixtieth part—of the tariffs "on all the merchandise that arrives by sea to the port of Naples, or the wharfs of Amalfi or Sorrento, but also on the products that arrive by land or which are exported from the same port or which are purchased in the city and weighed on its public scale (*statera*)." With an overall revenue amounting during the Swabian years to two hundred *oncias*. Revenue that was still being taken in at the beginning of the Angevin era, so much so that in 1269 the king ordered that the customs agents and warehousemen of Naples hand over that sum to the representatives of fifty-seven families of *milites* who had the right, it was said, "by venerable custom," to receive the two hundred *oncias* deducted from the fiscal revenue. An assignment of revenue that remained in force until at least 1341.[6]

Fifty-seven families: the core of Neapolitan nobility. Of the men of the clans who were gaining the upper hand. The protagonists of this extraordinary transformation that came about amid the transition between the ducal era and the Norman era. When what had once belonged to the collective was now privatized, to be bought and sold. And the city, its defenses, and the soul that had ensured its survival, from *res publica* to *cosa nostra*. Belonging to a great many individuals whose profiles matched that of the families, the clans, the coteries. Those individuals had names: Boccapianola, Caracciolo, de Aversa, Boccafingo, Oliopesce, Capece, Tomacelli, Minutolo, Brancaccio, Bonifacio, Scriniario, Caputo, Fellapane, Poderico, et cetera.

The process of privatization of public elements of power is a common aspect of much of the medieval universe. A process that in the Neapolitan case constituted the cornerstone upon which the entire edifice of urban society was built. That process became customary to such an extent that, for instance, the very shares of fiscal revenue received by the families became subject to inheritance, as well as commercial transactions, assignment, donation, and even fractional inheritance. With examples that echoed from the Norman era to the Swabian period and then up to the Angevin times, with aristocratic control of shares of the fiscal revenue registered on the *piazza maggiore* or the wharf known as the Molo dei Capece, controlled directly by the family of that name (which represented one of the many forms of enrichment of the clans, along with the workshops and farmland cultivated outside of the city).[7]

This matter of the private management of certain public resources, such as defense structures, is one of the elements of the environment in which, much later, we'll see the men of 1343 swimming, like fish in the sea. A transition that was clear to their contemporaries, and that has been documented even by those who've studied the history of Naples of three and even four centuries ago. One such scholar was Camillo Tutini, who writes with succinct clarity that the nobles "took care to reinforce and guard not only the gates but also the towers of the city during times of war and pestilence," adding that "where every *seggio* took care to guard its own gate, with the assistance by day of the nobles of that piazza along with the common folk, and taking great care in the evening to make sure the gate was shut tight."[8]

The System of the Seggi

And so here we are, face-to-face with this object, so obscure and by and large unknown to the majority: the *system of the* seggi. Different terms are used to define them. *Tocchi, sedili, teatri.* Pieces, seats, theaters. And of course *seggi.* Benches.[9] To the untrained eye, simply meeting places. And locations for interactions.

Connivance and collaboration. Which is what they are. That said, let me reiterate, only to the untrained eye. Because, to quote from the writings of Tristano Caracciolo, there's a minor nuance we can't ignore. It would be more accurate to specify that it's not merely an ordinary meeting place. Not a place of leisure or amusement. No, it's more a place of *consensus*. A place where an assembly makes a decision. The people of a neighborhood. A *rione*. An area. A neighborhood, or a quarter. What exactly were these *seggi* like? It's not as if there's a model. People gathered wherever was most convenient for the nobility of the quarter. Under the porticoes or along the *supportici*. In the cloister of a church. In an atrium of said church. In the passageways of a monastery. Next to *estaurite*. Or *diaconie*. In the vicinity of ports and towers. Wherever they developed, there necessarily had to be one basic trait: they had to consist of two separate parts. One larger section, for the *nobiles*, to which everyone could gain access and where it was possible to meet, gather, and discuss, but in all likelihood not actually make binding decisions about the business affairs of the quarter. Then, next to that space, there was a small room. Private. Small. Rather dark. With a table and a few benches. Going into that room was not a common prerogative, open to one and all. Because it was the exclusive domain of those who were in command…

Heads of households. Super-noblemen. Namely, as we were saying, the *nobiliores*.

Just when this form of social aggregation and control came about is not clearly established. In the thousand or more documents from the ducal age that it has been my pleasure to read over the last thirty years, no mention is ever made. Because, naturally, the *seggi* were a superstructure that came into being and developed after the end of the duchy and that sank its roots into this new family-based social fabric, reduced to parcels and subdivided. Before that, the city seemed to have been split up differently. By regions, such as Marmorata, Summa Platea, Ficariola, Portanova, Domunova, Balnei Novi, and Calcarie. The *regiones* didn't follow a subdivision with any clearly defined boundaries. No: everything looks pretty flexible. Pretty arbitrary. Starting in the fifth decade of the twelfth century, within the context of this age-old subdivision, like mushrooms, we start to see these unusual things, the *seggi*, spring up. In 1146 the Tocco dei Cimbri, in 1150 the Sedile Furcillensis, in 1170 the Tocco di San Martino, in 1177 the Tocco de illis Acciapaccis, and so on. In the end, there would be no fewer than twenty-nine. Which spread over the age-old topographic network in no particular order. In an anarchic fashion. With only the vaguest of connections with the *regiones* where they stood. For instance, in the region around Somma Piazza there were three. In the region around Porta San Gennaro there were three more. But in the region around Santi Apostoli there was only one. And around Marmorata there were more. Some of the names of the *seggi* are linked to churches and chapels where in all likelihood the families gathered. In other instances, they hearken back to the name of the old region, or else the name of a gate or a tower. In many other cases, on the other hand, what prevails tends to be the names of the family groups. Those clans grow and tend to mark the territory with their presence, as if to say: this area belongs to this or that family, the second area belongs to another family, the third to yet another, and so on: Cimbri, Acciapacci, Saliti, Malaci, Calandi, Cannuti, Mamoli, Mannocci, Zurli, Loffredo, Caputo, Gattola, Pistasi, Griffi, Costanzi, Donnorso, Carmignani, Franconi, Rocchi…

The *seggio* becomes a natural center for supervising the quarter, fundamental in terms of internal matters but also for interactions with the other city *seggi*. With a size that could certainly vary from *seggio* to *seggio* but that never encompassed single-family aggregations, save in a single case, that of the Griffi family. The purpose, therefore, was to incorporate into each of the *seggi* as many families as possible, with understandings among the heads of families. For instance, in the Capuana region, the *seggio* of Santo Stefano included eight families while that of the Melati included two. In the region of Montagna, eight *seggi* (of the Calandi, San Paolo, the Mamoli, the Cannuti, Somma Piazza, Porta San Gennaro, the Ferrari, and the Saliti) included forty families, ranging from a minimum of two for the *seggio* of the Calandi (the Calandi and Cotugno families) to a maximum of eleven for the *seggio* of Somma Piazza. In Nido, in the *seggio* of Arco, there were eight families, while in the *seggio* of Fontanola, there were six. In Forcella, in the *seggio* of the Cimbri, we find a record of seven families; in that of the Pistasi, three, and so on.[10]

It often happened that one clan would prevail over the others and take on a role of command. That would increase the clan's impact on society at large and its military capacity. The most notable example can be found in the history of the Capece (or Cacapice) clan of the *seggio* of Capuana, which in 1266, during the civil war for supremacy in the quarter with the Caracciolo, chose this strategy once it realized that the Caracciolo had greater strength in sheer military terms. The chosen solution was to *stringere lega* (make an alliance), which is to say absorb into their core group as a clan other families from the same *seggio*, substantial but of lesser nobility: the Aprano, the Bozzuto, the Latro, the Piscicelli, the Minutolo, the Scondito, the Tomacelli, all of which would end up representing the various branches of the Capece family. Thanks to the absorption of these new families, the Caracciolo were pushed into a corner for a while, and a sort of gigantic power structure was created. It takes no stretch of the imagination to envision their resulting influence over municipal matters. This surely constituted a factor favoring equilibrium and reorganization in the power relationships within their quarter.[11] Other times, a clan might fragment into a thousand smaller rivulets, something that was not uncommon when a family expanded to an excessive degree, overflowing its jurisdiction and branching out, developing a great many subgroups, or arms, like the goddess Kali. These arms would frequently break away from the main body. In their turn, they would engender many separate core groups, now autonomous, forming new branches. These might exist on what appeared to be an independent basis, with no connection to their origins, but in reality these were still core groups intimately connected to each other. This is what happened with the Brancaccio family, *copiosissima d'huomini e ragguardevoli massimamente nell'esercitio dell'arme* ("numerous in their men and especially noteworthy in terms of their use of weapons"):

> Some of them, on a whim or a caprice, or as a way to stand out or differentiate themselves from the other, or to denote some honorable enterprise or heroic action performed, whether in peace or in war... with a variation in some part of their coat of arms, with some addition made or with appellations (*soprannomi*) added to some of them, names that continued down the generations in their successor as was customary in olden days to add names either as a joke or a pastime or to denote in them some quality of the soul or the body or to distinguish themselves from others, or else by some dignity obtained, and over the course of time they came to form out of a single trunk and different families various separate branches and lines.[12]

Soprannomi. Nicknames and appellations. Signs of distinction. Distinguishing features that wound up establishing the differences among lineages. These are the elements that Carlo de Lellis indicates to describe this phenomenon, which I'd describe as something like a schism within a schism. If you ask me, it's nothing more than an extreme symptom typical of the expansion of the presence of certain clans in an urban fabric that tends to expand in accordance with the family's corresponding ability to grow and compete. With branches that progressively grow, until they take on their own distinctive appearance. As was the case, in fact, with the Brancaccio clan, which germinated at least a dozen other clans: the Imbriaco, the Dullolo, the Fontanula, the Briele, the Impelloni, the Zozi, the Casillo, the Abate, the Foschi, the Cardinale, and the Vescovo. While a very similar situation unfolded for the Caracciolo and the Siginolfo.

In the fragmentation bound up with the emergence of these family groups in search of prominence and moving in to conquer

municipal power, the establishment of a *seggio* with their own
name or else a climb to power within the ranks of life in the quarter, meant in either case, for a clan—and for its clientele and its
acolytes—not only the attainment of the prestige of a given status but "the effective tool with which to solidify power acquired
into political heft, in order to enjoy the benefits of having a voice
among the members of the apparatus that controlled and directed
the city's life and fate."[13] In other words, anyone who led the *seggio* also led the quarter: the physical location where the clans ran
the zone's administration; they established the criteria of external
defense and the tasks relating to the public order; they monitored
and protected public morals and customs; they established com-
pacts of a religious nature; they settled matters relating to justice
and the law as well as inheritance and estates; they mediated feuds
and disagreements between clans, except in matters of life and
death.[14] That was the framework within which the members lived
their lives, from cradle to grave, from birth to death. Here a profound solidarity bound together the clans that formed part of this
system. And each individual, man or woman, was assigned a role
that they performed to the best of their abilities.

But the *seggio* was more than that. It was a meeting place, an
assembly point, somewhere you could idle away the hours or cel-
ebrate with parties. And the system of the *seggi* worked, because it
was clear to everyone that only the ruling families and their clans
were responsible for assuring the city's governability. They were
also responsible for solving one of the thorniest problems for social coexistence as a whole, which had to do with the guardianship of underage orphans. Which is something we should stop to
consider, however briefly.

Being a minor demanded certain forms of guardianship. The
one thing was, though, that in accordance with the tradition of
Roman law, there was more concern with guaranteeing the minor's patrimony than the minor's own well-being. To prevent
abuses of property, it was customary for the public authorities to
appoint a guardian, who was entrusted with the administration

of their ward's property. In the city, for centuries, this task of appointing guardians was carried out, as we can certainly guess, by the duke, who chose a guardian, or as the term ran, an *advocator*, a responsibility that was imposed and mandatory. It seems strange perhaps in our era that such great importance should have been assigned to such a thing. But important it was. These weren't superficial problems, these were substantial issues. Matters relating to management of public and economic life, given the importance of the property that was at stake. Usually, what was at stake was land, the central issue in all economic interests for any citizen of the Middle Ages. And as long as the ducal family preserved its power, it never budged on its rights in this matter and exercised its role without a break. Indeed, the last administrative act performed by Duke Sergius VII was to choose a guardian to safeguard the interests of several underaged members of the noble de Abatissa family.

In this case, too, we would have expected to see that function be handed over to the new Norman power. And so it was. But in only one case, dating from 1141, when it was Peter, the new *compalatius*, the representative of Roger II in Naples, who supervised the selection of the guardian. Immediately thereafter, though, something happened. Perhaps it was a disagreement within municipal society with respect to the royal representative. Or else it might have been something as simple as a call for adherence to the terms established by the Neapolitan nobility in the agreement stipulated with King Roger II. The fact remains that after this case the control of minors and their property became once again a responsibility of the city. And specifically of the *seggi*. It would in fact be the leading representatives who took on this task: the *nobiliores de regione Sancti Pauli maioris, de regione Signa, de regione Portanobense, de regione Capuana,* and so on. The Neapolitans, in other words, expected to and did in fact preserve their autonomy in a matter of such supreme importance. They demanded exclusive jurisdiction in this matter, without any potential obstacles from any central power. A solution—as you can easily see—that was very much a sign of the times. Because, once again, it dismembered and modified one of the principal and original municipal jurisdictions, exactly like what happened with the Publicum, which had been broken up and subdivided among the various groups, the various *seggi*, the various clans, without there being any longer a single organic authority to turn to.

In the city there existed other points of family aggregation above and beyond the *seggio*, and they tended to involve the sphere of the sacred. It was here that ties of solidarity between one family and another were reinforced, cementing alliances, bonds of kinship, and wedded unions. Like the *estaurite*, from the Greek *stauros*, cross. If we want to try to understand what they were, we'd need to imagine something that approaches the votive shrines that you can still see as you walk through the most ancient parts of Naples. These are altars that stand permanently at street corners, where they served to collect offerings and donations to be used "for the benefit of poor maidens in order to allow them to get married, for invalids, the imprisoned, in other words, to help with all needs those who were members of their own district," as Giuseppe Sigismondo wrote in 1788.[15]

Their construction was bound up with the worship of the cross, an ancient cult widely practiced throughout all of Christendom and focused on two holidays in particular: May 3 (*inventio*, Feast of the Cross) and September 14 (*exaltatio*, Exaltation of the Holy Cross), without overlooking the Adoration of the Cross, which took place on the occasion of the processions around Easter. This very same period was, for Naples, the season of the greatest celebrations, dating back as early as the ninth century, if not earlier, in part due to the notable influence of the Eastern churches on the city. Palm Sunday was the crowning moment. The archbishop, along with the chapter of canons and the other clerics, would arrive at the church of San Giorgio Maggiore (Saint George Major). He would stop in the square, or *platea* dei Cimbri, where he was awaited by crosses covered with blessed palms from all the *estaurite* of Naples carried by their respective priests. Two of those, that of the Santi Quaranta Sant'Erasmo (Saint Erasmus), upon the archbishop's starting call, would run a race, and whoever won was awarded a prize.

What was the origin of the *estaurite*? They originated spontaneously. Every quarter, in much the same way as what happens now with the votive shrines, encouraged the creation of an altar in accordance with their own will, spirit, and devotion. Nonetheless, they began to represent something more than their original idea. From centers of religious gathering, they were transformed in the new family system into yet another organism for social control, in which, for instance, it became possible to express through offerings (and the control of the same) the privileged status of one family with respect to another, or the most senior of all the clans with respect to all the others. And the life of the *estaurite*, which at first consisted of the spread of the cult of the cross and the exercise of charity, resulted in the development of two new factors. In other words, they became "a powerful instrument bonding together the families who took part and they stimulated the religious activism of the lay members, who soon hoped to extend their control from the *estaurite* to the churches they belonged to."[16] An activism that had one precise objective: to allow the family clans to have a role in the selection of the clergy. This provoked quite a few conflicts with both the ecclesiastical authorities and with the religious entities that demanded the rights of patronage over various city churches. And so it turned out that the *estaurite* became a further institution of family control of the quarters. Comparable to that of the *seggi*.

Another place where the clan recovered its identity-based roots is in the family churches, recorded historically as far back as the ducal age, when there were a great many of them, more than thirty. Many of them are dedicated to the Virgin Mary, marker of a cult that was already widespread as early as the year 1000, with titles that contain references both to the Madonna and to the family group, such as Santa Maria de Merulo Comite, Santa Maria de domino Atriano, Santa Maria de domina

Galatea, Santa Maria de domino Reclauso, Santa Maria de illi
Bulcani, Santa Maria de illi Pappacavallo, and Santa Maria de illi
Paracefali. It's plausible that these were one of the earliest places of
social gathering and interaction where alliances were sealed, not
only based on blood ties but also on other factors of broader commonality, dictated by creed and faith and shared identity with the
same rites. What we can say for certain is that these churches fit
into a model that was quite widespread in the city: the visible and
material aspect of a location where *parentes*, members of no special
organization, were qualitatively transformed into associated *consortes*. That is to say, into groups that, through the ownership of a
church, could now aspire to assimilation into the city's elite. How
should I describe them? The formula that springs most easily to
mind is that they were status symbols that further embodied the
family's prestige within its own context of identity and affiliation.

In the formation of the private churches, there never appears
with any clarity a single-family nucleus dominated by a prevalent
surname. Actually, what we already see in the pre-Norman period is the presence of a great many nuclear families, understood
to be, among them, a set of *parentes et consortes et domini*, who
shared out among themselves, collectively, the ownership of the
church. These family groups formed consortia whose origins, unfortunately, have proved impossible to track back on the basis of
existing documentation, even though I believe that both religious
factors and family solidarity guided the decisions. Let us not forget the economic motivations, as attested by several episodes: the
control of a church meant, for one or several families, also taking
possession of its assets, which either provided substantial revenues
or else could be rented or sold. So much so that the churches themselves might be broken up into shares (*sortes, portiones, uncie*)—
which then matched up with an economic equivalent, generally
speaking, land—each parcel of which could easily be transacted
or marketed. That fact attributed a nature, so to speak, to each of
these churches that remained, as it were, no longer solid, but now
liquid,[17] thanks to the use of shares as tools of exchange.

A reality, the world of the private churches, of which we have much less evidence in the Norman period. And that is for one objective reason: the documentary discrepancy with respect to the ducal period, with a sharp tilt in favor of the earlier period. In any case, the phenomenon of the private churches persists, with some significant examples to offer. For instance, that of the monastery of San Gregorio de Regionario, which in 1152 belonged to a consortium that included several powerful families of the urban aristocracy, including the Bulcano, the Brancaccio, the Morfisa, the de domina Mira, the de domino Lamberto, and the de domino Catio. These clans were joined later by others that surfaced at the end of the ducal period and under the new Norman domination, among them the Summonte, the Caetani, and the Sergonata. Family groups that in their control of the entity operated "in their own name and in the name of all their relatives and consorts," as the traditional formula informs us.[18] A continuity that on the other hand can be ascertained for the Angevin period, when the phenomenon of family patronage of churches is documented as truly numerous.

Clans and Monasteries

The theme of the monasteries directs us to one of the leading scenarios for confrontation between the clans in this period. To consolidate one's authority, in fact, meant for many of them using their own people, both men and women, to penetrate into the lives of the cloisters, driven not only by motives of a spiritual nature—though make no mistake, those had considerable power. But in this peculiar and distinctive amalgamation that we now call the Middle Ages, where the religious and the secular were so intimately intertwined, so much so that it frequently becomes impossible to spot the differences between one side of the divide and the other, participating in the life of a monastery really was a significant objective for a clan. To enter into its *sacri dittici*, or sacred diptychs, to obtain prayers of suffrage for the soul of a head of a clan of particular prestige, or to become a consort and parent of the same saint, male or female, to whom the monastery was dedicated, through offerings and donations that publicly highlighted the power attained by the group in question, meant a great deal for any given family. Equally important was to have that relationship with the abbot or abbess. It meant: we're at the top, and at this level we see ourselves and only a very few others, and higher than this it's not possible to go, inasmuch as our clan has established through the monastery's intermediation a direct relationship with the divine.

A power from which all other powers naturally descended, though they might be more prosaic in nature: the exaltation of a status gained, the option of controlling the enormous patrimonies owned and enjoyed by the monasteries, the forceful emergence into the very dynamics of the cities, where being able to speak out in an assembly might mean a great deal, such as being able to exploit that potential as a further flywheel of government over the city, but also over the hinterland.

The history of certain monasteries was closely bound up with the larger Neapolitan story. Among them was the Monastero dei Santi Severino e Sossio (Monastery of the Saints Severinus and Sossius), established in the aftermath of the stormy events of the year 902, when the city had almost fallen prey to the Muslim troops led by Emir Ibrahim, when it had been necessary to carry off in haste and fear the relics of Saint Severinus of Noricum, which had been held on the promontory of Pizzofalcone—another location that was central to Western history, being the last residence of the last emperor Romulus Augustulus—to within the safest circuit of city walls.

The number of monasteries was roughly thirty, which with the exception of just a couple were all inside the city. The vast majority of them were based not on the Benedictine Rule but rather on the Greek, Basilian rule. The monasteries possessed vast estates, accumulated over time primarily thanks to an exorbitant number of donations that—a unique condition at least for the Tyrrhenian cities—had involved the entire populace, in a vast collective movement. The function that these monasteries served had been very important, and not merely on a social level. They had been responsible for encouraging the campaigns of colonization (or reclamation) of the territory, by means of contracts that greatly encouraged farmers. These contracts demanded of the farmers, in exchange for the right to cultivate and harvest their lands, relatively affordable fees or perhaps a portion of the yield from the harvests, a share that those same monasteries proceeded to offer for sale on the markets. Markets that, between the tenth and twelfth centuries, were thriving to a notable degree, as the larger trade across the Byzantine and Muslim Mediterranean continued to grow.

The monasteries had been, in particular, the great engine providing a linkage between the ducal dynasty and the urban world, with constant, symbiotic, dialectical union. As a result, many of them, one way or another, appear to have been subject to the ducal families' direct control. To name just one example, the foundation of the monastery of Santi Severino e Sossio, dating from 907, was a joint venture on the part of Duke Gregory and Bishop Athanasius. The two extra-urban monasteries of San Salvatore *in insula maris* and Sant'Antonio *in scapula montis Pausilipensis* belonged to the ducal family, especially San Salvatore. Likewise, the powerful monastery of the Santi Sergio e Bacco (Saints Sergius and Bacchus) also appears to have still been under their aegis in the first few decades of the twelfth century. The dukes were in charge of life there, down to the details of their organization, as was the case with the Cenobio dei Santi Gregorio e Sebastiano (Cenobite of the Saints Gregory and Sebastian), a single entity created in 1009 by Duke Sergius IV through the fusion of four earlier monasteries. For the consecration of that monastery, the dukes selected a formula that brought together a reminiscence of the classical city, a hint of patriotism, the aid of the divine, and their current concrete political power, in which Naples becomes its predecessor, the ancient Greek settlement of Parthenope, and the city is "a Deo protecta *nostra* civitatis."

In order to encourage the monasteries, the dukes were willing to deploy all sorts of donations, offerings, exemptions, and privileges. They conveyed substantial portions of the public lands and were compensated in exchange by a service similar to the service we find recorded in Byzantium as being performed for the emperor: a prayer to honor the duke and the nation that said duke embodied, as, for instance, Sergius III required around the turn of the millennium. An attitude that translated into the handover of a part of the Publicum but that, in the perverse circuit that developed between the ducal house and the monasteries, still remained in the hands of the dukes inasmuch as they were the masters, or *domini*, of the monasteries. The donations, until around 1050, are generic in nature, unaccompanied by any detailed descriptions of what was donated. The proportions change with Duke Sergius V, who rules for more than twenty years, from 1050 to 1076, a period in which this process of conveyance of wealth, titles, and rights undergoes a radical transformation. Exactly what is the turning point? A privilege dated 1075 with which the duke conveys to his Monastero del Salvatore (Monastery of the Savior) the entire southern line of the city walls, all included: walls, towers, gates, breastworks, described as *iure nostri publici*, under public control. Also, among the last donations made by Duke Sergius VII, there's the entire handover of all that remains to him of the by now heavily chipped away at Publicum to the monastery of the Santi Severino e Sossio (Saints Severinus and Sossius): in all, fifty-two items, including fields, farming hamlets, vineyards, and lots more, all located in the hinterland, including the farmers with their families. A patrimony that outlived the duke and was transformed between the twelfth and thirteenth centuries into lands that the monastery rented out: and these were the boom times that marked the definitive liftoff of the religious institution's economic wealth, an estate that lasted for many centuries yet to come.[19]

This entire story that I have insisted on recounting down to the smallest details does, in the end, have a point. In the new transitional phase, how should we characterize the relationship between these religious entities possessed of such enormous potential, so crucial both to the city's economic life and its social life, and the new family order being established in the city? Very simply, the clans recognized those entities' role and their resources, and they understood that one of the ways to lay their hands on those resources and get control of the entities was, to put it plainly, to invest money. Lots and lots of money...

Let's see what happens at the powerful nunnery of San Gregorio Armeno (Saint Gregory the Armenian). Beginning with a matter that is only apparently marginal in nature: the amount of land that it purchased over the course of the twelfth century. Between 1133 and 1138 the monastery acquired only a few pieces of land. And it invested a capital of 116 *solidi* into gold *tarì* (the coins then accepted as legal tender in the city, as they would continue to be for the entire century).[20] That situation reversed, in a way that smacks of the uncanny, beginning precisely in the year 1141, when there was a sudden and substantial surge in land buying. The purchases increased tenfold, and in fact the monastery spent no less than 1,647 *solidi* in gold *tarì*! What is the explanation for this shifting of gears from a small-scale land policy to such an incisive investment involving such enormous sums? Was there someone behind all this? And if so, who? The money for these investments didn't come from donations. No, it seems to have come from appanages, a further reflection of exactly what's happening on a symmetrical basis in the city. What exactly are we talking about? Not everyone could afford to send a daughter, a granddaughter, a niece, or another female relative to become a nun in a monastery of such great social prestige as San Gregorio. It was really quite expensive. In fact, each woman, on becoming a nun, was required to perform an act of great economic significance: purchase an asset (ideally a well-cultivated parcel of land). And they would do so with money received as a gift from their family. An asset that, as a rule, was maintained during the nun's lifetime as her own source of income. But the moment that she died, that land became part of the monastery's patrimony (or, as was frequently emphasized, part of the *infirmarium*, the structure designed to provide assistance to the sick). It did not return to the family. And the monastery's estate thus grew considerably.

The appanage was beneficial both to the nuns and to the nunnery, or monastery. For the latter, it was a sort of long-term investment that could be collected on the nun's death. As it were, deferred to a later date. For the nun, it was a guarantee of a sort of pension—a form of rent—on the property purchased by her family, with the possibility of feeling like a landowner and therefore in a certain sense autonomous and independent, in a condition of superiority over the other nuns, for the rest of her natural life.

This phenomenon of the appanages was a substantial one. And it was one that families climbing the social ladder threw themselves into. It was a large-scale game, with many implications and connections, and it developed like a spiral that spread as it rose. The more the monastery increased its ability to exert pressure on the city's vital ganglia, the greater the number of clan members eager to become part of it. The greater the increase in demand for entry into the monastery, the fiercer the competition among the families to see who could purchase more valuable land to donate to it. It turned into a battle that brought together economic capacity and social prestige, where the final objective was inclusion in one of the key locations of urban life. And the families paid for lands— handsomely cultivated lands, rich, complete with houses, stables, facilities for winemaking, and lots more—in cold, hard cash, solid gold coins, at an average of more than one hundred *solidi* per transaction. The protagonists were the families we know, all members of prominent clans, all boasting names of ancient nobility: among them the de Domina Maria, the de Domino Pandolfo, the Capece and, most prominent of them all, the Caracciolo. Alongside them were also other families who were trying to make their way into the Neapolitan elite, such as the Frezza, a family of Amalfitan merchants, who thus manage to carve out for themselves a slice of social visibility in the municipal environment.

That created, basically, a system *ad excludendum* to which only the members of the more prosperous classes could gain access, with a hierarchical makeup based on wealth, thereby configuring the marginalization of families and groups that, lacking capital, could no longer hope to gain admittance to a religious institution of such charisma and authority. The protagonists of this new form of exchange were dynamic operators, such as the Amalfitans, who glimpsed an opportunity in their acceptance into the ranks of the monastery for a further aggregation into the city's elite. And then there were the members of the most powerful and prosperous clans, among whom we find those who were most flexible and open to change and who chose to use the monastery as a passkey for their further social climbing; by the same token, there were also those who, in a more conservative mindset, found that the space of the cloister offered a reassuring dimension of continuity.

The whole thing was steeped in a logic of concatenation and interdependence in which, for the entire urban society, the growth and consolidation of individual monastic institutions were perceived as elements of growth and prestige for anyone involved in them—be they families or individuals. With no contrasts in interests and with a substantial commonality of visions, lifestyles, and values.

The relationship between the monasteries and the leading members of the families might also express itself in another fashion. By encouraging different types of relationships—where if today one was controlled, at some future date one might also hope to become a controller. The story of what happened between the families of the *seggio* of Calcara, not far from the sea, and the monastery of San Salvatore *in insula maris* is truly significant. And it really does explain a great deal about the abilities of certain clans to insinuate themselves into well-consolidated traditions of social management, eroding them from within until, in the end, they were able to devour them whole.

Located where the Castel dell'Ovo now stands, the monastery was the beneficiary in 1075, as I have previously described, of a donation of an extraordinary nature: it received from Duke Sergius V the walls, gates, breastworks, and towers distributed along the part most strategic to the city's defense, namely the port. The monastery, which was under ducal dominion, wasted no time and set out to contribute, so to speak, to the collective effort during the long resistance against the Normans, by encouraging financing for the reconstruction of the waterfront area, which had been so heavily hit by the siege. Under the monastic government, the area grew, because San Salvatore managed to operate simultaneously as an element not only in the coordination of religious life but also of social and economic activity. The monastery owned workshops, it owned the gates through which passed goods subject to tariffs, and it owned several churches, including the church of San Bartolomeo—an *obedientia*, which was a sort of subsidiary of the monastery. Dedicated to San Severino (Saint Severinus), it was the operative branch of a main entity that stood some considerable distance away, outside of the city, on the islet of Megaride.

The siege by Roger II in the 1130s did nothing to undermine this power, which persisted, with an intensification of the collaboration of a number of families in the quarter—in a logic, once again, of coordination and mutual aid. While the monastery managed and ensured support that was more than spiritual in nature, the families operated on local and practical terms, safeguarding everyday life, under what we might describe as the benevolent gaze of the monks themselves. This bond grew and strengthened with a barter of a religious nature resulting in the foundation in 1179 of a congregation connected to the church of San Bartolomeo. An extensive group of families worked to create a *communitas et fraternitas* and to provide their help for the construction of an edifice *cum Dei adiutorio*, with the assistance of God. All the noble families of the area pitched in. That included all the heads of family—no fewer than thirty-nine of them, from Giovanni Pentalaro to Piero Pulderico—of the *seggio* of Calcara. In those same years, though, some of these families decided that this state of equilibrium was no longer acceptable. And among them, there was one clan in particular. The name was Caputo. They, too, had participated in the creation of the Confraternita di San Bartolomeo (Confraternity of Saint Bartholomew) and they had grown up in the shadow of San Salvatore. Under its power. But the new social and political dynamic now pushed them into action. They were no longer satisfied with moving in the wake of the monastery. This role of leader played by the religious entity was becoming a burden. Whereas they as a clan were growing in number.

They were further driven to take action by their ties with another clan that formed part of the congregation of San Bartolomeo, members who not only lived in the same quarter but actually in the same building. One clan on one story, the other on a different story. They were called the Gambitella. Some of them were actually the most powerful men in the quarter, speaking in military terms. It was in fact no accident that they lived right inside the Calcara gate, or Porta di Calcara. They were, in other words, the cutting edge in terms of the city's self-defense, summoned to protect this crucial element of the city walls. On a permanent basis. Established in their ancient and traditional abodes. Absolutely uninterested in moving from that spot, averse to the idea of going to live in other *regiones*, or other *platee*. Because "as relatives they almost never left their quarter or their street, loyal to it not only because of blood ties or shared interests, but most importantly bound by the need of bringing efficacious and concerted actions in the cause of defending against the city's enemies."[21]

And the Gambitella were not alone. They expanded, establishing other alliances that indirectly strengthened the Caputo. Their relatives were men in other important clans, such as the Mastromaione and the de illa Portella—a name that, in and of itself, constitutes quite a program, in the way that it indicates their roots in the local area. And the four families created between them an imbrication made up of marriages, ties of friendship and camaraderie, and descendants. The *compari*, the cousins, the uncles, the godfathers were too numerous to recount. The clan was forming, and the heads of the clan were the Caputo. It boasted a clear and well-defined hierarchy, where they were the leaders and everyone else was a foot soldier. So what did they do? They went straight to the heart of all power in the area, which was the monastery. And they took that monastery apart, dismantling it little by little. They asked for the rights to use houses and workshops from the religious entity, all of them in the area around the Porta di Calcara, especially at the time of the institution's greatest weakness, when it was being channeled into the monastery of San Pietro a Castello.

These assets, we should emphasize, can be found a few decades later in accounts that no longer describe them as property of San Salvatore but of the clan alone. And once the clan had made its money, it also started to buy houses all around the area, expanding the size of its landholdings. With a compactness of property that became increasingly well defined. Until the clan had stamped its imprimatur on the entire quarter, which thereafter began to lose its original topographical connotations. Until finally everything had become the unrivaled dominion of the Caputo, who had thus established themselves as one of the most important clans in the city (and so they would remain for a very long time).

A transformation that was quite normal for the contemporaries of this era, when it was common for streets, gates, and houses to lose their original attributes and take on others better suited to the aggressive new arrivals. But here, in the area around the port, the onslaught really was something. The gate, the Porta di Calcara, became the Porta dei Caputo. The *seggio* that once had the same name as the gate now became the Porta dei Caputo. The principal tower, adorned with statues from the classical era, became known as the Torre dei Caputo. The street that runs through the district, or *borgata*, became Rua dei Caputo. The Caputo family became *numerosi e prodi nelle armi* (numerous and known for their prowess with weapons), the owners of an agglomeration of houses that Carlo de Lellis described as "quite grand and magnificent,"[22] a settlement that rose up from the seashore and ran all the way to the present-day location of the Convento di Santa Chiara (Convent of Saint Clare). It stretched westward, nearly all the way to the landholdings of the Castagnola family, the clan that owned the powerful tower known as the Torre Mastra, beside which stood the *estaurita* that belonged to them. Or the houses and the family *seggio* of the Griffi. Meanwhile, in the other direction stood the tower of the Romeno family and the landholdings of the Bonifacio and the Costanzo families, among which, in the Angevin era, there emerged the none-too-welcoming figure of Giacomo, familiarly known as Spatinfaccia ("Sword in the Face"), who, true to his name, was one of the most violent protagonists of the period.

The center of the Caputo's power was, naturally enough, their family *seggio*, the former *seggio* of Calcara, now, of course, the Seggio dei Caputo. It was surrounded and therefore guarded by the clans of the Mastromaione, Gambitella, and de illa Portella, whose houses were all dotted around it. It had been built directly atop the age-old gate, now the Porta dei Caputo. Let me make myself perfectly clear: when I say atop, that's what I mean. Atop. Not next to or inside of. Just try to imagine it: sitting directly on this massive, squared-off structure that looms over the port. Perhaps featuring porticoes or loopholes opening out toward the beach. At once a place of physical observation of the stretch of waterline and of the layout and social makeup of the quarter. The first documentary record we have of it dates from 1193, but it was surely much older than that, by at least thirty or so years. It was possible to enter it through a series of steps connected by one or two catwalk terraces, lined with gates, doors, and loopholes that were most likely guarded by sentinels and watchmen who made it impossible to attack. Impregnable. With a large hallway that allowed entrance to the main room, which had been donated in perpetual concession by the monastery of San Pietro a Castello to the Mastromaione family themselves.

The Caputo weren't the only ones to experience dynamics of this kind. Let us take, for example, the Vulcano, who controlled a real pinch point, masters as they were of an enormous square

tower that commanded one of the most important intersections
in the urban road network. Or else the Costanzo, who, *viri armi-
potentes et strenui*, "having joined the militia of the sea, chose to
move down by the water to live on a street that, even now, is still
called the Vico de li Costanzi," in an area not far from the Porta
dei Caputo. A family that grew in power, with a major naval and
military role, that, as we learn from accounts of the time, controlled a "great clientele of Neapolitan people, which gave them
the right to meddle where and when they pleased in all Neapolitan
business."[23]

What about the central power? Could the Norman king not
intervene in any way? Of course he intervened, through the person of one or several of his representatives, such as the *compalazzo*
or the *comestabuli*. They, however, were often denizens of the system of the *seggi*. As we can clearly see from an eyewitness account
dated 1226, in the heart of the Swabian period, when during a
very serious clash between the Genoese community and the Pisan
community, to which I shall return on a more specific basis, the
ones deciding the outcome of the matter were, aside from Matteo
de Acerra, seven *comestabuli*, all of them members of the militia:
Giovanni Trentademoni, Sergio Tortello, Sergio Guindazzo, Ligorio and Sergio de domino Landolfo, Tommaso Aldemari, and
Pietro Caracciolo.[24]

Loyalty, Honor, Memory

The character of the clans leads us to delve still deeper into the
physiognomy of this municipal world. We shall do so in such a
way as to draw closer to our objective of designing an Identi-Kit,
as detailed as possible, of the "ideal Neapolitan type." Because
thus far I have focused, lingering extensively, on the formation of
that universe and on its fundamental structures. But what about
the attitudes? What about the behaviors? Is there anything we can
say about the mindsets, the mentalities? The political and social
conditions that produced this Neapolitan society had their sunset

long, long ago. That said, beneath the surface, there continue to flow moods, feelings, and passions that have settled, creating layers of sediment, and even turned gangrenous, dating back to that extremely productive twelfth century.

With a process that would slide from structure to superstructure. Neapolitan society at that time was a society long since based, as we have seen, on the idea of military defense. The man who counted most in that society was a *miles*, a knight. It seems that he wasn't guided by a written code of rules, but rather a series of simple guidelines. Camillo Tutini offers a few indications:

> When a Neapolitan noble in the old days was about to receive the honorable title of cavalier (knight), he was expected to meet six conditions. First, he could not be a *negotiatore*. Second, his family of birth had to be examined. Third, he was expected to swear an oath of loyalty to God, the prince, and the republic. Fourth, he was expected to wear a sword. Fifth, he was expected to bear the sign of the militia, and sixth, he could not be a minor, in terms of age.[25]

The *miles* is distinguished from the rest of municipal society, from the *populus* or from the *mediani*, a fluid social class from which, at intervals, a few families might break loose with aims of entering the aristocratic elite on the strength of their newfound political or economic importance. The status of the *miles* was based on certain tangible elements that differentiated him from the crowd, such as the fact that he wore a sword in public, or other signs that are not specified in this case but which we can try to imagine: special attire, colors, insignia on his shield with the family emblems, et cetera. Then there are other restrictions: age, which cannot be younger than twenty-five, meaning a well-consolidated maturity with respect to a society that skewed very young, as Neapolitan society must indeed have been. He could not engage in discreditable professions, such as engaging in trade, an ignoble pursuit befitting only deplorable individuals. A limitation that in all likelihood only referred to people who actually had shops and dedicated themselves to the purchase and sale of inexpensive items; it probably did not concern the work of major merchants, especially if we consider the continuous intrusion into the ranks of the nobility of members of the merchant trade of Amalfitan origin. With one stunning example of assimilation, from the early decades of the eleventh century, and involving Sergio di Pardo Amalfitano.

He came from the coast and was a merchant with interests extending along the entire Tyrrhenian coastline between Amalfi and Naples, a landowner with assortments of farmland, buildings, castles, forests, orchards, and slaves, and who could afford to deal in luxury objects from all over the Mediterranean basin, ranging from Spain to the south of France, from the Byzantine and Muslim worlds; in his last will and testament, dated 1025, the only interest that he expressed—and he practically shouts it to the sky—is that he wished to be considered for all intents and purposes a *miles*, an active member of this municipal world. A knight belonging to the Neapolitan military force.

Sergio knew that such a connection, perhaps more than his landowning and his economic wealth, would be the one element that, in Naples, would reinforce social consensus in favor of himself and his family. And so he wished his children to continue along this path, helping to "soldier and defend by serving as knights in accordance with the customs and usages of this city." And for that reason, he divided into four quarters his collection of horses, weapons, armor, and vestments (*omnes armas et loricas et caballos cum illorum paraturis*), one quarter for each of his four sons. And he ordered that this equipment, which was fitting and proper for the militia, should never be scattered or given to anyone else, but always remain in the possession of his sons. Because we can imagine these signs, the family arms, painted with the colors of the clan—these are the marks that distinguish them, those who are *milites*, from all the rest of the citizenry.

In the final analysis: the military prerogative was to remain obligatory and exclusive for the principal branch of the family tree, and it was jealously preserved, as an element distinctive of its status. A branch that would later establish a bond with the clan of the Capece, considering that Sergio's granddaughter Mira would marry a certain Sergio Capece, bringing with her a sizable dowry and unmistakable benefits to the rise of that family.[26] The other element was the pairing of loyalty and honor: toward God, toward the king, and toward one's own city, the *res publica*. Loyalty and honor were first suckled along with one's mother's milk. With the very first rudiments taught while one was learning to handle arms and armor. Felt on the skin before absorbed by the brain. A pairing of qualities that constituted a sort of secular religion to be consulted from time to time, every day. A full-fledged pedagogy, as Todeschini writes so effectively, certainly not concerning our context but in words that lend themselves perfectly to the Naples of the time, "the separation of *animal* men from *spiritual* men."[27] A *regime of conventions* where those who failed to comply with them, those who tried to deny them or subvert them or who behaved in ways that failed to correspond to the existing and previously established schema, were therefore disturbing the moral order that underlies general rules of behavior. Such a thing, of course, absolutely could not be allowed. So anyone who did it was out on their ears. Rejected, segregated, pushed away to the outer darkness of the social sphere. Such a person was—to use a term that is popular still today to indicate a traitor, a breaker of oaths, the *pentito* of the clan—the *infame*.

The code was the element of distinction that defined the spaces of social inclusion and exclusion. Which established who could take part in the larger life of the community as a whole. With a scale of values and functions that conferred a degree of prestige, no longer bound up with the individual as such, but rather to his membership in the group. Belonging to a group of families (the Pignatelli, the Caracciolo, the Romeno, the Brancaccio, and many, many others) was what conferred identity. And the greater the degree of participation and proximity to the top of the pyramid (in a hierarchical scale that went from clients to relatives, family

members, blood relations, comrades of various sorts—*compari*
and *comparielli*—and clan chiefs), the more one enhanced one's
personality, one's visibility, the perception that others had of you.
Because, in Naples, "belonging" meant "being." In a universe
where recognition of status—that is to say, in a comparable fashion
with other shared settings throughout the Europe of the time—
was not so much bound up with the way we see it nowadays, with
individual merit, the logic, as it were, of the self-made man, but
rather of the group, the clan, the family, and in particular the position and the profile that each individual took on in that context.

This was the situation in Naples, that of "the social order, that
is, within the sphere of the distribution of honor,"[28] according to
the ever-valid expression of Max Weber, with a lifestyle that is,
in every way, in keeping with the ethical norms of that environment. Where group discipline penetrates every aspect of everyday
behavior. This makes it clear that whoever is in charge sits high
above everyone else (as stated, *lo capo di tutti*). Superior, powerful, and what matters most, immune to the control of others, even
that of the established authorities. Each of the *nobiliores* was, in
fact, the absolute chief of his quarter. *Rex in Regno suo*, the king in
his own kingdom, limited only in his choices by the general rules
of behavior. Made different from the mass of the citizenry by two
specific factors, already identified succinctly by Tutini: bearing
arms, that is, the ability to exercise the monopoly of violence; and
the ability to rely on a genealogical memory that could be identified by one and all (through the possibility of *examining his family
tree*), the seal of approval that assigned the definitive prize of a
recognized social authority.

Concerning the first point, we'll offer just a few words, given
that the entire consideration that we've provided thus far regarding the development of the control in military terms of municipal spaces assigned the monopoly of force to the clans. This was
accepted by one and all as legitimate, with an equation: being
strong meant being powerful. Through this monopoly, the clans
maintained their supremacy and a command over weaker groups,

whose members found themselves reduced to positions of dependency and subordination. In order to emerge from that situation, there weren't a lot of paths available: You could either allow yourself to be co-opted, as was the case with the aggregated clans of the Capece, creating a new solidarity based on an expansion of alliances. Or else you could react. Show defiance, in a quest for reinforcement. Do one's best to climb over the heads of the clans and the heads of family at their command. Thus creating parallel alliances. And therefore unleashing war.

Instead the sharing of this monopoly had another, inverse effect: it solidified the bonds of solidarity between the chieftain and the foot soldier, with a powerful relationship between those who commanded and those who obeyed, based in Naples as well upon pacts, sworn oaths, and unswerving loyalty. Bonds of solidarity that also manifested themselves, for that matter, in the 1343 raid.

All the same, in this situation, where force was the differentiating element that could change equilibriums, modify relationships, and transform alliances, there was an unmistakable risk that violence would be taken up as the best way of solving all disagreements. There can be no doubt about the fact that Neapolitan society was a universe in which quarrelsomeness was chronic and not episodic. Suffice it merely to consider the disagreements and quarrels that pitted Neapolitans against Neapolitans, laymen against clerics, monks against noblemen in the documents dating from the age of the dukes, so much more numerous than those that have come down to us from Norman times (unfortunately a great deal rarer). These are a useful litmus test for understanding the successive long-term trends: to be clear, I'm not saying a genetic characteristic, that would be too much; but at least a leitmotif that we encounter constantly during the Norman and Swabian periods. Or else, what shall we say about the clashes between the most prominent families and those that were trying to find a little space for themselves, the *mediani*, clashes that in 1156 were transformed into a full-fledged battle for control of the city? An episode that, as so often happens, had as one of its chief effects the destruction of those very same official documents that served to ascertain the power of the elite. A revolt that was harshly suppressed by the noble clans, who thus, with great emphasis, reiterated once and for all the status quo as far as they were concerned.

There's one thing that's especially striking: namely that the further we progress in reading about events in municipal life, the clearer it becomes that in this social climate based on physical might, violence became the agreed-upon tool to settle all disagreements. It was an element of everyday action that became the norm, for a wide array of reasons of all kinds—from private matters to issues affecting the group and the clan. Behind the stabbings, brawls, and feuds, underlying the apparent senselessness of the motives that triggered them and the savage cruelty of the blows, the violence and murders that each group inflicted on the other, there was still something very precise. A signal: that the rules of this strange coexistence, built on a code often made up of intentions, unstated messages, simple glances and looks, had been broken. That a pact had been disregarded. That an alliance had been shattered. To say nothing of the fact that a feud is also useful as a tool to tighten the circle of one's own group, reinforcing the bonds of solidarity and companionship against the enemy clan. Adding the sums to reach the total. We'll come back to this in greater depth later...

The other distinctive element has to do with the origin. As far as that's concerned, what comes into play is memory understood as a singular segment of the collective identity. There is a single underlying fact: to preserve a memory in Naples has nothing to do with playing at heraldry, a very popular hobby back then and every bit as much nowadays. Instead, it means performing a profound civic duty (as was the case from the ducal period on, with a continuity that is difficult to follow for the Norman-Swabian period, but that was there, believe me). Because it's not so much a matter of sitting down and writing the history of one's own family, as is the case in the Tuscan *Ricordanze*. No, instead, it's all about preserving: papers, documents, privileges that attest in a special way the substance and extent of given patrimonies, the properties, the sale and purchase of properties, transfers of ownership, donations made or received, et cetera.

There are a great many small or large family archives in Naples, and they correspond to a need that we can summarize as follows: since the core of power—both economic and social—lies not only in the clan's military force but also in the matching parallel entity constituted by landownership and real estate, preserving the memory of the ways and means that lay at the root of the family patrimony constitutes a fundamental social process. To that end, what is needed are neither genealogists nor genealogies, nor extended forms of memory, as was the case, for instance, in medieval Amalfi. What counts, instead, is storing up documents and written accounts, legally recognized attestations whose weight and efficacy lie entirely in the *heuristics of evidentiary proof*, to borrow Paul Ricoeur's expression.

To be the owner of a family archive is by no means an unusual thing in the context of medieval southern Italy, where we find an abundance of secular references to *chartaria* and *tabularia*. Here in Naples, however, the phenomenon of lay archives takes on unexpected dimensions, in terms of size and spread. This is attributable to a great many factors, which I'll refrain here from exploring in depth: one in particular might be the city's affiliation with a cultural *koine* of Byzantine influence based upon both written records and a guild of notaries, the *curiali*, guarantors of the rule of law. There was a constant reliance upon these professionals to confirm, validate, and reinforce one's rights of ownership. And those rights were not merely economic in nature, inasmuch as they also constituted the memory of a laboriously attained identity and social role. After all, in any dispute, when it is a matter of adducing evidence, then defense is based not on words but facts. Well-documented facts. Whereupon one is expected to "show the documents," to *ostendere chartulas*.

From the last decade of the eleventh century onward, this formula has been replaced by a more general and demanding one. The new formulation underscores the requirement of preserving documents and making them available when requested, not at just any whim, but *for the purposes of the city* (*per usum istius civitatis*). The practice in question, then, previously left to the goodwill of the individual, underwent a further evolution, becoming institutionalized. It was transformed from a nuance into a social undertaking. It became a collective necessity. An awareness and a conscience that the *civitas* had of itself, configuring the role that the city itself assigned to families, repositories of a historical memory with an important role in the continuity and survival of civic institutions; a need for preservation that was a by-product of a conscious ideological determination.[29]

The majority of family archives constitute, all things considered, a complex structure in which each individual brick of documentation, every single holding of papers, becomes an essential component of the construction of the larger edifice of society itself. Structures that are bound together, forming the larger scaffolding that supports a mindset and a lifestyle within which the city becomes one enormous archive, fragmentary and broadly distributed. On the whole, these are small, or in certain cases extremely small, family holdings that might contain two, three, or perhaps four documentary testimonies, offering a narrow memory of possessions and how the estate came about. But there are also more substantial instances. Archives that contain five documents, but even more, at a certain point amounting to as many as twenty, and more than that. With numbers of testimonial documents preserved that grew in lockstep with the family's economic power and importance in society, an archive that certainly made it possible to trace out an extensive history of property that attested to the legitimacy of its dynastic vigor. Such was the case in 1015 when the married couple Maria Diletta and Pietro Gerpa, members of the aristocracy, presented eleven documents (*chartulas*) that, unbelievable but true, make it possible to work our way back to the very formation of their pool of property, conceded as a donation at the very beginning of the tenth century by the dukes Giovanni II (Ioannes) and Marino I (Marinus).[30] Eleven documents that quite explicitly declare: This is us. Here we are, ready and willing to explain to anyone in Naples who cares to listen that this married couple are noble because they're *venerable*, with property given them more than a century ago by two Neapolitan dukes. What could possibly offer a greater nobility shored up by a venerable and long-standing property?

In substantial archives like this one (though it is a common feature in others as well, such as the archive of the wealthy and aristocratic Inferno family), of course, we find numerous commonalities. Identifiable shared denominators. And what is the principal one? A reference to the family's progenitor or forefather. The first founder of the family fortune, who is naturally mentioned in the oldest document in the archive. What that reference means to the family is pretty self-evident, I'd imagine: it's the bond joining head to tail of a larger family organism. An element of concrete reality that creates a correlation over time, not one of chance, but a link of clear function. A prompt for family cohesion, a link in the chain of hereditary transmission of the landed property. Testimonials that do more than merely establish the physical existence of a family estate, but indeed extend well beyond that significance. Documents that take on other meanings. They become tiles in the larger mosaic of a family's formation, the foundation of its wealth and its status. Thus, a deed drawn up by a notary, through the exercise of shared memory, becomes a crucial moment in a longer, more expansive family and collective saga, possessed of social and intellectual value.

This original preservation of memory presupposes people who recognize that value of the written word. That is to say, people with a rudimentary knowledge of how to read and write. We shouldn't think of Naples as a city of illiterates. Rather it was a city populated, at least on the level of the elite, by a vast class of functional semiliterates, endowed at the very least with the ability to interpret (to some extent) a written text. More important, they were capable of recognizing the value and importance of written text as an emanation of an authority with ancient roots, a foundation based in the city's very history. Testimonials that confer prestige, dignity, and authority upon whoever possessed them. Instruments of a largely illiterate society, but one that, to borrow the words of Petrucci and Romeo, "preserves within it specific functional spaces for writing and written texts."[31] In the final analysis, the description of this widespread patrimonial memory constitutes a further ingredient for our understanding of this complex Neapolitan family-based society, whose sensibility finds one of the driving forces of its identity precisely in an understanding of its own history and in the memory of its past, experienced as a family and collective exercise of preservation and transmission of the documents that concern each family.

Then there is the city's landed wealth, based in large part on a myriad of small plots scattered all over the territory of Naples. It is from these that the families drew their basic subsistence, as well as the eventual surplus that they could always sell on the burgeoning Neapolitan market, where, as we shall see, the demand for agricultural foodstuffs was highly fluid, with demand extending to various areas of the Mediterranean basin. And the commerce engendered money, which could then be reinvested in many different ways: to bolster the channels of luxury and prestige or else to increase the possibilities of ostentatious display of privilege obtained by embellishing, renovating, or enlarging one's home, for instance. We shouldn't rule out the possibility that there were other factors at play, in a broader scheme that becomes clear over the course of the fourteenth century: namely, that with the capital attained, invaluable alliances and friendships could be outright purchased; and that they might be able to favor the entire group that sprang up around the clan, thus financing the individuals and families of *clientes* (as they are called in the documents, or also *stipendiarii*) who lived in the shadow of the founding father, enjoying his generosity. Another kind of bond that should not be overlooked in this history.

The *miles*—or knight—must also be a devout worshipper of God. A follower of His cult and His saints. To have a private church, to build an *estaurita*, to participate in the life of the monastery—all this does in fact have a strong social connotation. But behind it all, there is God. The Virgin Mary. The cult of the cross, with its various processions. The awareness that what is beneath is an isomorph of what is above. And that between eternal life and earthly life there exists an inseparable channel, where the earthly is a preparation for the eternal. And so people trust in saints. How can we help but think of San Gennaro, also known as Saint Januarius? The ancient cult of a warrior saint, which may perhaps be why that saint was so popular with the Neapolitans. So much so that as late as the fourteenth century, we can imagine children gathered wide-eyed around the fireplace, and the family members who were considered the finest storytellers focusing on the saint's great ability to defeat enemy armies. And they'd repeat the legendary and felicitous account of the Muslim attack of the year 958, when the Neapolitans, "with great and copious streams of tears and sighs began to pray" to Saints Agrippino (Agrippinus) and Gennaro (Januarius), "who, like them, with their merits and prayers succeeded in freeing the city from the flames of Mount Vesuvius, and so they must provide aid against the rage of the infidels." So what did the saints do? Did they just sit there twiddling their thumbs? No, they did not:

> The aforementioned blessed saints, martyrs and bishops, appeared one night to a Greek prisoner at that time in great affliction for Naples, and asked him why he shed such copious tears and so greatly despaired. And he replied that *crai* [tomorrow] early the city of Naples would fall to the enemy and that there would be a great bloodbath.

In the face of all this desolation, Agrippino and Gennaro could hardly just stand there and watch. And so they comforted the Greek by telling him that God would never allow "such evil to befall." When the night ended and day dawned, the Saracens approached the city and, lo and behold, then what happened? The

Saracens, pushing great movable towers before them, drew near to the gate of Porta Donnorso and threw scaling ladders up against the walls. Then all the Neapolitans came running. They were accompanied by the two saints, who headed straight for their ships, especially the one of the largest tonnage, and by some miracle sent it straight to the bottom of the sea. Whereupon, terrified and upset, the Saracens withdrew, raising the siege and abandoning the city.[32]

A vivid story, designed to strike the listeners' imaginations and offering the confident belief that powerful saints, stronger than any other, capable of defeating both Mount Vesuvius and a Saracen invasion force, was on their side. With that saint's assistance, the listener's clan and his city would be mightily reinforced and emboldened. This was a saint that had nothing meek, mild, or merciful about him, but instead closely resembled this *gens napoletana*, this Neapolitan tribe, who identified with him and glimpsed in his behavior a thread that pointed to the idea that the use and logic of force and violence was perfectly legitimate, especially if they were employed in order to defend their homeland, the Neapolitan *res publica*.

When Tutini speaks of *respublica*, the Latin for "republic," I chose to translate it as "city." And I'm quite sure that I was right to do so. Loyalty to Naples is the throughline that transforms these citizens of just one of many settlements in southern Italy into a *Neapolitan nation*. Because, as I have already stated, even if the rule was that the city was broken up into quarters, neighborhoods, and communities, with clans and other loyalty-based associations, those various fingers of the Neapolitan hand clenched tight into a hard and powerful fist whenever they were called upon to defend their common interests.

A Laborious Coexistence

The year was 1190: fifty years after the fall of the duchy, those very same energies began to emerge. This happened in increasingly convulsive phases, in which the identity first began to poke its nose out of the fertile soil, and then, in time, demanded more and more for itself. As this newfound identity gathered more power, it took the form of both military and economic predominance. Let's take a look at the events that began to unfold in that very same year. The city had grown, so much so that Tancred, the king of Sicily, conferred on it important privileges related to freedom of trade and the right to mint its own coinage.[33] Sure enough, as is so often the case, the city began to take advantage of moments of weakness betrayed by their monarchic power. And just how? By trying to expand its own living space, its lebensraum, to use a term familiar from a later historical period. Loyalty to the city, in fact, meant working to ensure that it could enjoy the best opportunities for development and growth.

The character who emerged to pursue that objective was a major one in the Neapolitan environment, strengthened by the support of his own family as well as alliances with other respected clans: Aligerno Cottone. Of course, he wasn't operating solo. He wasn't a dictator. No, he governed in a collegial manner, in close coordination with other members of prominent families. And together they created a directory. A directory of consuls. These were the families involved, who were configured as the leading clans in the city of those years: Griffi, Falconario, Donnobono, Crispano, de Licio, Buccatorio, Mormile, Stelmatio, Pignatelli, Comino, Teofilo, Mastalo, Picozza, de Arbata, Marcodeo, Imperatore, Bossio, Spada, and Rudicella.[34]

A powerful group that was experiencing a critical moment of transition. A time of struggle for control of the Kingdom, pitting Tancred against the emperor Henry VI. The Neapolitans were quick to choose. And they chose Tancred, for plausible reasons. First of all, of course, loyalty to the dynasty already in charge, to which Tancred was an heir, though a spurious heir. But there were more concrete reasons as well, based on the growing autonomy ensured by the Norman king. What about Henry, what would the attitude of the emperor be? Choosing him would have been a leap into the void, buying a pig in a poke. So they decided to take certainty over uncertainty. A guarantee of safety certainly beat an unknown future with dangerous possibilities. And so Naples became a fundamental, strategic salient in the resistance that Tancred was putting up against the Swabian troops. His *milites* and his fortifications were second to none in the Kingdom.

The siege began under the command of the emperor in person. And it smashed up against the city's defenses, unsuccessfully. The Neapolitans were simply too strong. Peter of Eboli (Petrus de Ebulo) and the miniaturist who painted the illuminated manuscript of his poem depicted, as in any self-respecting graphic novel, some of the most outstanding moments of this siege. The commander of the Norman-Neapolitan troops, Richard, Count of Acerra, being shot in the eye with an arrow. A Neapolitan hurling large rocks down on an attacker from atop the stout circuit of walls. And that same Neapolitan mocking the emperor, left hairless and without troops as a result of the epidemic that was raging through the imperial encampment, while instead hailing the success of Tancred, who had proved himself to be capable of giving the emperor a drubbing and a good shearing to the sheep that followed in his lead.[35]

That siege turned out to be a success for Naples. Because it was a disaster for the emperor. Who turned tail and hurried back to Germany. While Tancred's forces counterattacked, setting out from Naples and proceeding to retake Capua, Aversa, and Teano, culminating with Montecassino. Order was restored. The Neapolitans had paid the dearest price and now expected to receive their just reward. The biggest benefit fell to their hero, Aligerno, along with his clan: one of his brothers was assigned the county of Fondi; while his son, Giovanni, demanded from the archbishop of Naples no fewer than twenty churches located in the city, plus a number of prebends taken from the revenue stream formerly due to the capital.

But then, in 1194, Tancred died. And with his death, the entire web of power and alliances collapsed. His son, William III, turned out to be a weakling. William's mother, Sibylla of Acerra, was every bit as weak as regent. And so Henry VI returned to the charge. He invaded the Kingdom, with the support of the Genoese and Pisan fleets. In Naples, it became clear that this was no time to mock their foes. The situation was stark, and the city was isolated. The idea of holding out was sheer insanity. Negotiations got underway with the Pisans. Who in turn mediated with the emperor. In the end, the Neapolitans threw open their gates and welcomed their enemies in.

Do you imagine that at this point everything changed? It did not. It was no longer as it was back in 1137. Henry was nothing more than an episode—a parenthesis. There was a change of leadership, but no change in the underlying substance. And so there were no deep-seated changes in the life of the society. Still, something did happen. Something immediately contingent. The experiment with the consuls was tossed overboard. Still, when all was said and done, it had never been anything more than an experiment. More decisively, there was an attempt to demolish the one element upon which the city's strength relied. Henry first and foremost ordered Conrad of Querfurt to knock down the walls of Naples. Perhaps that decision was prompted in part by the whistling sound that still echoed in his ears from the insults and jeers that had poured down upon him from atop those walls. All the same, we cannot say at this remove just how much of the walls was actually demolished. Perhaps nothing was torn down but a few gates. And here and there a turret or two. In other words, it was only a partial demolition, which did nothing to alter the city's potential. Most likely, the structures were rebuilt immediately, though perhaps not in the same location.

The fact remains, however, that this marked the beginning of a new season. A Swabian season. Which the Neapolitans largely disliked. The "wake of a tradition of liberty"—as the Neapolitans' determination to run their own lives, along with their families and their clans, has been somewhat baroquely described—was now suppressed. But only on the surface. Deep down, the old dream smoldered. And it smoldered good and hot. Self-rule: that was the dream. And the idea of a *homeland*, a *Neapolitan nation*, gets all tangled up with the dream of independence. Which means, first and foremost, reinforcing the safety of what matters most to Naples. Namely, its hinterland, its essential source of survival. And so the interests at play expanded.

Already, over the course of the fifty years of Norman rule, the clans had shifted the territory of dominion northward, toward the little city of Aversa. Here, possessions were held by, among others, Aymario and Pietro Capece, Guglielmo de Abenabulo, Sergio Balzano, son of the *miles* Donadeo Brancaccio, the *miles* Giovanni de Napoli, Ligorio Gauderisi, and, naturally, the Cottone.

Unexpectedly, in 1197, Henry VI died. And in the blink of an eye, all the enemies of the new ruling house raised their heads. It was sheer chaos. With Costanza (Constance) and Pope Innocent III on one side, guardians of young Frederick, the future Frederick II. On the other side, a sprawling crowd of other protagonists: pretenders to the imperial throne, great feudal lords, other cities, and so on and so forth. All of them trying to outmaneuver this new power. And Naples? Thanks to its particular ruling class, it took another shot at it. It tried once again to develop a political approach, more or less independent, and one that would, most important, promote its own particular and private interests. Twenty-three rather strange years, from 1197 until Frederick II's return to the Kingdom, in 1220. During which time it seemed that, in Naples, there was a wavering movement, starts and stops, but actually a persistent movement in a direction that involved not so much a break from the Kingdom (such a thing would not even have been conceivable) but rather a further reinforcement of the city's role and presence as a minor regional power. All this with just one objective: that it become clear to all the other cities and surrounding communities that Naples was their better, more powerful than they and ready and able to unleash its fury if anyone ever ventured to strike at the city's vested interests. All this without any diplomatic posturing.

Are there any examples? Yes, there is one, and it's as hard to miss as the side of a barn. The attack on Cuma, where the intentions of all the clans converged in favor of the safeguarding of the hinterland's shared resources. It was 1207, and the countryside around Naples was infested with renegade German soldiers and brigands eager to prevent necessities from arriving regularly in the city: wheat, flour, oil. There was one thing, above all others, that they found unacceptable. Namely that the castle of Cuma, which had stood for centuries as one of the defensive bulwarks of the Neapolitan territory, should now lie helpless, infested by gangs of highwaymen. Gangs that were taking advantage of the safety of that fortress to put the rich surrounding farmland to the sword, along with the stretch of the Phlegraean coast. A sort of Tortuga avant la lettre, a pirate island, godforsaken and lawless, so bad that the bishop himself was forced to take to his heels.

The Neapolitans decided that things could not continue at this rate. With a situation further aggravated by the fact that Cuma was no ordinary settlement. In fact, it possessed a treasury of holy relics that could hardly help but motivate the devout Neapolitans to try to help. One almost has the impression of hearing the heated, vehement words of the archbishop of Cuma, Leo, who fled to Naples, where he harangued the *nobiles*. Reminding them: "Beloved friends, have you possibly forgotten that it is there, in Cuma, that the earthly remains of Saint Juliana now lie? As do those of Saint Maximus? What are we going to do about it, leave them in the hands of those pirates, or has the time finally come to take action?" But we must take into account motives other than those that were merely religious. There were other competitors casting covetous gazes on the territory of the Phlegraean Fields and on Cuma. The city of Aversa. As well as a feudal lord, Goffredo di Montefuscolo (Godefroi de Montefuscolo), one of the many adventurers who, in a momentary power vacuum and period of political disorder, was trying to clear a space for himself, in a bid for personal power in the area.

Given their basic nature, do you think that the Neapolitans, well aware of their identity, eager and willing when it came to war and conflict, and having only recently fought imperial troops to a standstill (something that must have filled them with pride…), well, do you think they could have stood for it? Of course they couldn't. And so, the *milites* set off from two different starting points, from the *casale*, the farming hamlets, of Giugliano, not far from the Phlegraean Fields, and from Naples itself. They arrived at the castle of Cuma. It took little time indeed to evict the highwaymen and brigands, who were good only at strong-arming the weak and helpless. In the face of armed Neapolitans, the dispute was quickly settled. But that was not all. The *nobiliores*, having carried out their military action, met for an assembly, as was their custom (*habito consilio*). And they discussed an important point: So far we've been lucky, and Cuma failed to become a poisoned thorn stabbing our sides. And that's because those governing it were simply so many buffoons, capable of extorting the countryside and nothing more. But what if someone else were to take possession of the fortress? Some powerful feudal lord? Since these people were not prone to dithering, they came to a rapid decision and proceeded to burn and ravage everything in sight. It was the end of Cuma. They went home afterward, accompanied by the words of praise of the hagiographer who wrote: the Neapolitans returned joyfully and in pomp and circumstance to their homeland. Homeland: a word that was used advisedly, not chosen at random. Naples, in fact, could only be described with the swelling emotion and pride of those who acknowledged its antiquity and glorious history, renewed now by the power of their fellow citizens. With the exaltation of a city which was no longer merely Naples, but rather the ancient Parthenope, "Parthenope civitas gloriosa."[36]

We should devote our wholehearted attention to this episode. And it should not be underestimated. Because it clearly explains a mode of behavior, typical of the protagonists, of the hegemonic clans. Which at this moment of the utmost precariousness, stepped forward to vouch for and ensure the safety of their

fellow citizens, inasmuch as they were leading and prominent figures in the communities that they governed. Communities of the
Neapolitan nation. A modality that, understandably enough, also
serves to explain the hidden impulses, the drives and thrusts that
push under the skin of the protagonists of that long-ago November 1343. With a perception of the roles that, both in 1207 and in
Naples at so many other points in time, was quite accurate. Understood by the very *nobiliores* of the quarter, who commanded the
mass of the *milites*, their foot soldiers, and the population at large.
Who in their turn understood that it was possible only to solve
problems by turning to them, their lords and masters: *Signori dei
Seggi*. In their great numbers and with their great power, the masters of the city.

And if the central power, in this phase of Frederick II's royal
minority, was weakened in the Kingdom, the presence of the Neapolitan clans was reinforced, within and without. It was further
established that the *milites* garrisoned not only the city but would
need to be ready for battle outside of it as well. And that wasn't
all: their strength and their ability to protect the city needed to be
made clear to one and all. They needed to be sensed as a powerful
influence wherever the city's influence could be felt. And even in
the villages outside the city, in the very farming hamlets, everyone needed to know that there was an authority—the authority
of Naples and its families, that they were all summoned "to withstand the city's enemies and to defend its farming hamlets and
possessions."[37]

The Neapolitan *milites*, at the outset of what was going to
become the exceedingly tortuous thirteenth century, could
be defined as follows: individuals driven to act by a now well-
consolidated organization in the system of the *seggi* and by the
common expectation, based on their own personal concept of
honor and loyalty, that it was their responsibility to defend their
own clan, their own *rione* or neighborhood, their own city. Tough
guys in an everyday reality made up of violence. A world that operated on just a few rules that spread by word of mouth, punctuated

by the teachings of the elders, which took the form of an iron-bound upbringing and education imposed upon the young, who were raised on the strength of these precepts, with very strict retribution for those who failed to stick to them, up to and including the accusation of being a turncoat. A society in which one of the nobility's most important prerogatives was the right to carry weapons and exercise the monopoly of force, the foundation of all forms of control.

The *milites*. Well aware that their very existence could by now be expressed in a project that extended well beyond the city walls and hurtle off into an elsewhere, that, as of now, had not yet been clearly defined, but which was gradually emerging. The concept of a Neapolitan nation that aspired to a greater role in the general history of southern Italy.

And a great many things seemed at this point to take on an ambiguous form. For instance, people were pushing for greater degrees of independence. On the other hand, it was impossible, it was unthinkable to allow oneself to be excluded from the life of the Kingdom. It existed, and life had to be lived inside of it. The important thing was to understand this Neapolitan *power without a state*, divine exactly what game it wanted to play; and just what it wanted to be when it grew up. Then, in 1211, Naples played its cards. The Neapolitans didn't like the Swabians. Better to have Otto IV of Brunswick. International factors weighed in the decision-making. But the immediate objectives provided a certain clarity: for instance, Aversa was with the Swabians, and Aversa was a tempting plum desired by the Neapolitans. Then there was an overriding fear: the Normans had blandly participated in Neapolitan affairs, whereas the Swabians hadn't. There was a shadow cast, hinting at the possibility of the imposition of a royal rector, who would shatter a system of government by the *seggi* that worked wonderfully well in the city—and that, above all, worked perfectly for the city's clans. The Neapolitans must have thought to themselves that it would be better to form alliances with anyone, even with the devil himself, rather than let anyone into their home who might demand all power for themselves, with a subsequent concentration of that power. Entitling them to make life-and-death decisions for them and about them.

Then, however, Otto was defeated at the Battle of Bouvines, on July 27, 1214. Followed by Frederick's return. And Frederick had plenty of things to take revenge for. Above all, he needed to make it clear with every tool at his disposal just who was in charge. In Capua in December 1220 and in Melfi in 1231 he took measures that only a great monarch, with the utmost authority and political instinct, could hope to promulgate. With an overarching framework: to offer an institutional and normative organization for the Kingdom as a whole. The *milites*, in this scenario, appear to be out of control, loose cannons that defied all attempts to master them. For instance, a number of years would have to pass before it became clear exactly what services they were expected to render to the emperor.[38] But it was difficult to stipulate their exact role. Restarting the machinery after many long years out of political power was complicated for a Kingdom that was busily reorganizing itself administratively. If on the other hand there was only the scantiest level of cooperation, really only the most minimal efforts made, it must obviously have been laborious and difficult to keep accounts and impose policy decisions.

Certainly, Frederick wasn't kidding around. For any city, the control had to be ironbound: one had to limit severely any administrative autonomy; appoint plenipotentiary representatives (on the model of their Norman counterparts, the *compalazzi*); and impose absolute centralization. The principle of absolute power had to abide over all, *plenitudo potestatis* of divine derivation. Quite a problem, for those who wanted to go on wallowing freely in their own pond. Measures to which not everyone proved willing to submit: one need only recall what had become of the Muslims in Sicily...[39]

Likewise in Naples it was clear that the direction had changed. Frederick came to the city on more than one occasion. He certainly felt no contempt toward the city, quite the contrary (and in fact he ordered the establishment of the Studium, the university, in Naples). He reinforced the city's port, inasmuch as Naples lent itself particularly well, given its location, as a harbor and naval base for the royal fleet. He also ordered the reinforcement of the city walls and strengthened the castles, both Castello Capuano and Castello del Salvatore (nowadays, the Castel dell'Ovo), one to the east and the other to the west of the city itself, certainly in accordance with an overall logic of military maintenance and reinforcement of the Kingdom as a whole, but also with a view to the internal control of the city, adding his one personal garrison. And with him, on his various expeditions, he brought several representatives of the militia—it's reasonable to assume those he felt were most effective, valiant, and loyal. Then he took the next step: he brought his own *compalazzo* to the city in 1224. That was emblematic of a specific political choice because, being familiar with Naples and its general ungovernability, he was not about to put just anybody in charge of things. Indeed, his choice fell upon one of his finest functionaries: Enrico di Morra, who had previously occupied the much more elevated and responsible position of *maestro giustiziere*, or master justiciar. On paper, therefore, this was a *diminution*, a drop in rank. But in reality the shift concealed an objective that was clearly thought-out. Frederick wanted a man of distinction, with years of experience, who could manage Naples, this bizarre world of knights and city quarters fragmented and divided, but ready at the drop of a hat to unite if conditions demanded it. A world of warriors ready to unleash violence, because if there's one thing they knew how to do well, that was violence. And above all, a world of those who detested meddling in their private affairs. And who wanted to keep their independence, as they had managed to do with their Norman kings.

Therefore, it wasn't a matter of privilege, as had been written. Rather, it was a matter of realpolitik. The management of a power ready to boil over, a force that needed to be sedated and kept under the whip. In a city that in the meantime continued to grow and amounted to—including its farming hamlets—no

fewer than 4,068 hearths (i.e., fireplaces) and over 24,000 residents, while Capua, the second-most-important city, barely managed to boast 1,124 hearths, and something on the order of 6,744
persons. And Naples possessed an urban society that, albeit in accordance with the peculiar logic described above, began to feel it
was increasingly part of a Kingdom, rather than a single cell float-
ing unattached in the void. A center of commercial and cultural
attraction for an entire region that was starting to turn to it in a
clear acknowledgment of its allure, in part thanks to the creation
of Naples's university, which brought new contributions in the development and propagation of knowledge, exchanges, relations,
and culture.

And the city continued to exert its own political attraction, for
those who had no love for the Swabians. Was it or was it not the
one force that had held out against Roger II? Was it or was it not
the one force that had halted Henry VI? And now Naples needed
to be kept under close watch. Limited in its seditious impulses.
But it was also necessary to understand its potential and ensure
that it flowed in the right bed, like some mighty river, because it
could bring major advantages to the German monarchy. In other
words, it was going to require a twofold approach, smiting those
who proved too ambitious but showing fair treatment to those
who proved collaborative with the new regime.

All things considered, Naples appeared to be the fulcrum of
a control that might allow Frederick to project his power across a
regional scale, until it could be extended from the city to the rest
of the peninsula controlled by the Kingdom. In Castel Capuano
and in Castello del Salvatore, the sums of the taxes collected
not only in Naples but also throughout the district were deposited. And that district extended all the way to Molise and the
Benevento area. Not only the *compalazzo* but also the *camerario*
(chamberlain) of Terra di Lavoro came to live in the city—one
of the leading officials of the Kingdom's bureaucratic machinery.
Wines, foodstuffs, weapons, and cloth all came and went through
the port of Naples . . . Lombard prisoners arrived, and ships laden

with wheat departed for Pontremoli and the Lunigiana region. In short, Naples was Frederick's eye on the Tyrrhenian Sea, with a view that stretched all the way to Genoa, to the French coasts, and to the great island of Sardinia, coveted by Frederick's son Enzo, and to Sicily, with which the bond was strongest and most abiding.

And there were Neapolitans who loved things exactly as they stood. They could aspire to public offices, to state positions of employment. They could hope to participate in a dynamic that could hardly remain isolated from its context. For instance, there were many clans who liked the Swabians: first and foremost the Capece, who readily placed themselves at the dynasty's service; the same applied to certain members of the Filangieri, Caracciolo, and Vulcano families. Nonetheless, these were exceptions. Because the city as a whole remained intractable. Most of the families were intolerant of this new political situation. They didn't like new and unfamiliar people in their streets. They didn't like seeing fortifications placed out of their control. Powers that dwindled in the face of new institutional figures who disregarded them and answered solely, and without intermediaries, to their emperor-king, Frederick. They could feel the breath of these new functionaries hot on their necks. And that certainly didn't make them happy.

In the meantime, for many, the atmosphere became increasingly unbreathable. All of the privileges obtained under the Norman monarchs were being canceled. One at a time, without any ostentatious emphasis. One day it's one thing, another day it's another. But the rights were being methodically eliminated. The only customs and traditions that were kept alive were those that failed to contradict the new constitutions. Every writhing surge of revolt was immediately repressed by the garrison that stood ready and loyal to Frederick, stationed in the two castles: Castello del Salvatore and Castello Capuano. For them, it was a walk in the park to rush out the sally gates and spread rapidly throughout the city... the city's *libertates* were being undermined. And loyalty to Frederick became the discriminating factor even if what you wanted to do was simply get married, as certain members of the *nobiliores* learned to their own dismay, among them the Protono-bilissimo and the Tomacelli families. In fact, when they wished to marry women from other clans (the Vulcano clan, or the Capece *de monacho*), they were first required to pass the emperor's evaluation and receive his approval, or *placet*. A certification of approval that had absolutely nothing to do with the would-be bridegroom's moral rectitude or upright lifestyle; it was entirely bound up with his degree of faithfulness to the monarch. An unmistakable signal on the emperor's part, who knew that, even behind a marriage between noble lineages, there might lurk expansions of alliances between clans hostile to the Swabians.

Everyone, both Neapolitans and imperial allies, was keenly aware of this steadily more scathing atmosphere, growing from red to white-hot. And that unleashed a violent, under-the-table form of byplay. The Neapolitans sharpened their weapons: and not in any metaphorical sense. No, the physical whetstone was turning in reality. While the imperial forces did their best to get those sharpened weapons out into the open, and in 1231 they actually issued an edict against anyone who concealed weapons illegally, as well as against arms smuggling. An edict that, as best we can determine, was simply sidestepped. And that must have been the case, for those clans that kept weapons and used them as a tool of power...

The Swabian garrison stood ready to put down any rebellion. Fear was lurking everywhere, amplified by the propaganda spread by the clergy, the monks, and the friars preaching against Frederick. People stopped to listen. And day by day the conviction grew that this situation really couldn't go on much longer. Tensions worsened. And finally the horrible event unfolded. A number of Saracens from Lucera stationed in Naples (though just why we do not know) clashed with a group of Neapolitan noblemen. On both sides in that brawl there were fighters not interested in the details of military gallantry. The brawl turned bloody. There may have been a death or two. Blame was placed on the Neapolitans.

Especially on one, a certain Matteo Griffi, who was ordered to lose a hand to the executioner's axe.[40]

Resistance

All the same, these were only warning signals. Nothing major had happened yet. A brawl isn't really all that momentous. It's just a passing episode. And after all, Frederick was still solidly ensconced in power. Who had the nerve to rise up against the Wonder of the World, *stupor mundi* himself? No one did. No one had the strength or energy to overthrow him. But then, on December 13, 1250, in Ferentino di Capitanata, the emperor died. Whereupon tensions exploded. All the enemies of the German ruling house rose up as one. Neapolitans, Capuans, the residents of several Apulian cities. It was as if they had all awakened out of a deep sleep at once, in unison. And to make things even worse, with no need of papal incitement. All that it had taken was the report of the emperor's death. The alliances were reinforced. The secretly established networks suddenly came out into plain view. And hatred ruled the day. A great many who had been luxuriating just the day before in the emperor's benefits and attentions now suddenly went over to the other side, joining up with the rebels.

In Terra di Lavoro it was the Neapolitans who opposed Manfred. They put up an impressive resistance, harsh and determined. They were the leaders of a coalition that included the cities of Capua and Aversa and a number of feudal lords, such as the Count of Caserta. Manfred passed around Naples. He tried to lay siege to the city. He was attempting to push the militia to accept battle in an open field. But the city refused to take the bait. Manfred decamped without having been able to lay his hands on his primary intended prey, the most tempting mouthful. Meanwhile, things went back to the old ways in Naples. It was as if thirty years of Swabian rule had washed away without leaving a mark. A generational leap without the slightest transformation. The clans reared their heads again. The Cottone made their appearance. Among the others who emerged, there was a well-known face who had been on good terms with the Swabians, Riccardo Filangieri, the son-in-law of Pietro Cottone. He could claim the prestige of the venerable old clan that had distinguished itself in the days of battle against Henry VI, but also that of the clan in which he had been born, one of the noblest anywhere in the city.

Riccardo became the *podestà*. The only case in the city's history. He didn't rule alone. Aided by the usual council of the *seggi* and the families. The city, in any case, had become an autonomous municipal township. Freed of all bonds and guided by a junta with a *podestà* as leader. Riccardo had been one of Frederick's men, and this was known. But that proved useful now in the war against the Swabians, given his political and military skills. After him, in keeping with the tradition of the communes of north-central Italy, Gallo de Orbellis was named *podestà*. The only Milanese to have ever ruled Naples. I have to wonder what the Neapolitans thought of him. A question of only relative importance, given that he ruled for a very short time. A true meteor in the larger panorama of civic power. His presence hovers as something of a curiosity.

Meanwhile, the war was progressing. And bringing fear with it. Naples seemed to have turned back into the city of a previous century. The Naples that put up resistance to Roger II. Everyone readied themselves. With a new level of awareness: that they were defending their homeland and their nation against the aggression of the Other. Of the enemy, the representative of the Antichrist, if not the Antichrist himself. From the hinterland, people came to seek shelter in the city, which was still surrounded by the stoutest walls in the Kingdom.

The year was 1253. Conrad IV was arriving. The new pretender. He knew that this was the rotting center of the resistance to his rule and his supporters. This marked the beginning of a truly heroic phase. The *milites* showed even greater courage than they had in the past. The city was surrounded, by land and by sea. Siege wagons were deployed. Tunnels were excavated in order to enter the city from underground. The stated objective was to seize the city and throttle it. The siege began. And it was the harshest siege of the three that we have described. A siege that turned the city inside out and upside down, transforming the Neapolitans into wild beasts, stunned by hunger and dazed by incessant combat. Saba Malaspina, the chronicler, tells us that there was nothing left to eat. Nothing but the carcasses of filthy creatures, corpses that aroused disgust and revulsion at the thought of touching or eating them. Weeds, plants that not even animals would touch. Nettles, branches from fig trees and other varieties of tree bark that did little or nothing to alleviate the pangs of hunger. Getting into the city wasn't easy, even for the besieging forces, who found worthy opponents in the Neapolitans. A relentless opposition. Continuous fighting. Rampart after rampart. Battlement after battlement. Tower after tower.

Until Naples finally surrendered. Once again, it wasn't because the city's walls had collapsed. No, what collapsed was the willingness or ability of its populace to hold out. And Conrad chose to take vengeance in full. He wanted to clear the streets, decimate his foes. Let Naples serve as a chilling example for any other city that chose to rebel. The clans that had put up the most-spirited defenses of the city walls against the continuous assaults by German and Saracen forces were those that most painfully felt the impact of the Swabian war hammer. And exile was the punishment meted to those who, from the city fortresses along the coastline—fortresses guarding gates, such as the Porta dei Caputo, or towers, among them the Torre Cinta, the Torre Mastra, or *seggi*, such as the Seggio di Porto, the Seggio dei Griffi, or the Seggio del Barbacane—had done the greatest harm to the besieging forces. The men of the clans who had grown up and lived in those fortifications and redoubts. As had their grandfathers and great-grandfathers before them. And to whom those sections of enclosure wall, those cast-iron grates, those loopholes were not something anonymous and chilly, but rather a part of their own lives, their everyday existence. A reason to live, in a way, because to lose them would have meant abandoning their own home, with all the memories of important events, familiar stories, and abiding identities that they contained. This is the world that Conrad wanted to tear asunder. And so it was "farewell Naples, hello exile," for these families: Filangieri, Caputo, Griffi, Macedonio, Ligorio, Cafatino, Spinelli, and Maramaldo.

After seeing to his actual enemies and their *damnatio*, Conrad turned his attention to the walls. And this time, he really did dismantle them, especially along the coastline, which had been impossible for invaders to breach before that. The Porta del Caputo vanished. In its place was a vast gash in the wall. All around it, a desolate spectacle of houses reduced to rubble and land left uncultivated. Even worse, the Torre Mastra disappeared, a great tower that had stood there ever since the seventh century, looming high over the sea, on the slopes that ran down to the port, as if to say to one and all: "Come on and do your worst, try and take Naples, but you never will." Instead, there was one warrior who succeeded... Namely, Conrad: who brought with him the terrible image of a character *di natura crudele et inhumano*—cruel and inhuman by his very nature.

Exile and destruction, however, did nothing to stop Naples. Because even though they understood that the battle was lost, they could still hope to win the war. Over the course of this stark episode, in fact, the *seggi* came back to life. And defeat had quite the opposite effect. It failed to depress, but if anything revitalized "the city's age-old territorial understructure, with the interlocking positions of command along the enclosure wall."[41] In other words, the people of the *seggi*—the families, the clans—could still be seen there. Tenaciously locked onto their roots, like a mussel gripping the rock face of a shoal. And there was no wave powerful enough to sweep it away.

The experience of Conrad's siege woke people out of their sense of complacency. Now the clans needed to decide what to do next, whom to support, before it was really too late. They needed to find a political solution that would satisfy them, a way to get rid of their Swabian enemy once and for all. And they found it. Because in the meantime the pope in Rome was taking steps. As was Louis IX, the king of France. They put forward a new pretender to the throne of the Kingdom. Someone to combat the Antichrist, who had now become Manfred. A pretender who turned out to be the brother of King Louis, none other than Charles of Anjou. And Charles began to ready himself for action. He was powerful: he had the pontiff on his side, he had the finest horsemen of Europe, and—something that never hurts—he had the unalloyed support of the bankers of Tuscany and Florence, who by and large underwrote the expedition.

So what did the Neapolitans do? As far as they were concerned, this was the perfect solution, a candidate they embraced and supported wholeheartedly, accepting him enthusiastically. God was on the side of the Anjou. Manfred was the enemy, the *unjust usurper of our Kingdom*. Certain Neapolitan families detested him violently, the fruit of an ancient, inveterate hostility. A hatred that had run through their veins for more than fifty years, ever since the era of Henry VI. Opposition to the Swabians had finally been channeled into the proper conduit. It was time to provide the greatest possible support to the Angevin ruling house, which in the meantime had begun to move, marching southward. And that support was much more than mere lip service. The clans were offering all their potential, in weapons, soldiers, and money, and they arrayed it entirely at their new allies' disposal. And there was something striking about this new alliance: membership was unanimous. There were few dissenting voices, practically no one was classified as *proditores*, or traitors. Infamous rats.

All of the clans understood that this was the right opportunity. The best circumstance to take the great leap. In order to ensure that once and for all the Neapolitan nation should become a protagonist in the Kingdom's future destiny.

Along this path, energy brought new energy. The first ones to provide support were the Amalfitans residing in Naples, who immediately sensed the advantages that would come from this new outlook. They were possessed of capital that came not so much from commerce but rather from the management of public works contracts and administrative offices. And they loaned cash, by the bucketful, to the Anjou, often with no hope of seeing returns. But they knew that this money wasn't scattered to the four winds. That it was an investment. Among the families, we should mention the Frezza, the Coppola, the del Giudice, the d'Afflitto, the Muscettola, the Spina, the Cappasanta, and the de Bonito.

These were communities that had close ties of blood kinship, familiarity, *comparaggio* or membership in the numerous Neapolitan clans. Clans that, in their turn, moved in lockstep: Scannasorice, Ferrillo, Venato, di Costanzo, Pappansogna, Macedonio, Capuano, Alopa, Aprano, di Capua, di Gennaro, Rosso, del Doce, Celano, Caputo... A mass of people. And then what should we say about their military intervention? The Caputo were shipbuilders, readying war galleys. The same work that the del Giudice family did. They provided horses, weapons, and lances. A tangible and extended source of support that continued over the course of the first few decades of the Angevin monarchy, when the dream of a Kingdom that extended to both sides of the Mediterranean seemed to become concrete.

For that matter, what was Naples becoming? What remained now, in the middle of the thirteenth century, of that small city, a pale shadow of the great Byzantine empire? Not much. Traditions, customs, laws, usages, rites, and ways had gone downhill. But a solid base had been preserved. That base consisted of the city's families. The clans of Naples that, little by little, in a lengthy evolution, had been capable of carving out for themselves a leading role within the municipal context. And in that context they had left their footprint, which consisted of a pervasive social control, capable of creating a cohesive, unitary, triumphant universe, based on clans and family groups that had found in the *seggi* their guiding element of coordination and collective control for the government of the city. Clans whose subsequent evolution was forged in the shared resistance against the Swabians and the shared objective of taking part, with the House of Anjou, in the assault to become masters of the new Kingdom. A Kingdom where Naples, in the brief period of just a few decades, grew to outstrip any other rival city. It was now the supreme city of peninsular southern Italy in terms of wealth, demographic dimensions, and economic potential. No other city was so dear to the hearts of the new monarchs. Naples had supported their efforts and was continuing to do so. And now the Neapolitans, their families, their clans, the groups of *parentes, fideles et consortes* that surrounded them, were asking only one thing in exchange: for the city to become the Kingdom's capital. The proper conclusion to more than a century and half of history, demanded loudly by a society that felt it was a winner, ready to offer its help in the effort to create a Kingdom with solid, robust foundations, extending upon a genuinely Mediterranean scale.

The Procession of Corpus Domini

And, as we know, Naples became a capital. And it was a great capital, one that regularly held a festival with ancient roots. The festival of Corpus Domini. The festival that was taking place on that very day, back in 1343. A festival that has a great deal of sacred ritual to it, with the maximum display of the holy of holies. But behind the liturgical scenes, this was the moment when the *seggi* celebrated themselves. Where in the background, one after another, the nobility of each quarter would hand off a *palio*, a sort of wooden baldachin, hoisted aloft on poles or clubs, each to the next, as the procession passed through the city and its various zones:

> The nobility, along with the common folk, agreed to carry the *palio*. The first ones to lift up the poles of the *palio* inside the archbishopric were the noblemen of Capuana, given the fact that the church of that name had been built within the precincts of their jurisdiction. And that procession wended its way toward the church of Santo Stefano in the direction of the Seggio Capuano, descending the narrow lane, or Vicolo delle Zite, and

as they left it and continued toward the church of Santo Agrippino, they relinquished the clubs, which were taken up in their
turn by the noblemen di Forcella, and they carried the *palio* all
the way to the Palagio della Zecca, the mint building, where
in the marble wall a sculpted cross can be beheld, a sign of the
boundary of Forcella and the beginning of the jurisdiction of
Portanuova, and so those noblemen took the *palio* and carried
it to the church of Sant'Agnello dei Grassi, and from there it was
the noblemen of Porto who took it, passing through the Seggio degli Aquari, adjoining the Piazza di Porto, and thence carried by them all the way to the wall of the Monastery of Santa
Chiara where, in that building, another marble cross has been
carved as an indication of the beginning of the jurisdiction of
Nido; so that the noblemen of Nido took up the poles of the
palio and entered the church of Santa Chiara, whereupon, passing through their own piazza, they continued up toward Arco,
which had in the past been a *seggio* united with Nido, and there
reaching the lane, or *vicolo*, alongside the Chiesa de' Morti
[Church of the Dead], the *palio* was taken by the noblemen of
the Montagna and, passing through their own *seggio*, the *seggio* of Talamo, San Paolo, Mercato Vecchio, and de' Mamoli, it
was carried on all the way to the Vicolo de' Panettieri, the lane
of the bakers; whence it was again taken in hand by the noblemen of Capuana and returned with them in procession into the
Duomo, the cathedral.[42]

The *palio* would move forward, wobbling, dancing, in a continuous forward progression. From one end of the city to another.
Entering and exiting. Making its way up and down steep slopes
and inclines, the notorious *pendini* of the city. Streets that wid-
ened and narrowed, until they became practically impassable for
the crowd. Churches. Crossroads as ancient as the festival itself,
bedecked with marble and crosses, where the *palio* stops and
waits. Perhaps with some specified movement, some turn or spin
of the baldachin. A way of expressing honor. A way of expressing

reverence. A way of expressing homage. And then it would move on. Moving on to *them*. To the *seggi*, the institutions that are still there, still alive, the beating heart of every quarter. And in honor of the memory of those twenty-nine *seggi* that that day, during that festival of 1343, no longer existed and were, at this point, nothing more than a memory, made up of a few stones and a few chipped and battered walls. Forgotten traces. Traces that the festival was now stitching back together. Bringing it back to the surface, with a ritual as remote as it was full of meaning. And all this means, basically, to those who are present, to those who follow the procession, two things about life in this Naples of the *seggi*: that the strength of these *seggi*, entirely hidden, tucked safely away in the *palio*, belongs to no one but also belongs to everyone—and that, for this very reason, the *palio* is never stationary in the hands of one single *seggio*, but instead that it proceeds and slides from one to another—and that the men of one *seggio* can only carry the *palio* with them, bearing the evil-averting power that it contains, until they reach the boundary of their own quarter. It is forbidden to continue any farther. It would mean crossing borders that are not established by human beings alone. Those limits are set by time, by memory, by the spirit of the city. It would therefore constitute sacrilege, infamous hubris. A misbegotten curse.

In this ancient festival, there was someone who wasn't just there to make a spectacle. Someone who was on the margins. But who was managing things. Someone who helped to coordinate the passage of the baldachin. Someone who waited for the procession to stop at the crossroads. And with that procession came the devotion of the men and women of this and of the other quarters. An intersection that the local families had renovated and polished and buffed until it looked like new. Shiny: an ostentatious appearance. Under guard by the men of the district's clans. Who were in their turn watched over by the one who governed it all, though doing so required nothing more than brief gestures: the *mastro di festa*, the master of the festival, who was also probably the most venerable nobleman of the zone. A personality who was paid high honors as the *palio* went by. Who in return paid his respects to his own *nobiliores* and the *nobiliores* of the other quarters who had come to see it. And who waited until the *palio* was held high before giving the order. To set it down, now, with a jarring thud. To hand it over to the men of the following quarter. Who then lifted it up and took it away, for the new round.

The last round would be completed by them. The last shift of the *palio*. The noblemen of Nido approached the noblemen of Capuana. Among them were Matteo Aldemorisco; Tommaso Imbriaco; Andrea Carafa; the Brancaccio family, with Lisulo and Boffilo; Giovannello Cappasanta; Tommaso Capuano; and Giovanni Pignatelli. They picked up the baldachin and they handed it to the people from Capuana, who with bows and gestures of respect raised it to their shoulders for the final circuit, all the way to the archbishopric. Among them were Guglielmo de Tocco; Nicola Galiosa; Landolfo Minutolo, also known as Schiavo; Tommaso Filomarino; the Caracciolo family—with Giovanni, Giacomo, also known as Cafaro, Marino, also known as Simon, and Lisulo; Lisulo Siginolfo; Giovanni Cossa; and Giannotto Seripando. All of them noblemen. All of them *milites*. All of them children of this lengthy season that had begun with their fathers' fathers' fathers, with a siege back in 1135. Now, all of them implicated in the new Angevin monarchy. With titles, honors, and prebends. All of them men of great authority, before whom the entire quarter parted way to let them pass. And honored them. Children of the same rules and the same morality, which had been built up through a lengthy process of development. Heads of families and heads of clans.

Every last one of them.

Members of the party. And to a greater and lesser extent, participants in the November 1343 raid.

IV

THE TWO WORLDS

Birth of a Capital

There's something about the night of 1343 that grates badly to our ears. Considering the names of the protagonists, there's one basic thing that eludes our understanding. They represent the crème de la crème of not merely Neapolitan society, but really of the Kingdom at large. They are counts, barons, feudal lords, owners of *casali*, farming hamlets, in the hinterland and of castles even farther outside the Neapolitan territory. Prominent citizens who can safely aspire to stand beside monarchs, such as, say, Marino Caracciolo or Tommaso Imbriaco, who were the king's *senescalli*: his seneschals.[1] They were, as we might say in modern times, members of cadres. Personalities of the royal court. People who took an active part in the doings of the royal house. Who recognized its power and worked within its projects, expectations, and opportunities.

And yet it would seem that, when faced with dire necessities, like that of violent famine, they hesitated not at all before literally tossing all this loyalty into the briar patch. And roundly indifferent to all and any established authority, they decided on their own what to do next, according to a framework of behaviors and rules, an organizational and decision-making scheme that had not the slightest link with the larger idea of a government that guaranteed a state of public order, ready to serve the needs of the populace through an orderly structure of functionaries, administrators, and officials. The attitudes and behaviors of the noblemen of Capuana and Nido veered far, far away from any such logic. Instead, it belonged to the mindset of a *stateless power* that weighed in to solve problems that it really had no right or jurisdiction to solve. And this unfolded without a flicker of disappointment or objection from the community that surrounded them. Quite the opposite: that community looked on and, above all, expressed its approval. The truth is that all of them, the chiefs, the foot soldiers, and the spectators, all came from a single dimension that was radically separate from the institutional context. A dimension that was not an underworld but rather a parallel environment: another social world. One that survived with its own norms and principles, its own institutions and authorities, even in the presence of the established sovereign power. And there, in that Other World, the clan and the family were the true link between the individual and the state.

Two worlds. Two realities. Frequently separated, but never entirely independent. And those two realities, and perhaps this is the greatest paradox, necessarily had reciprocal need, one for the other, in order to ensure the general stability of the larger community. A coexistence in which, as soon as it became possible and the boundaries of political action allowed it, each one willingly eroded the sphere of power of the other: when one of the two showed itself to be weaker than the other, less capable of operating or devoid of sufficient security to be able to go on acting. This was by and large the schema that brought together and faced off the monarchy and the denizens of the system of the *seggi* on that night of November 1343. This unfolded in a relationship that was, most often, one of alliance, complicity, and mutual assistance. As it was also a dynamic of conflict for the hegemony within a larger municipal theater of operations that over the course of the fourteenth century underwent numerous disturbances. This process stemmed from one specific point: the ways in which Naples became a capital.

Naples's promotion to a capital took place immediately. After defeating Manfred at Benevento in 1266, Charles came to the city to begin actually governing the Kingdom. And he chose it as his capital for unmistakable reasons of political strategy: "Having chosen to reside in this city and take it as his home, both to aid in matters relating to the pontiff and the Guelphs as well as for convenience in relations with France, since he was closer here than he would have been in Palermo, where the other kings had been accustomed to reside."[2] So, clearly, the initial choice of Naples was political and diplomatic. Dictated by the convenience of its location: not far from Rome and the pope. Where the envoys from France could arrive more easily than in Palermo, which had been the capital during the time of the Norman-Swabian Kingdom.

That is what Summonte wrote in the seventeenth century, and he added: Consider, though, that, ever so slowly, Naples became *almost the chief* of all the other mainland cities and, since it already served as a royal residence, it became, de facto, the principal executive center of the Kingdom. With an immediate disruption of the traditional social settings. Because the city began to take on a dimension of political and commercial attraction that, hitherto, it had possessed in only the smallest proportions imaginable, unlike anything that would come later. The king is there, many thought to themselves. So we need to be there too. And so they began to pour into the city, a river of advantage-seekers that steadily grew, barons, administrators, men of the law, professors of the Studium, or university, arriving from other parts of Italy, men of the cloth and men at arms, people from the world of the courts, jurists, legal consultants, et cetera. And that wasn't all: what should we say of the businessmen, the merchants, the retailers, and the artisans who flowed into the capital of all Italy, in the hope—and the expectation—of new investments, earnings, opportunities, and meal tickets?

Naples was modifying its appearance. Powerful city that it was, however provincial, it grew sharply in just a few decades. It grew from its just over 30,000 residents in 1266 to roughly 40,000 at the end of the century. Above all, it became more international. A great many new inhabitants arrived. The foreign colonies in town grew much larger. Especially the enclaves of the Genoese and the Florentines, who set up housekeeping next to the port, where their loggias stood. But along with the monarchs who came from north of the Alps there also came a mass of Frenchmen that grew under the protective umbrella of the Anjou. Frequently rapacious, these Frenchmen hurled themselves upon the Kingdom and upon Naples in search of fortune. Here many of them married members of the families of the *seggi*, and those marriages brought with them alliances, property, and feudal landholdings. In a form of connubial bliss that reinforced both sides. There is a rich case history of such unions. Matrimonial strategies that allowed the rapid rise to political careers. Let us take, for instance, the Siginolfo family of the *seggio* of Capuana, which has been studied by Giuliana Vitale. They joined forces with the de la Gonesse, the Etendard, the Joinville, the Lautrec, and the de Millac. They operated with an exogamic tendency that proved to be a great revolution, because it put an end to the tradition according to which marriages could only be accepted within one's own identity group (with common rules on succession and marriage in the *seggi* of Capuana and Nido). Those marriages were launching platforms for the clans, driving them much higher in part due to the added degree of visibility acquired in court circles and in part due to increasingly powerful internal consensus.

For that matter, it was also possible to find instances of a French family joining together with various local family groups, as in the case of the de Bourson, where Jacques, in three different marriages, was wedded first to Ilaria, the daughter of Riccardo Filangieri, who brought him a dowry that included numerous of her father's feudal landholdings; then Philippa de Joinville, the lady of Corigliano and Balvano, the widow of Philippe Echinard;

and Giovanna dell'Aquila, the widow of Louis de Mons. A welter of marital bonds that truly becomes intricate, if you consider
that the children from the first marriage then proceeded to marry
children from the second and the third. In a dynamic that only
seemed to be confused and tangled, but whose entirely rational
objective was clearly to increase the family fortune through successive marriages. And, where needed, to preserve the unity of
that family fortune through the marriage of stepsiblings and half
siblings.[3]

So there was a new cosmos that demanded to be fed. Not
merely in terms of primary needs. There was a pressing and in-
sistent need for luxury, in a crescendo fed by a court that was becoming one of the principal houses of Europe. And out of a whole
social universe that surrounded it, attracted by new fashions, symbols, and forms of ostentatious consumption. All of which varied
depending on one's own degree of implication and involvement
in the circle of the ruling monarchs. Here's just one example, to
better understand the atmosphere: that of Princess Isabelle de
Villehardouin, who was married in 1271 to Philip of Anjou, one
of Charles I's sons; a woman, as it happens, who had a very un-
happy life, since her husband died in 1277 and she remained, a
widow, at court until 1289.[4] It is highly relevant to note the way
that as a function of one's position within the court the use of fabrics changed, as well as luxury garments, *parures* (sets of matching
jewelry), according to changes in the woman's own condition, as
she progressed from young bride to fresh widow: a situation that
demanded changes in habits and attire, as well as a fixed duration
of the requirements involved in the period of mourning. Depending on occasions that rolled around according to the calendar,
women were expected to make use of different fabrics in terms of
fiber and color. The variety ensured by the provenance of artisans
and merchants made it possible to stage a climactic scene where
taste and enjoyment of luxury matched up, suiting the princess's
particular status. Even as a widow, inasmuch as she was the king's
daughter-in-law, she still enjoyed a privileged post at court. And so

the woman regularly received finely tanned hides, drapes in scarlet wool, silk, jewelry: in brief, products much sought after in the West and now also in Naples. These were items that only people at court and the nobility could afford to indulge in, given their truly very elevated prices. With a hierarchy of their use bound up with the social role and the position held in the identity group to which one belonged, with fabrics and colors that might only be possible for the queen to wear, while others might also be accessible to princesses, and others still by ladies of the court, damsels, and so on. All with costs that, of course, varied in a context where, in the absence of local production, the market depended exclusively on imports. A sector in which there were a great many actors, extremely varied, with a prevalence of Tuscan and Florentine businessmen, whose number was destined to grow. These merchants grew extremely rich by exploiting the very noteworthy opportunities that this new demand for luxury products offered.

Now let us return to Naples. After the execution of Conradin, Conrad IV's sixteen-year-old son and Manfred's nephew, on the Piazza del Mercato, and the end of the war against the Swabians, Charles I began his long campaign of transforming the city into a capital, with the objective that was unmistakable, to borrow Summonte's words: to command "this city in grandeur and magnificence." To give it, in other words, an appearance befitting the role that had been assigned it by the new monarchy.

This was a vast, gigantic operation, begun by Charles and taken up again afterward by his heirs, involving multiple generations of laborers, stonecutters, artisans, architects, and artists, among whom we need only cite figures of the caliber of Pietro Cavallini and Giotto to gain some understanding of what we're talking about. An initiative that had extremely high costs, so much so that it virtually bled dry the very coffers of the government.[5] To track the progress of the public works undertaken by the first of the kings of Anjou is much like following the silhouette of a young girl who is transformed and develops into a lovely woman. The signs are alluring to behold. There is the development of the

harbor strip, with the expansion of maritime equipment and public works. The tower, the Torre di San Vincenzo, is built where the
"ancient wharf once stood for the safety of the vessels." Several
stretches of walls were restored and expanded, which the scholars
inform us was the sixth expansion of the circuit of the city walls in
Neapolitan history, with a significant modification: the circuit of
walls now encompassed the Piazza del Mercato in the same location it occupies still. Work began upon the cathedral. Construction was undertaken and completed of the churches of Sant'Eligio
al Mercato, Sant'Agostino alla Zecca, and Santa Maria del Carmelo, better known as the Carmine.

But the project that made the greatest impression on the
contemporaries and the city's collective imagination was the
construction of the castle-palace of Castel Nuovo. "In Charles's
conception," wrote Giuseppe de Blasiis, "it was meant to be both
a palace and a fortress and stand outside of the city, in a healthy
and pleasant location, close beside the sea, where if needed it
would offer free passage to rescuers or for escape."[6] The new residence was intended to possess a twofold nature: it was meant to
be a massive defensive structure, from which it would be possible
to thrust back enemy attacks if necessary. At the same time, it
would be a building of magnificent beauty. Something diametri-
cally opposed to the residences that had hitherto been the homes
of the king in Naples. Because they had all been either too small
for the needs of a growing court with an international character,
as the Castello del Salvatore had been. Or they'd been unhealthy,
as was the case with Castel Capuano, where the pestiferous air
of the surrounding marshes made it impossible to live there with
any serenity.

The Maschio Angioino, or Angevin Donjon: here was a new
home with surprising characteristics. A unique structure with an
extraordinary impact on the appearance of the Neapolitan landscape, "symmetrical with everything that, in political terms, the
advent of Charles I was to mean for Naples and for the Kingdom,
and in the relationship between the capital and the provinces."[7]

The most stunning new development of an urban world in the throes of transformation: majestically rising above the sea, to make it clear to one and all that now, in the Mediterranean and in the West, there was a new great state, under the rule of the Anjous. The symbol of a metropolis that was growing at a truly astonishing speed, as it expanded toward the port and the sea, even at the cost of sacrificing what society and the urban layout had managed to preserve of what was customary and habitual. And so there was a continuous opening of new space. Demolitions of existing structures. Gardens around the castle, full-fledged paradises with exotic animals, fountains, chapels, carved grottoes, hunting lodges, delightful retreats, shade trees, all described by Boccaccio, who writes about "lovely young saplings with luxuriant green branches, warding off the rays of the great hot sun."[8]

And the palace became the central axis of all political dynamics, of a great kingdom of international breadth and scope that could interact as a full-fledged peer with all the other monarchies then in formation. And around that palace there orbited an open and lively city, a companion piece to the older city, constrained, narrow, and parochial—by now completely outmoded. Which served as a counterbalance to it, substituting a more linear grid to a chaotic urban plan. An area that was enlivened by large squares, such as the Piazza delle Corregge, the site of the horse market and, on holidays, games and tournaments. With broad streets and imposing residences: the homes of the members of the court, a number of nobles, and, most important of all, the members of the royal family.

An area that profoundly modified the city's appearance, upending its arrays as it shifted westward from its older city center, toward what is even now the central driving force of Naples, where there stands not only the palace but also the seats of government, the Camera Rationum, or countinghouse, and the court of the Ammiragliato, or Admiralty. A renovated dimension that tended to attract, with a multiplier effect. Among those clustering close were knights, clerics, priests, *officiales*, valets, domestics,

Norman-Swabian Naples

N

0   250   500 m

1. Cathedral
2. Palazzo Augustale
3. Sant'Arcangelo de illi Morfisa
4. Donnorso Gate
5. Mastra Tower
6. Caputo Gate
7. Barbican
8. Herculanensis Tower

9. Castel Capuano
10. Area of the Seggio dei Griffi
A. Via San Biagio dei Librai
B. Decumano Maggiore, or Great
     Decuman (Via dei Tribunali)
C. Largo delle Pigne (Piazza Cavour)
D. Piazza del Mercato (Market Square)

ambassadors, squires, merchants, students and professors from the Studium, doctors, artisans, and artists, working incessantly on the continuous renovation of the castle. An energy that drove a steadily growing urban plan that took over the slopes of the hill, the Collina di Sant'Elmo, moving toward the coast, down toward the beach of Beverello, where the tower-lighthouse, Faro di San Vincenzo, stood. Reaching all the way to Pizzofalcone. And later, farther on, all the way to the promontory of Posillipo.

Under Charles II, as well, this policy continued. There was more construction of "well-leveled and straightened roads." In 1302, the king ordered work to begin on the construction of a new port basin, larger and more secure, not far from Castel Nuovo, in the area of the Pisan port. There was need for it due to the growing needs for loading and unloading areas, and in order to handle large volumes of general commercial activity. An exceedingly costly operation, to cover which a new tariff had been imposed on wine exports, to the extent of two *tarì* a barrel—a tax that was replaced in May 1306 with the so-called *gabella del buon denaro*—the good money gabelle, or tribute. The whole area was disrupted by the work. Pozzolana, ash used to make a kind of cement, came from the Phlegraean Fields and from Pizzofalcone. From the farming hamlet of Ottaviano, not far from Mount Vesuvius, came plenty of lumber: for the coffers, for the construction of foundations, for construction in general, to stoke the kilns for the production of lime. To bring this material, 1,030 carts were utilized, provided not only by the capital (which purchased 200 of them) but also by the cities of Capua, Aversa, Caserta, and Maddaloni.

There was a general feeling of immense enthusiasm for the project. That said, progress proved to be extremely slow. Not merely because of the vast scope of the project, given the fact that it also included two large areas for the safe docking of ships, one beneath Castel Nuovo (the Sottopalazzo) and the other in the so-called Loggia dei Marsigliesi. Natural causes played their role in slowing and interrupting construction. One such cause was a great tempest that struck the construction site in 1305, hammering the port so fiercely that marble columns and stone blocks were dragged out to sea and only salvaged with enormous effort. A project that Charles never lived to see completed. But which offered great advantages to Charles's son Robert, "who was able to attract commercial shipping from all over Italy."[9] And work continued. In 1305, construction began on a new arsenal in the same location as the old one, but built to suit the new dimensions of the capital and the Kingdom. As a result, a new artery was called for, a thoroughfare that in 1308 set out from the side overlooking Castel Nuovo and ran all the way to the commercial area, a section that occupied the older part of the port, in the Barbacane zone, which was crossed by the city's chief commercial street, the so-called Rua dei Cambi.

We are in the presence of a full-blown urban design that would have as its champions and impresarios Charles I, Charles II, and Robert, and that would be carried forward, albeit with a lesser outlay of resources and with much reduced objectives, by Queen Joanna I of Naples as well.[10] The project would take further form with the construction of a series of cathedrals and churches that brought with them revolutionary effects in terms of landscape. In the short span of just seventy years, the Angevin monarchs encouraged, directly or indirectly (with bequests, assignments of money and land, donations, and outright purchases), the construction of twenty-three churches. A revolution that bears the unmistakable façades of the churches of San Lorenzo Maggiore, San Pietro a Maiella, San Pietro Martire, San Domenico, the Naples cathedral and, most important of all, Santa Chiara. If in fact Castel Nuovo is the city's political and administrative fulcrum, Santa Chiara symbolizes the by now complete fusion between the *gens d'Anjou* and the Neapolitan populace; the sacred depiction of French power in the city. In short, then, the monument of state, the royal sanctuary that contains within its structure the bodies of the late sovereigns, lying in pomp and state.

It is interesting to note that in this general operation of reordering and modifying the city's face, one central problem was that of disagreements over sanitation issues. Some observers might point out that there is nothing new under the sun. The Angevins, in an attempt to solve the problem of difficult environmental conditions in a city struck especially harshly by such endemic diseases as malaria, did their very best. And they devoted time, money, and expertise to the solution. Often, however, with the result of watching all their hard work go to naught, and in short order be swept away by neglect and larger crisis.

Work was underway on reclamation of streams in and outside of the city, as well as the hygiene of potable water, with the reactivation of the Formello aqueduct, begun in 1268 with an investment of one hundred *oncias*. There was a general reorganization of the sewer system, when Charles II ordered on April 11, 1301, "that rainwater be channeled into great reservoirs inside the city, offering free drainage beneath the paved surfaces of the streets, which were plagued with puddles, mud, and all sorts of filth." In 1304 work began to flush the sewer conduit of Capuana (the *clavica de Capuana*), because rainwater rushed violently through it, only to reach the mouth of the sewer, where garbage and refuse piled up, causing floods that badly damaged the surrounding houses.

The most spectacular intervention, however, was that of the transfer of the crafts activities of leather and linen processing out of the city. Those transfers were implemented forcibly, without consulting the citizenry in any of the decisions, and with the transfer of manufacturing activities involving manual workers and skilled artisans from one part of the city to another. Starting in 1300, work began on the dismantlement of a series of basins for the maceration of linen flax located near Naples, at the bridge, or Ponte della Maddalena, in Santa Maria a Dogliuolo, and in the village of Terzo. The justification was that those basins "brought about corruption of the air": an *infectionem aeris* that had damaging consequences for the eastern section of the city, where malaria was already particularly widespread. The operation was undertaken with eminent domain, resulting in expropriations of the owners, who were either members of the *milites* class or else city convents and monasteries, though they were offered some monetary compensation. This is an episode to which I shall return.

Likewise, the transfer of the leather tanning facilities from the urban neighborhood of Pistasio to the suburban area of Moricino unfolded with a fair level of tension and protests. In June 1301, the master leather tanners, whose activity "rendered filthy a large section of the city, infecting the air even *in umbelico dicte civitatis,*" were ordered to leave the *platea Pistasie,* through which ran one of the city's main sewers, and to move to another area, farther out of town. The extra-urban zone of Moricino, not far from the Convento del Carmine, was chosen as their destination, and the leather tanners were invited to set up their ateliers and workshops there.

The idea was that this was a benign, uncontroversial choice, something that would harm no one, on a strip of land between beach and sea. Unfortunately, no one had taken into account the views of the friars of the Carmelo monastery. They launched a sort of community uprising, involving all the inhabitants of the area, in an act of NIMBY avant la lettre. An uprising that resulted in operations involving armed force, but also maneuvers of both a legal nature and affecting property ownership. For instance, the friars made it impossible to purchase new parcels of land along the waterfront. All the same, the choice of Moricino was practically obligatory: there was the particular configuration of the area, on the outskirts of the major urban concentration, enabling a continuous interaction with the center of the city; and also because the reorganization of port and harbor structures as well as traffic arteries along the coastline allowed for appropriate integration between productive and logistical structures.

Then there was the day-to-day problem of hygiene and rubbish, which must have been quite a challenge in a city that was densely inhabited in many areas. The attempt was made to resolve this on an urgent basis with the rationalization and reclamation of certain areas invaded by wildcat construction that needed to be reined in. A great many streets were paved, and stone for that purpose was used that had been salvaged from the ancient Roman flagstones of Pozzuoli or of the Appian Way, or else with stones quarried from the Phlegraean grottoes. As a part of this larger reclamation project, we also find the renovation of some of the more overlooked quarters of Forcella and the port, a welter of buildings and narrow lanes plagued with miasmas. One part of this renovation involved the demolition of the *pennate*, wooden structures that extended between buildings, making the quarter even more sordid than it already was, as well as partially dilapidated constructions that gave the entire neighborhood a tumbledown appearance. Or else drastic prohibitions were issued against "the disgusting custom of not only going to leave one's bowel movements in little used alleyways and lanes, but also of tossing out windows unclean waters and other filth." Also, in 1313, King Robert issued directives that the streets be cleaned and also that the paving be restored to a good state, because he was unwilling to let his *delitiosa civitas* be sullied by the "reek of corrupt air and poisoned by garbage," a condition that was also thought with great certainty to be the cause of disease.

A challenging struggle, as we were saying, in a world much less ready and able to deal with environmental challenges than ours is. This was so much more the case in a city where—and as we push past the first decade of the fourteenth century, we shall see this clearly—problems bound up with a general crisis of the city's social environment were so overwhelming that they swept away even what little had been done in the fields of public decorum and hygiene. So the chronicles remind us, filled as they are with references to the general condition of desuetude that plagued the urban fabric: covered with waste and rubbish, especially in the older neighborhoods, crowded and densely inhabited as they were. And so, as a result of "the pooling into wallows of waste waters and the accumulation of heaps of filth," on November 23, 1312, the city was termed to be "sickened with miasmas." On August 20, 1321, the air had become unbreathable because "garbage and filth are scattered throughout the drainage channels" (*in canalibus immictunt immundicias*), resulting in "emanations of terrible fumes." On September 4, 1322, mention is made of *aquas immundas et alia sordida* that, once again, in defiance of royal prohibitions, "are tossed out of windows and doors," defiling the streets and making them practically impracticable. And people complained about it. The inhabitants of the *platea de Albino* demanded that drainage gutters be built in their street to deal with the pooling waters, so deep that they prevented the progress of horses and pedestrians. Or else, "in unanimity, the people, both *milites* and ordinary citizens who are still inhabitants of the *platea di San Martino*, demanded in 1304 the reconstruction of a gutter *commonly known as a chiaveca*, i.e., sewer." And so on, in a succession of documentary evidence of management difficulties that, as the imbroglios plaguing this capital in a state of crisis grew increasingly out of control, made it impossible to intervene with policies that might reduce or limit the general state of deterioration.[11]

The King and the Other World

In the city government there was an even greater shoal to be cleared. An obstacle that had everything to do with its people. The Other World, to use the metaphor referenced previously. That is to say, the old group of the *nobiliores* who had subscribed, en masse and enthusiastically, to the new French leadership. The men of the clans and the *seggi*, men who now wanted to count for something. Who wanted to play a part. Now, with the new monarchy, they were going to have to figure out what power relationships there were going to be between these two poles of authority, one of which constituted both state and law, while the other represented custom and tradition. There was a difference from the past. A large and substantial difference. Namely, that the Normans and the Swabians had been imposed from without. Not so with the Angevins. They had been yearned for, *invited*. The Neapolitans had contributed to the rise of this monarchy, with great spending of resources and energy. And if Charles had chosen Naples, well, that had at least in part been their doing. Ready as they had been to supply the substrate upon which to construct the political edifice of the Kingdom. In a relationship that from the very outset possessed an ambiguous overtone. There was collaboration, but it had its limits. There was dialogue, but it entailed attempts, where it seemed possible, to undermine one's counterpart in order to gain personal benefits.

Charles understood this immediately, and once he'd entered the city, he made use of the *milites* to resolve and pacify any and all sorts of social tension or turmoil. Well, he must have asked himself, are they or are they not the people who run the city, the guarantors of public order? In that case, let's make room for them, but let's also immediately reduce their power. And so the first thing the king tried to do was to shatter the alliances. Especially those between the nobility and the common folk, which meant the elite and the working classes, artisans, and merchants, and which had previously been a strong and active bond. One that had seemed unshakable. So much so that anything the king proposed for the city they rejected ("nothing that he put forth of his own conception appeared able to be done"). And so what did the king decide to do? He tossed all the papers in the air and overturned the table, so to speak. As Summonte wrote, "to make ruling his realm easier, he split the unity of government, the nobles from the populace." Let me repeat those words, which had an extraordinary impact: *to make ruling his realm easier.* In short, there was an awareness in Charles that we must truly consider surprising. He knew that the government of the city wasn't completely under his control. And that if he wished to rule, he would have to split, to separate one class from another, create divisions between those who, until then, had been unanimous in their choices of what measures to undertake.

Alongside the old standby of *divide et impera*, there was another way of depriving the clans of the Other World of their strength and power: strip them of the land where they live and multiply. Their breeding ground, their broth culture, to use a term associated with bacteria, consisted primarily of the spaces where they gathered and organized their moves. Those places needed to be eliminated. How to go about doing that? In as drastic a manner as could be: by demolishing what constituted the greatest danger in the context of a strategy of institutional control of the city. And once that danger had been removed, by building on top of it something new that could completely scramble the original social and topographic network, resetting the environment and shattering that traditional tissue of connivance that had served as the humus, the fertile soil in which the families of the nobility had first sunk their roots.

A truly radical process of urban renewal and transformation of the ancient sectors and the traditional warp and woof of clan dominion. There were a number of different episodes of this nature, all of them quite significant. The construction of San Pietro a Maiella and San Domenico Maggiore modified an entire area in a substantial fashion. With the first church, what vanished was the ancient city gate of Donnorso, which had long belonged to the family of that name, resulting in an alteration of the urban layout and the gate itself being moved, after which it also lost the association with the family name. The construction site of San Domenico Maggiore, on the other hand, absorbed the age-old church of Sant'Arcangelo de illi Morfisa, one of the many private churches in the city, which involved not only the Morfisa family but also other families in the area. Santa Maria la Nova was built on the ruins of the Torre Mastra, which had long been the property of the Castagnola family; an operation that also swallowed up the family *estaurita*. Beginning in 1270, the church of Sant'Agostino alla Zecca was built, requiring the demolition of the venerable old tower the Torre Herculanensis. In order to build Castel Nuovo, property was taken from the Griffi and the Carmignano clans. A broad expropriation plan was drawn up for the construction of the Convent of Santa Chiara, and that involved the property of the nobleman Tommaso Guindazzo, several members of the Brancaccio family, a Ravignano, the doctor Guido Viola, and most of all, a number of the Caputo, who therefore saw their entire real estate holdings vanish in the space of a single decade; those holdings had been the basis of their power in the portside quarter. It also resulted in a topographic revolution, given the disappearance of all and any references to streets, porticoes, or gates bearing the name dei Caputo.[12]

The last event had to do with the church of San Lorenzo Maggiore. Something that offered an especially stark indication of what sort of strategy the royal government was following. Let's hear what Carlo Pecchia has to say:

> In Naples there was a royal palace where the *milites* as well as the other citizens came together for business of the city. Charles of Anjou found such a union to be dangerous: he therefore decided to separate not only the *milites* from the populace, but also *milites* from *milites*, and the first step he took was to destroy that palace, laying on the ruins of it the foundation of a magnificent church of San Lorenzo [Saint Lawrence].[13]

This history is reported by a great many sources. From Summonte to Celano, all the way up to the nineteenth century. What is the story? That the king, finding it *too dangerous* to allow the *milites* to assemble and meet with the members of other components of the city's power structure, potentially to build an opposition party against him, had the whole thing demolished, thus destroying the chief municipal decision-making forum, the Palazzo Augustale. An intervention that, once again in this case, upset the traditional array based upon the clans, thus striking brutally at one of the families with the oldest presence in the quarter, the family of the Marogano, who owned houses, courtyards, churches, and workshops. A governmental decision that didn't end with the demolition of the Palazzo Augustale, but continued with the beginning of construction on one of Naples's loveliest cathedrals, the Franciscan church of San Lorenzo, which rose atop the ruins of this ancient fortress, a center of family power.

Naturally enough, these various demolitions and interventions were prompted not merely by objectives of repression. They also owed their origin to the more general trend of transformation sweeping Naples as it grew from a city into a capital, in accordance with a policy pursued by the Angevin sovereigns. All the same, the urban renewal and the construction of the major churches and monastic complexes had the parallel effect of unhinging and devastating the load-bearing structures of an entire world, namely the world of the clans. So much so that demolitions were the natural topic of discussion when urgent interventions on behalf of public safety were called for, in order to put down violence, internal strife, and wars among clans. The most spectacular case had to do with the Griffi clan, in 1331. This imposed a draconian repression in the aftermath of a bloody running feud that ensued following the murder of Lorenzo Castagnola. In retaliation the house of the clan chief Carmayno Griffo was torn down, and then on August 15 the venerable old family *seggio* was razed to the ground, "not merely as a symbol of the past, but also as an organism of power and the cause of recurrent tensions and disorders."[14]

In any case, the expropriations were not merely intended to undermine the urban landholdings, the solid and acknowledged element of ownership that established the clan's strength and power. There existed other strategies, and they were no less effective. Among them was the tactic of striking directly at financial resources and estates, landholdings that were made up of parcels of land, working farms, and structures for the flax maceration in the making of linen. I've previously described the reclamation efforts designed to eliminate linen-making manufactories from the city precincts, with a stated objective involving public hygiene. But behind that decision, there lurked another aspect, one we should not overlook.

For centuries linen had represented one of the principal Neapolitan exports, along with white wine, also known as *vino greco*, or Greek wine. For a long time, Naples had produced raw linen, as well as fabrics and finished garments and textile products, involving a scattered distribution of artisans working across the territory. This linen industry had a certain success in the markets of the Middle East and North Africa. Its export business, however, came to a halt between the twelfth and thirteenth centuries, on account of the fabrics being produced in north-central Italy at a more affordable price. The result was this: the production of finished garments and other sewn articles came to an end, but not that of raw flax, used in the making of linen. Flax was grown widely around Naples, and the resulting production found a profitable outlet in the areas of textile production in north-central Italy.

Raw flax for linen, in other words, was highly profitable. The only drawback was that it had to be treated and steeped in special tanks known as *fusari*. These tanks were for many years arrayed in the same corner of the port of Naples, with a harmful effect on the surrounding environment. That fact resulted in orders being issued, from the Norman era onward, for the linen maceration tanks to be moved eastward, to the city's outskirts. At that point, the *fusari* became fundamental factors in Naples's economic life: a truly precious resource, given the fact that the entire volume of production of this fiber, which arrived entirely from the hinterland, was transported to this one area. This was an operation for payment that became increasingly profitable for the owners of the *fusari*, largely because the production was substantial and the tanks were few in number. That in turn pushed the cost of using them higher, increasing potential profits.

At the end of the thirteenth century, ownership of the *fusari* was in the hands of several clans. If, for instance, we take the ten basins located near the bridge called the Ponte Guizzardo or Ponte della Maddalena, we find a number of owners, among them the Caracciolo, the Minutolo, the Guindazzo, the Piscicelli, and the Protonobilissimo. They were all required to deposit in the state's coffers a utilization tax of fifty-one *oncias* and twenty-three *tarì*. The result was surely a substantial income, with numbers much greater than the taxes paid to the treasury, sums that were plausibly reinvested in the expansion of the various family homes. At the turn of the new century, however, everything changed. By order of King Charles II, work began on dismantling the *fusari*. The reasons, as we have seen, certainly had to do with solving the serious health problems they were causing. Still, at the same time, this constituted a sharp blow to one of the factors in the clans' wealth. In short: with a single intervention, two results were attained, one of them urbanistic in nature and the other political. Killing two birds with one stone.

The operation was carried out so rapidly that between 1308 and 1310, every single maceration tank to the east of Naples vanished. That state intervention must surely have met with the disapproval of the families that had owned them, who received only a one-time payment of fifty *oncias*, money siphoned off from the bread tax, and certainly less than half of what they could have earned in a year of production. Still, however, they were left with the land following the reclamation, and that land quickly became the site of either new construction or else agricultural crops, which offered an opportunity for new and different forms of income.

So this was a process of stripping the clans of their wealth. Depriving them of their economic lifelines. Uprooting them from their longtime territories. Deforming the physiognomy of the *seggi*, their traditional bases, introducing new families of new origins, among them the French, such as the Origlia, the del Balzo, and the de la Rath. Limiting the pressure brought to bear by the most prestigious groups. These were the methods employed, in a process of domesticating an aristocracy that could be loyal when it chose, but which was also every bit as likely to be unbridled, argumentative, and given to violence and wholesale aggression. A class that needed to be brought to heel. Was this enough? Not entirely. Frequently these steps turned out to be little more than palliatives. In that case, the government chose to adopt a craftily targeted political strategy designed to put an end once and for all to all these old subdivisions by quarter. And it aimed directly at the big target, that is, the age-old system of the *seggi*. In the end, the decision was made to reduce the twenty-nine ungovernable, chaotic family *seggi* scattered throughout the city to just five major aristocratic aggregations that were intended to channel the entire aristocracy into a few clearly defined groupings that would be easy to control and manage.

What was the context of that decision that was clearly, narrowly, and entirely political in nature? The point was this, that the state must prevail over disorder and anarchy, and the state absolutely needed, especially in the capital, to maintain a tight control over public order and those various forces that might create problems and tensions that might affect the general peace and stability of the Kingdom. These aggregations, in the end, continued to preserve their original traditional configuration, and they were still called *seggi*. And they adhered more or less to the same original divisions of territory into regions, taking the names of the *seggi* of Montagna (or Forcella), Capuana, Nido, Porto, and Portanova. Plus one more, the *seggio pittato*, of the common folk. Entities that revolutionized the traditional municipal apparatus, with the imposition of a new order that would go on to have a very long history.

This was not a choice settled once and for all, but rather, as Monica Santangelo has explained, a process first begun, if we are to accept what is handed down by oral tradition, in the earliest years of the Kingdom under Charles I and then continued, with a great many vicissitudes, all the way up to the 1380 formalization under Joanna I.[15] A complicated process that had everything to do with the administrative attributions, the management of how tax burdens fell, the collection of the gabelles, as well as tensions within the ranks of the nobility, where they were struggling to preserve their age-old prerogatives. But the strongest drive behind this revolution was, unquestionably, institutional in nature, an attempt to reduce the critical elements that could induce fissures and cracks within the general system of municipal management.

A lengthy process of development, then. Within which, it wasn't as if the old aggregations disappeared in a puff, or were dissolved willy-nilly, by force (except for the *seggio* of the Griffi,

but in that case, it was about public order, and therefore impera-
tive...). The development was slow and gradual. The smaller *seggi*,
as Summonte recalls, were invited—or, probably we should say,
obliged—to be recomposed into one of the principal *seggi*, according to the following operative scheme: when "matters of public
government" were at stake, each small *seggio* met separately to
thrash out its own attitude about the matters at stake. Only after
these meetings was a general assembly held of the principal *seggio*
that also comprised the smaller *seggi*. Therefore, no longer a fragmented welter of *seggi* scattered throughout the city, but instead,
for an extended first phase, a constellation of *seggi* that clustered
around the larger, institutional *seggio*, "like so many bishops, or
perhaps we should say limbs acknowledging their head."[16]

The *seggi* would go on to manage the city, running it with
the five political and administrative articulations of Montagna-
Forcella, Capuana, Nido, Porto, and Portanova. Units endowed
with specific judicial, religious, and sumptuary jurisdictions, as
well as their own magistrates, in connection with the capital's
other *officia*. Every *seggio* would go on to select an *eletto*, or chosen
member, from its nobility for the Tribunale di San Lorenzo, the
city government made up of six noble *eletti* (Montagna and Forcella had two, but only one vote); and, in alternating turns, also an
eletto from the *seggio* of the common folk, or populace.

In conclusion, the old articulation into *seggi*, which had represented the city's spirit for more than a century, was broken under
this new system. Careful, though: we're in the presence of a substantial operation, but also a cosmetic one. Because it's as if they'd
trimmed away so many dry branches, withered and dried out by
the passage of time along with new and developing historical conditions: suffice it to consider that many *seggi* by now represented
no more than two or three families, often reduced to poverty and
devoid of any real influence over the business interests of their
quarter. Basically they had no real representation in the political games of the municipality. A slimming down and efficiency
that everyone could agree on, because it skimmed off the cream.

Sifted and sorted. Split up so that the *nobiliores* of the *nobiliores* were allowed to rise and emerge, in a situation that broke down into two macrogroups: on the one hand the aggregation of Porto, Portanova, and Montagna-Forcella. On the other hand, the protagonists of the raid of 1343, the noblemen of Capuana and Nido. A distinction into different areas that was more than merely administrative, one that had a much more profound and articulated profile, since it divided the city into two different settings, with customs, traditions, and practices that varied from one zone to the other, with the steady emergence and rise of the clans boasting greater political influence, such as the Caracciolo, the Carafa, the Brancaccio, and the Minutolo.

With a role for the *nobiliores* of Capuana and Nido, to distinguish them further and more completely from the mass of the Neapolitan nobility. Sufficiently to allow them to feel superior, thanks to the royal decree of King Robert that in 1339 entrusted them with two-thirds of the civic honors. Let's read what Camera has to say:

> King Robert, in order to put an end to quarrels and demands, decided toward the end of June to summon to his presence all the parties involved; said parties, having agreed to submit wholeheartedly to the will and determination of their sovereign, heard that Capuana and Nido would enjoy two-thirds of the honors, thus the remaining honors were to be divided among the remaining three *seggi* and the common folk (a decision that was difficult for the other three to swallow, who determined to bide their time, hoping for a modification, which came in 1380). Aside from this resolution, it was also determined that in the elections of the royal officials and ministers, and in the management of public affairs, the *seggi* of Capuana and Nido were asked not to communicate with the others, but rather separately, so as to ward off all and any scandal, disturbance, et cetera.[17]

Capuana and Nido, very simply, formed a separate political entity. One that would go on to clash repeatedly with the other *seggi* in order to establish its preeminence, its capacity for initiatives, its own military capability. An expression of the most powerful family clans in the city, clans that now found themselves further aggregated, organized, and strengthened by the natural selection that had, meanwhile, been produced by the slow elimination of the less prominent *seggi*. In a city where, to paraphrase Orwell, "all of the nobles are equal, but some were more equal than others." A de facto condition attested by King Robert himself, who four years prior to the episode of the raid against the Genoese ship was forced to acknowledge that the two *seggi* not only had priority over the entire system but were also separate from the rest of the municipal aristocracy. A separation that would become even more massive, just a few years later, as a result of the series of dotal *consuetudini*, decided *more magnatum*, according to the indications of the most important families. That decision was destined to carve a deeper trench between Capuana and Nido on one hand and the rest of the city on the other.

That was the attitude of the state and the monarchy toward the social milieu, especially that of the elite. And if I were to name the traits that characterized the ensuing political intervention, they would have to be selection, reordering, and repression. Three elements to which I should add a fourth, which casts a spotlight on the families and the clans. I've said it before and I'll repeat it here: there is no doubt about the fact that the Angevin adventure represented for the Neapolitans the opportunity of all time. A national turning point (which begins in 1266 and comes to an end with the Unification of Italy) in the initial phases of which the Neapolitans played a very specific role: one of encouragement and impetus, which translated into logistical and physical assistance to the French monarch.

Now they were no longer the residents of just any old city: now they lived in the capital. They therefore belonged to a new game, one in which they were going to need to be quick on their feet and find a place for themselves: first of all, with respect to the newly central role that Naples had taken on as a new pole of attraction for the Kingdom at large, a keystone in both administrative and institutional terms and the seat of the royal court. What's more, with respect to the opportunities offered by this very central role, and in terms of new developments in the opportunities for social climbing, chances within the world of bureaucracy and offices, feudal privileges, direct contact with the sovereign, no longer distant and inaccessible…

These were new things, previously unimaginable. Things that now transformed into opportunities. The chance to be a leading element in this exciting new order. The ruling elite of not a city, but an entire kingdom.

A New Ruling Class

Just imagine something along these lines. One of these men who was there to witness the dawn of the new chapter of Angevin rule. Someone who, for his whole life—*his* life, just like the lives of his forefathers—had always lived within the perimeter of a closed precinct. A circuit as safe as a placenta, a place he knew stone by pebble, every single wall and corner, every tower, *his* gate, *his* private church, his surrounding family, kin, and ilk. A man who had never traveled farther than a hundred footsteps from his own local piazza. Who had never even cast eyes any farther away than that. And now look at him: projected out into a universe of unimaginable opportunities. Things that, until thirty or forty years earlier, couldn't even have been conceived of. Certainly, there had been the possibility of rising to Norman and Swabian administrative posts. But the path had been ever so narrow. Open only to a chosen few. And even then, Naples was just a city like any other, not the capital of a kingdom…

Now a revolution was underway—in both psychology and mindset—that involved the Neapolitan nobleman (though not him alone). A horizon was opening out, a road leading to greater honor and wealth. A path that might catapult him out into one of the outlying provinces, where he could form a structure of personal prestige and a different and much broader reputation. Opportunities that could put him into direct contact with people from far away: from Marseille, or Catalonians, Genoans, Florentines, Tuscans... people who could show him, with their words and deeds, that the world is so much bigger than the *contrada* (neighborhood) of Portanova or Montagna, and so on, where he—and his father, his father's father, and so on back in time— had always lived their lives.

So these individuals grabbed tight and held on to this new array of opportunities. They shaped themselves to comply with the new demands of the capital city. So true is this, that they formed a Neapolitan class of functionaries who, little by little, acquired positions of ever-greater prestige. A condition bound up with the sovereign's conferral of *familiaritas*, a badge of intimacy and friendship that nearly all the municipal clans could boast about. It was always associated with the role of *consiliarius*, something that isn't entirely clear to us in terms of what it actually constituted: most likely it meant the possibility of gaining access to court and, to some extent, to frequent the court. An attribute, *familiaritas*, that was granted very frequently by Charles II and that was analogous, as he himself stated in his will, to a pension corresponding to a hierarchical order that matched the ranks of the cavalry: forty *oncias* for the *milites*, twenty *oncias* for the *scutiferi nobiles*, twelve *oncias* for the non-noble *scutiferi*, six *oncias* for foot soldiers (*pedites*).

All of the most important families plunged into this new adventure, which transformed their members from prominent individuals in a clan or a group into tiles in the mosaic of a bureaucratic universe then in formation. These were the names: Brancaccio, Minutolo, Guindazzo, Siginolfo, Griffi, Caputo, Piscicelli, and so on. From the 1270s on, they appear on the rosters of professional posts of various kinds and importance, from military ranks to administrative and diplomatic positions. We also see a number of these *milites* who seem to emerge for the very first time from within the four walls of their quarter, their family *seggio*. They move into new contexts. They head for a position that will allow them to lift off into something well beyond a limited, local domain. But it will represent a further element of distinction. To establish with even greater power the difference *between who I am and who you are.*

Let's begin with the Guindazzo family. An ancient family that had held positions of great prestige as early as the tenth century. And who'd belonged on an unbroken basis to the group of the *milites*, with all their clan. A great many of them had entered into the ranks of the royal administration. Even if I limit myself to the thirteenth century alone, beginning in the eighth decade of that century a certain Simone served as the *portolano* of Baiae and the *magister salis* in Terra di Lavoro. He also served as a knight under Charles II, who repaid his services by endowing him with a feudal landholding in Calabria. Pietro was a contemporary of this Simone. He was appointed *castellano*, or chatelain, of Castello del Salvatore, known from the Angevin era on as Castel dell'Ovo. Between 1269 and 1270, he served as vice-regent of the master of accounts, treasurer, and commissioner for loans to the crown in Terra di Lavoro and in the duchy of Amalfi. Sergio was the *magister passuum*, in charge of tolls and tariffs. Together with Sergio Siginolfo and two members of the Latro and del Duca families, he collected tariffs—of anything but secondary importance—on iron, steel, and pitch; and he ended his career as the *giustiziere*—or justiciar, administrator of justice—of Principato Citra. Bartolomeo was the *secreto* in Terra d'Otranto and captain in Barletta. Another Simone (we see the same names crop up over and over, not only in Neapolitan documentation but in medieval documentation as a whole) was a doctor, a pontifical chaplain, and of course a *familiare*, or intimate, of the king. And so forth. We see the same situation for the Minutolo family, with Ligorio, from 1277 *portolano* of Naples and, from 1288 to 1292 *secreto* and *mastro portolano* of the principality. Or else Landolfo, also known as Saccapanna, *familiare* and *fedele, giustiziere* of the Capitanata. Or else for the Siginolfo, Caputo, Griffi, Caracciolo, Pignatelli, and Piscicelli families, indeed for all the families of the aristocracy at large.

Honors, no doubt about it, and considerable ones at that. But they bear some consideration. Because we shouldn't assume that all this is merely the result of a single group being assimilated into the meshes of the larger state. A process where what happens happens without shocks, a gentle, agreeable submission, *en douceur,* as the French might say, in which the Neapolitans accept and are grateful for these new opportunities they're being offered. Sure, that happened too, no doubt about it. But the interactions are far more ridden with dialectical dynamics than that. Let's start with the conferment of positions. It is natural that many should have been chosen from among the ranks of the city's aristocracy due to their personal prestige, family history, skills in administration and government, et cetera.

All the same, it didn't always go that way. Because unlike the case with trade, in which the people of the South proved that they, so to speak, lacked any noteworthy skills in their competition with far more aggressive rivals from elsewhere, when it came instead to public contracts, such as those for collecting customs fees, tariffs, taxes, and levies, certain families of the bourgeoisie showed unquestionable abilities. It was no accident that beginning in the Swabian Kingdom, public contracts had been the ladder leading to huge family fortunes. Those fortunes, for instance, were won by merchants of Scala and Ravello, many of whom had been transplanted to Naples, where they took on important roles in the financial administration of the Kingdom under Frederick II.[18] That tendency only became more marked under Manfred, when the financial administration, beginning with the highest rank of functionary, the *secreto*, and from there down, was entrusted with one-year contracts to businessmen from the Amalfi area. And those contracts were really quite expensive to acquire. For instance, the contracts for collecting taxes in Apulia at the beginning of the

Angevin era, in 1272, cost 2,400 *oncias*, which meant more than forty kilograms (nearly ninety pounds) of gold. So they must have brought in far more money than that. Otherwise, why bother to obtain them?

An interesting array, the men of the coast; largely endowed with skills at investment, perhaps not up to the level of competing with their foreign rivals, but still ideal for providing their sovereigns, first the Swabians and later, in particular, the Angevins, with the capital needed by a state in constant need of new financing. A role that brought them not only considerable immediate profit but also a reinforcement of their positions in the Kingdom's financial administration. It furthermore resulted in these families pursuing a lasting engagement with the machinery of state, thus consolidating a tradition that extended for many centuries and survived the change of dynasty in the fifteenth century.

That tradition served as an excellent example for the Neapolitans, many of whom lived cheek by jowl with these Amalfitans who had emigrated to the capital. The dynamic, in fact, worked as follows: they'd buy a public contract from the court, and they might do so at steep prices. Then the court gave them free rein to handle it as they saw fit, in absolute freedom, as long as they brought the court an established flat price at first. What that frequently meant was that they would squeeze every last penny out of merchants as they came through customs; they'd subject the populace to all sorts of taxes and surtaxes; they'd levy brutal fees on the producers who hoped to offer their goods for sale at markets and fairs. A situation of discomfort and difficulty that resulted in a storm of complaints and denunciations echoing endlessly: in Calabria, Terra d'Otranto, Basilicata, the cities of the Apulian coast, Capitanata, and Abruzzo. With local functionaries who often arrested, beat, and stripped the merchants of their goods, subjecting them to taxations that really came close to bankrupting them, with an unmistakable negative effect on trade in general.[19]

In the face of these situations the authorities had a hard time taking any serious measures. Because there were considerable immunities at play. And also because, in the meantime, the state had already received the money from its subcontractors. At most, the state might lodge objections. Or lecture. Or demand lawsuits. Though even lawsuits as often as not were dead letters. Here's one case that's pretty representative, an episode from 1285. Sergio, of the Siginolfo clan, was accused of having smuggled goods out of the port of Naples. A very serious charge, made more serious still by the fact that he was hardly a nobody. Not only was he a member of an important clan, but his father, the Count of Acerra, was an all-powerful figure at court, the *secreto* of Principato and Terra di Lavoro, a customs officer and *fondichiere* of the port of Castellammare di Stabia, and much, much more. Sergio himself was a *miles, consiliarius, cambellanus,* and *regiae marescallae magister.* And yet he certainly seemed to be the main operative of a network of smugglers who was involving other officials of the port, as well as leading members of other prominent clans or the families of important merchants of Amalfi. Soon they all found themselves under arrest in a sort of police sweep: members of the Minutolo, Scondito, Scriniario, Spina, and d'Afflitto families. All of them would by rights have been looking at serious penalties and an expedited judicial trial. Considering the status of those under arrest, however, and in order to prevent a chain reaction of further scandals, the "incident" was swept under the rug. The charges were dropped. And Sergio was allowed to resume his career undisturbed. In fact we find him again, four years later, at his usual post in the port of Naples, with the same cast of characters who had faced charges alongside him, among them Luigi Minutolo, Tommaso Scriniario, Riccardo Scondito, and members of the d'Afflitto family.

The system of competitions for public contracts had a practical utility, because both parties to the contracts derived benefits therefrom. On the one hand, in fact, it was useful to the state as a way of restoring vigor to the machinery of the Angevin regime, which—and this was a constant throughout the history of that dynasty—invariably tended to veer toward red ink. A constant that, we should point out, was by no means uniquely Neapolitan; indeed, it was a genuine common denominator of all the states of the ancien *régime*. Already, under the rule of Charles I, "the expenses to maintain an adequately articulated administrative apparatus, the troops and the fleets scattered across the map from Provence to Achæa, or the Peloponnese, the subsidies paid to support the Guelph cause in central-northern Italy, the programs for civil construction and the foundation or reconstruction of fortresses, farming hamlets, or new villages, as well as of royal palaces and churches in various parts of the Kingdom, and even the census that was required on a yearly basis from the apostolic see by the Angevin dynasty—all these things made the king a man perennially questing after money."[20] The state, then, became a full-fledged money-consuming machine. It continued to be a money pit under Charles II and Robert, in spite of Robert's notorious reputation as a skinflint. It carried a constant deficit that proved difficult to bridge with mere tax revenues and other income. It turned out to be so much easier to manage everything with advances on revenue, in other words, with loans. Which could of course be paid off with the assignment of public contracts.

For that matter, this system proved very useful as well to the *mutuatores*, those who loaned money to the state, among them families that we've already had a chance to get to know: Caputo, Castagnola, Griffi, Venato, Vulcano, Brancaccio, Guindazzo, Siginolfo, and so on: "All of them useful individuals who with their money were helpful to the King in the necessities of war." *Nobiles* who expected considerable returns from these investments. On the one hand, they expected to enhance their social standings in a scenario where the struggle for prominence could get quite intense, with levels of competition that spiraled in all directions, with new actors appearing onstage, rising from the lower depths and eager to climb the ladder themselves. On the other hand, they were in search of economic security in the form of public contracts, prebends, pensions, rents, and feudal landholdings. One vignette from 1348 offers an eloquent description of what was going on. In view of the revenues from a number of municipal levies—the gabelles of the *quartatico* and the *Bucceria*, the revenues from money changing, the revenues from Tintoria, the Bagliva of Ischia, the customs (Dogana) and trade warehouse (Fondaco) of Gaeta—Queen Joanna I decided to take a nice fat slice of money for herself, something approaching five hundred *oncias*, which she then rained down on various members of the corps of the *milites*: the Guindazzo family, notable among them Sergio, *miles, cambellanus*, and *familiaris*; the Carafa family; the Rumbo; the de Burgenza; the Impullone branch of the Brancaccio clan; and the Caracciolo. Also on two women, Maffea d'Aprano, the wife of the *miles* Filippo Siginolfo; and Belletta Cossa. In brief, to use the words of di Costanzo: "the nobility of Naples, indeed the entire city, was greatly elevated; because aside from the great number of counts, she also created a countless number of knights who lived on honorable pensions from the coffers of the royal taxes."[21]

This wholesale invasion of the royal offices—and everything that derived from it in terms of both status and economic reinforcement—became one of the most original interpretative elements allowing us to understand this new Naples as capital. Here, the gaming table upon which the clans were playing had a twofold meaning, both local and national in scope, on account of the singular role that the city now had in the logic of the Kingdom. In this context, the families we're examining experienced a profound transformation, inasmuch as many of their ranks changed their description entirely, setting themselves forward as *officiales*, components of a bureaucracy in the process of formation. In brief, they were transformed into a brand-new ruling class. At the same time, the monarchy entrusted them with what was dearest to its royal heart, this newly harnessed aristocracy, bound up in the new system of the five *seggi* and bound to loyalty through its involvement in the public administration: the day-to-day government of the city. Maintaining public order. Keeping the municipal peace. Ensuring that the two worlds fit snugly together. And so the family clans became the flywheel, the transmission between public policies and official directives and the actual reality of city life. In other words, the Angevin political will, in that challenging and vast sector of government that involved the management and control of Naples, once again passed, as was traditional, through the persons of the *fideles*, namely the heads of the major Neapolitan families, who operated in the twofold role of local administrators, expressions of the municipal populace and needs, but also officials of the royal state.[22]

The men of the clans had come a long way. And now, thanks to the sovereign authority, they were able to perform the duties on an official basis that they had already been carrying out for centuries on a de facto basis. That meant, very simply, ensuring public order. It might also involve police duties, at a time when the state was absolutely inadequate to the task of controlling the city with its own arms. For that matter, who else could the state turn to put a halt, or at least to some degree restrain, the violence, theft, and abuses that were the order of the day in King Robert's Kingdom? Necessarily, it had to turn to those who had full mastery of the urban fabric. The only ones who had the ability to restrain the excesses and careening outbursts that threatened the established order. An order that in this city had been established by the clans in the first place.

Returning to the issue of the administration, in the new Kingdom a context developed in which the *milites* were invested with long-term responsibilities, either specific or received on given occasions. In this state, still in the process of formation, we should not imagine there being any sort of rigid staffing; it was a far more flexible structure that availed itself of an extended circuit of *milites, devoti, fideles*, familiars of the king who were entrusted, from time to time, with certain tasks and responsibilities. According to the principle, first expressed by King Robert in 1329, that "public offices should not be entrusted to those who ask for them, but instead those who do not desire them in the least." And there was formed a core group that became increasingly stable with the passage of time, formed of trusted individuals, bound to the king by a knot of reciprocal assistance, devoted to the preservation and improvement of the Kingdom. With a special focus on the capital. Where the local aristocracy became the "irreplaceable hinge of the state, deriving its strength from the positions held in the city, and ready to mobilize effectually to perform and carry out numerous and varied royal services."[23]

And career paths became increasingly clear. There was a steady growth in the honors and responsibilities of a new class of *officiales*. People who were neither fish nor fowl, strictly speaking. Neither members of the feudal structure nor of a bureaucratic class of the kind we are familiar with now. No, they were something entirely different, pilfering their identity a little bit from here and a little bit from there but never seeing themselves as entirely comparable to either. Because they were made of a special stuff: they were *milites* of the old Neapolitan world, with deep roots in their urban environment. They were still distinguished by a single calling, that of warriors with strong ties to their own quarter, their own zone, their own *seggio*, their own clan. A universe that would weigh heavily on the foundational nature of the Angevin state, with its imprint of old-fashioned chivalry, in the sense of knighthood, not manners. One fundamental element of this identity was the monarchic institute of the military girdle, the official source of ennoblement that, in addition to encouraging political consensus and binding the greatest possible number of people to the dynasty, also expressed membership in the actual ruling class, with direct ties to the sovereign, and not merely in a symbolic manner. The core of that class was by and large composed of the old families that belonged to the Neapolitan militia.

As for exactly what was involved in the ceremony of the investiture of the girdle of knighthood, we have an excellent explanation from Matteo Camera:

> Being decorated with the *cingolo militare*, or girdle of knighthood, was the most eminent honor to which any patrician or personage might hope to aspire in those days. The solemn act of such an elevated knightly conferral involved the greatest men

of the Kingdom and demanded the most distinguished and sacred location. Only the sovereign himself could confer the honor of the girdle of knighthood; with his own royal sword he would touch the head and shoulders of the candidate knight and utter the words *May God make you a good knight.* After which, seven ladies of the queen's court, all dressed in white, would wrap his hips with the girdle that they held in their hands and that they had previously presented to the king; after which they fastened to his side the sword the candidate himself had taken from the altar.[24]

The ceremony continued from there. A number of knights would put spurs on the candidate's heels, dress him in a surplice of green woolen cloth, and seat him amid the other *milites* present at the service. Last of all, the bishop, who was also present, would receive the candidate's profession of faith and his oath of loyalty to his king. But it still wasn't over, because once he'd been admitted into the fellowship of the knights of the king, the individual thus admitted had to take a further step, namely...to pay twenty golden *oncias*, a one-time payment, as a donation. Once that was done, the new *miles* enjoyed all the privileges and prerogatives of the militia, such as being exempt from certain taxes, the penalties that could be inflicted upon the humbler common folk, and the obligation to fight a duel with anyone other than a knight. He also had the right to have engraved upon his tomb his own effigy, with his entire suit of armor and the arms that symbolized his status, beneath which were generally depicted two dogs, symbolic of faithfulness and loyalty.

The Sicilian Vespers

There is a moment in this tale of the relations between our two worlds that is one of rupture, constituting a line of demarcation between a before and an after. That moment is the War of the Vespers. War had been the dominant state of affairs since the arrival of the Angevins. The catalyst that harnessed enthusiasms, stimuli, and ferments, bonding together Naples and the Anjous in this sort of blood pact, a pledge of shared fate. The Kingdom, both under Charles I and under his son, was up in arms for years on end, and so Naples became the protagonist of the Angevin enterprises. With the *milites* who took part in it, on an active basis. And in so doing, they underwrote the political aims of the monarchy, taking them as their own.

These were international ambitions, aims that focused on the creation of a great Mediterranean realm. And there was an even greater dream behind that: the idea of pushing through Hungary to reach Byzantium. They would go to Tunis, Tuscany, the Balkans... with a tribute of energy and blood, the Neapolitans fighting for their king on land and sea. We find them in the expedition to Thracia. At the gates of Florence. In the battles of Corfu. Among them, some distinguish themselves as heroes. Praised directly by the king. For instance, Raone Griffo. An individual who turns up repeatedly in various theaters of war, where his military abilities were greatly prized. The same went for his brothers, Siginolfo, Sergio, and Bartolomeo, the last-named actually having been taken prisoner but redeemed through an exchange for an important personage, Giovanni Chiaromonte. Giovanni Guindazzo, involved in various military expeditions, and in recognition of the services he performed for the crown, was awarded the farming hamlets of Comite in Calabria; while the *miles* Sergio, along with a member of the Apocefalo clan, financed the fitting out of several ships for the fleet. Or else we could mention the vice admiral Landolfo Minutolo, also known as Saccapanna. And many others.

Behind all these expeditions and exploits, there was always the city of Naples. An administrative center but also a general headquarters, a construction site, a center for the logistics and preparation of operations. "The source from which the war actually takes its nourishment." It was here that the defenses of the entire

Kingdom were organized, their foundations laid. It was here that soldiers and sailors were recruited. Here that the fleet was provisioned and fitted out. The capital became the fulcrum of all initiatives, where everything converged, and from which everything unfolded. In an effort that grew ever greater and mightier. And which seemed to be able to attain the results hoped for, with a will for dominion that might vault far beyond the existing boundaries of the Kingdom.

But why war? Much of it, according to historians, was due to the personality of Charles I. A character who was, if we examine him closely, both insatiable and reckless. Who in the years between the late 1270s and the early 1280s was pushing far too hard, outstripping the resources of his Kingdom. Outstripping even his own capacity as a monarch, a king who ought to have learned just to say no, once and for all, instead of persisting, obstinately, questing tirelessly for new victories, new conquests. As Marino Sanuto the Elder tells us:

> Charles I had enjoyed many victories, triumphed in his campaigns, and killed King Manfred, defeated and ordered the execution of Conradin, captured Don Enrico, his brother and a relative of the illustrious king of Castile and Aragon, won back much of the part of Sicily that had rebelled due to the efforts of Corrado Capezzi...he had further reduced to the payment of tribute both the Kingdom of Tunis and its king...likewise made a tributary of the township of Pisa, created an alliance of great devotion, to himself and to his party, on the part of nearly all of Tuscany and much of Lombardy, acquired a part of, and the title to, the Kingdom of Jerusalem...he was on the verge of obtaining the principality of Morea...in short, this King Charles was virtually everything that he could be in terms of grandeur and power, and yet he was heard to say that what he possessed was a paltry thing for a man who aspired to be the monarch of the world.[25]

In other words, he could have stopped: that's what Marino Sanuto's voice is telling us. Don't think of Constantinople and what remained of the Eastern Roman empire. Be done with it. Enjoy your old age and the power you've attained. Just stay there, in Naples.

Matters went differently, however. The king couldn't get Byzantium out of his mind. That was his dream, his ultimate objective. Rumors spread. There was an eastern expedition being readied. Greater efforts were going to be required. It was going to be necessary to arm hundreds and hundreds of cargo vessels and battleships. There were thousands of knights ready, with their steeds. The king was working on a plan. He was focusing on an attack from the sea, from both sides of the Bosphorus. And in the course of that preparation, money was gobbled up at a dizzying clip, draining away into this enormous sinkhole of the eastward expedition. There was never enough money. And so new taxes were levied. As quickly as the words "new taxes" began to be heard, the answer "Enough! No more!" began to echo back. As a result, tensions deepened. Tumults ensued. The population was sick and tired of this, on either side of the Strait of Messina.

But it was the Sicilians who were champing at the bit, more than anyone else. With the advent of the new Kingdom, the island and its cities had lost their old role of centrality, importance, and vigor. They had once been the center of the world, and now they seemed to have been relegated to the outskirts. They felt colonized, excluded, and humiliated. What's more, they could hardly forget their great kings, Frederick and Manfred. And the horrifying act of the beheading of Conradin. They couldn't stand this imported dynasty, there only to squeeze money out of them to pay for expeditions and campaigns they had no interest in taking part in.

At a certain point, word began to spread throughout Palermo that brands had been forged, that whoever failed to pay their taxes would be branded with these irons, heated white-hot. The rumor was false, but what can you do when the populace's indignation is at a rolling boil, when the people only want to cry "enough," when they've had it with this king and this insane new enterprise? The Feast of the Vespers rolled around. The revolt erupted, caused, according to folk tradition, by the rape of Sicilian women by the French. It was March 31, 1282. The war began, and it would last for twenty years. A war that destroyed the unity of a monarchy created by the Norman kings.

Charles I only lived to see the opening phases of this war. The phases that were bitterest and most tragic for the Angevins. The revolt of March soon spread to all the rest of Sicily. In little more than five months, Peter III of Aragon was able to land unopposed in Trapani and proceed from there to Palermo, where he triumphantly took the Sicilian crown. The island had for all intents and purposes been lost to the Angevins. And the situation grew even worse for the Neapolitans, because the war rapidly spread. Like a widening oil stain. It became an international conflict. Starting from Sicily, it dragged in Aragon as well. Making nearly impossible any Angevin attempts to take back the island. And transforming what might have been nothing more than a simple revolt, easily put down in a short time, into a grueling war, with consequences of a scope that could hardly have been imagined in advance.

A war that, quite soon, had expanded well beyond the bounds of the Sicilian sector and spread to include peninsular territories. And it even came close to sweeping over the capital, seeing that in the waters off Naples, on June 5, 1284, there took place the first battle between the Neapolitan fleet, under the command of the king's son, the regent (and future Charles II), and the Aragonese fleet, under the command of the admiral Roger of Lauria. A battle that turned out disastrously for the Angevins, with the capture of not only many noblemen of the royal court but even the prince himself. Even worse, once the prince was taken to Palermo and held prisoner there, he came close to being lynched by the enraged crowd, still burning with the memory of the deaths of the last two Swabians: Manfred and, most of all, the young Conradin. Charles would remain for many years a prisoner in Aragon, only allowed to return to Naples five years later, in July 1289, after he'd been crowned in Rieti on May 29.

In the final analysis, the war, which had only been intended as a short-lived thing, was proving to be something far less than a bargain. It was clearly threatening the Kingdom's very existence and its delicate internal equilibriums. It was important to keep the situation under control, in this phase during which military defeat was casting long shadows on the Angevin political equation. Equilibriums that seemed to veer askew from the very outset, when the Neapolitan populace, which had been solidly in favor of combat before the battle actually unfolded, rose up, in fear of an Aragonese invasion and an ensuing sack of the capital. And just guess who came to put down that popular uprising, repressing with strong-armed authority and an iron fist. The militia, with the energetic support of the papal legate, though not without heavy losses and a clamorous en masse stampede of French knights from the city.

Charles I died at Foggia on January 7, 1285, and his demise brought an end to the controversial chapter of the dawn of the Angevin Kingdom that had transformed Naples from an ordinary city into the capital of a kingdom. But his death was not enough to put an end to the war. And the atmosphere in the city showed no sign of improving. "Deplorably," wrote Schipa, "with abuses of all sorts, there were ongoing quarrels and brawls and conflicts between citizens." What was the reason? It was the absence of a solid central power and most of all the lack of respect for the traditional rules (traditional customs, as the phrase went). I can't say exactly what happened. I can certainly conjecture that different groups were on collision paths, both the most venerable nobility and new and emerging clans, resulting in redefinition of the spaces for maneuvering and control, especially in terms of the redistribution of the tax revenues that, in the meantime, had been increasing. That hypothesis is supported by the reports of continuous denunciations and complaints about the taxes that were actually being paid. There were those who claimed they shouldn't have to pay, because of rights to exemption accorded *ab antiquo*. There were others, instead, who wanted either to eliminate those rights or gain them for themselves. With pitched battles between the various contenders, between those who, on the basis of either authentic privileges or long-established abuses, tried to refuse to contribute, whether to the payment of state or municipal taxes; and those who refused to acknowledge the basis of those privileges and the justification of their application. Hence supplications, lamentations, quarrels, and denunciations. Until the king, in 1293, in a bid to solve the problem and restore order to a governance that the representatives of the *seggi* were no longer capable of carrying out, chose to appoint six *apprezzatori*, or appraisers, who would be able to assign a value to the tax revenue that should be expected from each and every citizen, in order to ensure the greatest possible degree of equity. A solution that merely succeeded in putting a Band-Aid on a problem that remained terribly complicated, hopelessly tangled, and most important of all, a bellwether of tensions, quarrels, and clashes, guided primarily, as always, by the leading members of the principal Neapolitan families.[26]

Meanwhile, the war continued. And it was going very badly for the Angevins. In 1286, the Sicilian-Aragonese fleet showed up again in the waters off Naples. It occupied Capri and Procida. The enemy really was at the capital's doorstep. The *milites* were preparing to put up a stiff resistance. Fortunately, though, the threat vanished like a puff of smoke. But the raids continued, from the Cilento region all the way to Amalfi, and even up along the coastline of Latium. The following year, the same thing happened again: Roger of Lauria was once again lurking in the offing before Naples, and had soon won another naval victory. Result? Since weapons and warfare had been unable to resolve the matter, the decision was made to attempt a political solution. Or it might be better to say an economic solution. The admiral agreed to return home after the payment of a massive cash ransom. A solution that was humiliating to the pride of the Neapolitan people and their royal family.

An attempt was made to negotiate a peace treaty: in Tarascon,
in 1291. In Logroño. In La Jonquera, in 1293. At Anagni, in 1295.
In the meantime, however, skirmishes continued. Guerrilla operations. Pirate attacks by the Almogavars, exasperating an exhausted and already prostrate population and interfering badly
with transportation and commerce. And tensions remained high.
In fact, if anything they worsened, pouring new gas on the fire,
with the proclamation of Frederick of Aragon as king in January
1296 in Catania. More than an election, it was a provocation. Sure
enough, the war resumed, in all its vicious virulence. Frederick
didn't hesitate for an instant. He tried to strike directly at the territory of the Kingdom. And so, not only was he able to preserve the
strongholds and occupied lands on the mainland all the way up to
the northern boundary of Calabria, he even entered Apulia. Even
worse: on October 20 the pride of the Neapolitan fleet was put to
a harsh test, with the umpteenth defeat just off Ischia.

At this point, there was an unexpected plot twist. James II
of Aragon weighed into the hostilities, but on the Angevin side.
What could the reason have been for this sudden turnabout? The
main one was surely the papal investiture of Sardinia and Corsica.
The Sicilian cause was suddenly stripped of its most powerful ally.
Whereupon Roger of Lauria, too, changed allegiance, opting for
an alliance with the Angevin party. When Roger left, many others
went with him. And years later, it would be that very same admiral
who led the royal fleet against the Sicilian fleet off Milazzo, on July
4, 1299. At long last, victory.

The crisis plaguing the Kingdom of Naples seemed to have
come to an end. That same month the Angevins reconquered Ischia and the other islands in the Bay of Naples. But it was only
a passing illusion. The Sicilians, in Trapani, pushed back against
the Neapolitan troops and captured Philip I, Prince of Taranto,
the son of Charles II. And they resumed their offensive in the Bay
of Naples, this time with help from the Genoese. Once again it
took the military cunning of Roger of Lauria to beat back this new
threat, in the sea off Ponza.

The conflict went on, with varying highs and lows. With a new upbubbling of trouble: the attempted Angevin landing of a large contingent of soldiers in Sicily in May 1302. But things ground to a halt soon after. The two sides were beginning to run out of steam. The war had dragged on for too long, with an enormous expense of blood and energy on both sides, as well as staggering costs, both economic and in terms of human lives. And so we come to the Peace of Caltabellotta, on August 29, 1302. A peace treaty signed between King Frederick III and Robert, Duke of Calabria, the son and plenipotentiary of Charles II.

There were a great many conditions established by the treaty. First and foremost, Frederick would keep, for the rest of his days, rule over Sicily, with the title of King of Trinacria, which is to say Sicily. Second: following his death, his land would be turned over to Charles II or Charles II's heirs. Third: the occupied lands, reciprocally on the mainland or on the island, would be restored to their respective legitimate rulers. Fourth: all the prisoners would be freed. Fifth: Frederick would marry Eleanor, daughter of Charles II. On May 21, 1303, the peace treaty was ratified, with a single, final laceration. The Kingdom had now been split in two. On one side was Sicily. And on the other was the mainland section of the Kingdom. A separation that had a variety of effects. Allow me to point out here just two of them, which I consider to be the most important. The first was the sharp retrenchment of the House of Anjou's wild ambitions, which certainly were not about to die out but which had now dwindled somewhat in their rough impulsiveness after losing the possibility of dreams of broadscale Mediterranean expansion. The second was the birth of a new Aragonese Mediterranean power, which would play a prominent role in the political future of the South over the course of the fifteenth century.

After the war, what was the impact on Neapolitan society? There had been plenty of defeats, but there was also an equally powerful capacity for resilience and reaction. So many times the fleet had been beaten in battle, but each time Neapolitan forces had proved able to lash back and renew the attack, even after taking some crushing uppercuts. There were other positive factors that included a determination to keep going, a stamina that was strengthened by the Kingdom's sheer material force, which kept Naples and the monarchy from succumbing once and for all in the midst of the clash. Alongside these competitive factors, there was another, which shouldn't be overlooked: the ability of the sovereigns to preserve, even in the darkest moments, political and administrative control over the state, which never slid out of their grasp and was always maintained with an iron grip. As Giuseppe Galasso wrote, "at no point did Charles I or Charles II see before them the specter of a fate comparable to that of Manfred: namely, the loss of the entire Kingdom in the aftermath of a single defeat in battle, as was the case for the Swabian king, under the shadow of suspicion as to the loyalty of his own armies."[27]

That said, there can be no doubt that in the face of an enduring reaction, the Kingdom nevertheless experienced considerable wear and tear in those—more or less—twenty years of war. Now the horizon, with all its prospects, had changed profoundly. What would a veteran of so many battles, lost and won, have thought at the turn of the fourteenth century? He would have thought that the Kingdom he knew had undergone a radical mutilation. That it had been stripped of an important appendage, namely Sicily. It would have been enough for him to wonder what chances the Kingdom had, before and after the breakaway of that island. Surely the Kingdom's chances had been different, better by far, in the past, compared with its present situation. It was clear to one and all that an important pillar in the Kingdom's architecture had just been removed. One of its wealthiest regions. The region enjoying the greatest resources. Where a great many Neapolitans and Amalfitans had already sunk their roots, setting up their businesses and participating in the administrative life of the area as well. An asset in the form of a location, a position, a form of rent, now, sadly, long since lost. A genuine Waterloo for the House of Anjou, as the French historian Henri Bresc put it so concisely.

The Margin of Chaos

The atmosphere in Naples in the aftermath of the war appeared murky and toxic. As if the wake left by that long conflict was accelerating processes that were already underway. And that led to a change in the sort of social contract that had existed for such a long time within the clans. That reliable consistency based on specific coordinates, reflections, hierarchies, and mentalities that had functioned with reliable success. And that had found a foundational territory in the alliance with the new ruling house and the transformation of Naples into a capital.

This land, once so solid, was now crumbling. There were a great many symptoms, not necessarily of social disintegration but of the attainment of a threshold beyond which one could not venture, at the risk of utter collapse. It was the indicator of a *margin of chaos* that had been attained, after which lay only the fragmentation of social fabric or else a new path leading onward, with a structure that might stabilize an urban society shaken by the decline of political prospects of the Angevin dynasty: this is a key element that should not be underestimated in any analysis of this crisis in the Neapolitan situation.

A city that, in spite of the splendor of King Robert's court, appeared to objective witnesses such as Petrarch to be going downhill, a "horrendous animal, barefoot, head uncovered, short in person, rotting over time, broad-hipped, dressed in clothing so tattered and torn that we can easily see part of its flesh."[28] Full of young men at odds with the king's own system of values and customary way of life. Ready to ravish nubile young women. Or else causing scandal by their irregular ways of behaving and dressing, upstarts following eccentric fashions, untethered from established tradition:

> Among most young people, a startling new fashion has surfaced that among them calls for an uncertain style, a varied ritual, a different form of worship, strange and ridiculous movements.

Their head is held high, their hair left ungroomed, their face
almost covered by a thick and bushy beard, all horrible to behold rather than in any way admirable. The highest and lowest
parts that God gave to man they flaunt, and we really cannot
say truly with what feigned austerity, which they hypocriti-
cally call the simplest. The clothing that they once wore down
to the knee or even dragging on the ground, they now shorten
till the buttocks are uncovered; nor do they pay any mind to
the fact that they are offering shameful displays and that those
slender bodies are now rendered deformed and stout with bellies swollen by the volume of the knots that make them seem
either consumptive or dropsical. They sit sprawled on horses
and, to hold the reins, they extend both hands. Their helmets,
swords, and spears they judge to be too much for soldiers for
their tastes, and they wear their weapons short, going into war
with their limbs almost uncovered, offering their shoulders to
injury and baring their chest uncovered, preferring customs
that better befit little women to more virile usages. What is
more, and this makes them appear both stupid and foolish, in
their hair and beards they affect to imitate the same length that
was a privilege of the Arabs and an emblem of the philosophers.
As for what hidden guests are hidden in their sordid flesh, one
can only guess that their friends and the courtly gentlemen that
they frequent know well. No less than this is the madness and
the perversity of the old men who ought to set a proper example
but instead serve as mentors and masters to the young in these
novelties, and, tossing aside the hoods and caps that ought to
contain what little gray hair they still possess and at least cover
their disagreeable baldness, scorning the honest customs that
in the days of our forefathers ensured that the Kingdom mul-
tiplied and was fruitful, preferring awkward customs and de-
lighting in displays of their perversity.[29]

This truly remarkable description, where I feel as if I can hear
the voice of a prudish, elderly uncle who can't wrap his head around

the things that he is seeing around him in the city, isn't taken from a man-in-the-street opinion, full of disgust for these unorthodox tastes. No, it comes from a decree issued by King Robert himself, on January 15, 1335, which describes these unprecedented new behaviors as an *enormis novitas*, an enormous novelty, and behind the word *novitas* we can sense the lurking terror at the thought of innovation, which ought rightly to be rejected because of the unseemly effects of societal breakdown that it threatens to induce. A novelty that translates into the bad behavior and degenerate customs that seem to be waylaying, in ever-greater numbers, young Neapolitans and, with them, the young people of the provinces. Something that absolutely has to be stopped.

So just what is it that these young people are doing? If you read carefully, you can sense all their unease with the previous generation. Their resistance to the rules, the cults, and the rites, which they experience, but only reinterpreting them *contrariwise*. They move and they ride horses in the oddest ways. They dress in a bizarre fashion, altering their appearance so that if they are extremely skinny, they become fat, and vice versa as well. They display their naked limbs. They shorten their outfits. What is more, and this is the psychological datum that strikes us so forcefully, they show utter contempt for the symbols of the militia, of the cavalry. What good are helmets, swords, and lances? What good are suits of armor? To these young people, those are all *soverchie*, pointless tools, of no real use in any of the battles that, not to put too fine a point on it, their parents often lost. Far better a short sword, or a dagger. Faster. Easier to handle. Just a handy blade. And they are convinced that in warfare, people need to go uncovered. Presenting their backs to those who attack them. An approach that King Robert fails to see as a sign of courage, or defiance. Instead, he sees them as lunatics, or little old ladies, but certainly not brave men out to display *virile mores*.

We should not imagine that Robert had a direct perception of this deterioration of customs and warlike ways. All the same, if he was moved to weigh in on it, it is clear that it must have been

a social phenomenon that was beginning to have worrisome repercussions for civic life and the ever-present problems of public
order. He emphasizes that this youthful fashion, this wearing of
long hair and beards in which, as he writes, it's impossible to guess
what little insects or pests might lie hiding, this attiring oneself in
such a barbaric fashion currently shows no sign of coming under
control. Indeed, these young people's elders, who by right ought
to call their youngers to order and decorum, are actually allowing
themselves to be dragged down this same bad path, in a sort of
youthful aspiration that leads them to reject the wearing of hoods
and hats that might help to conceal the signs of baldness and advancing old age.

The king's greatest problem, let me reiterate, was the matter
of social cohesion and the censure of a fashion that might have
negative repercussions on the entire city. Which, indeed, undermined both dignity and decency, leading to a nostalgia for the
honest customs of the past, the ones the city's fortune was based
on, "and which in the times of our ancestors and our parents gave
the Kingdom continuous growth": the first driving force that allowed the Kingdom to develop. Customs that needed to be recovered by getting rid of these new fashions, which were *contrary and
perverse*. And by reacting to this scandal, which was throwing into
a state of crisis a formerly well-consolidated system, based on the
complementary relationship between generations and respect for
established forms.

A condition among the young people of *nonalignment* with
old customs, something that became even more dangerous inasmuch as it was public, evident, and open to the eyes of one and
all—something that everyone else could imitate, so that everyone
could take part in the transgression. And this, as you might well
imagine, was unacceptable. Therefore the behavior demanded
punishment. It needed to be sanctioned. Restored to the norms
of an obedience to the mores that governed everyone, both young
and old. In order to resolve this situation, the king sought methods of control of a canonical nature. He strove to restore a sense

of religion and a return to a moral order. And tried to establish an absolute imprimatur of legitimacy. Indeed, the edict makes reference to the decree of the Maccabees "against those who preferred the boast of Greek glories to the honor of their homeland." And, of course, the Old Testament. And from the story of Jehoshaphat comes the sanction against new things: "There was born a new king, who ignored the old king. An ungrateful new king, who ignored the benefits of the old king. A king who relishes new things is nothing but a new devil."

The message is clear: every form or way of life that fails to follow the established path is the fruit of the demon and must be cast out. Also because these excesses create in the king the greatest indignation (*indignationis nostrae*) so that it appears necessary to restore, as soon as is humanly possible, the old established order, the venerable and honest old customs (*pristinos onestos mores resumant*). Robert, in conclusion, like some latter-day Cato, summoned back to order an entire social group that was revealing itself to be restive and disorderly. Refractory. Hostile to tradition. And the rebellion against traditional customs had to be punished immediately by censuring these young people and ordering them to abandon this dissident fashion, with the imposition of fines, changes of clothing, and the cutting of beards, accompanied by the earnest invitation, honestly sounding a bit ridiculous, to shave frequently. An intervention that took immediate effect and that was intended to have the greatest and broadest publicity possible, so much so that it was posted on the gate of Castel Nuovo and the portal of the cathedral and of the Curia of Vicaria, that everyone might read it and comply with its injunctions.

A voice, King Robert's, that had some influence, though we cannot say how much. Perhaps it was listened to only out of one ear, lost "in the midst of the jolly bedlam that echoed around the royal palace." But the king's voice was bound to become even hoarser in the face of a youthful rebellion that soon deteriorated into uncontrolled, senseless violence. Petrarch wrote to Giovanni Colonna about Naples:

Walking about here at night is like making your way through a
forest filled with dangers. The streets are under siege by young
adolescents, members of the nobility, who walk around armed
and who cannot be subjected to any authority, nor do they follow the discipline inculcated in them by their parents, nor do
they pay any heed to the power of the magistrates, much less
the commands of the majesty of the king.[30]

Full-fledged mobs, *turme*, as a few years later Dietrich of
Nieheim would describe them after his visit to the capital city.
Mobs that did all manner of things, mostly the worst kind, such
as the young men of the Piscicelli clan, whose favorite sport was
to cause extreme and deplorable annoyance to the city's nuns.
The group was led by two sons of *milites*, Giuliano and Ligorio,
also known as Corasio, who moved about undisturbed, in a clear
condition of total impunity, surrounded by other members of the
household and supported in these adventures by young relatives
belonging to other equally bellicose clans. They were insolent
and aggressive, they broke into the convents and monasteries and
there insulted and outraged the nuns. There were two episodes in
particular that leapt into the spotlights of the chronicles.

In 1329, the two young men, followed by their *clientes*, on
foot and on horseback, forced their way into the convent of San
Gaudioso. They were searching for the nun Giovanna de Aufe-
rio, eager to avenge a wrong done to them by her family. Also
present, however, were her mother, Gaitelgrima Filomarino, and
her brother Boffilo. The two Piscicelli boys started insulting the
nun and threatening to kill her. They got down off their horses.
But Boffilo immediately stepped in. They started heaping insults
upon him as well. But they hadn't properly reckoned with whom
they were talking to. Someone much scarier than they were. Who
trimmed them properly for the holidays, as the saying goes, and
tossed them right out of the convent by main force. But the Piscicelli boys weren't done, and they set out on another excursion.
This time, they were reinforced by yet more staunch members

of the militia, the cousins and comrades (*compare*) Filippo and Gualtieri Caracciolo, the latter also known as Tirello. What was their objective? They were bent on making their way to the convent of San Gregorio Maggiore, where they hoped to make life miserable for the nuns there, on account of a feud—the umpteenth such quarrel!—with a blood relative of theirs, Aloara Piscicelli. So what did the *milites* do? They bided their time and waited for the auspicious day. Namely the day that they'd been told the nuns went outside of the city gates to tend to their farmlands. Down by the river Sebeto. And there they attacked them. They tossed them into the river. But then, as so often happens in mob dynamics, there was one guy who wanted to show off, add that grain of extra violence to incite and unleash the others, in a game that grew increasingly dangerous and out of control. Two of them went first. Then the others joined in, as if this were some fun game. They grabbed the nuns, hoisted them up by their feet, and dunked them headfirst into the water, practically drowning them. This episode roiled the city, stunning the townsfolk with this unusual sadistic bent. Nevertheless, the outrage remained, once again, unpunished by the state. There was no verdict or sanction issued against the Piscicelli clan, protected as they were by a shield of untouchability. They enjoyed the privileged status they could invoke because they were *milites* and, moreover, members of a clan that enjoyed protections in high places, among municipal institutions and also at court.[31]

Among the worst cases, then, let's examine this one, which involved all the families of the better society. It was 1332 and King Robert was summoning the nobility of the various *seggi* on account of the violent ill manners and lack of respect that was spreading through the city:

> In this city of Naples, there had already begun to spread a dangerous and pestilential form of abuse, which indeed we might better describe as a vile and detestable corruption. Certain lascivious and insolent young men of this city, driven by the flames

of libido and enslaved by the impetus of voluptuous carnality, set out to woo reckless and unsophisticated young women, and standing at their doors, with shameless and loose appearance, as well as deceptive deeds and false and persuasive words, they deceive them and carry them off, partly willing and partly reluctant, ravishing them forcefully from the homes of their fathers. Recklessly the natural order and the marriage contract are thus perverted, though said contract should always come before love, but is now postponed to sometime after the fact.[32]

Young men involved in *fuitine* (sexual kidnappings) or outright rapes, committed against young women who were either partly cooperative or blithely naïve. A custom that shocked families, inasmuch as it was perverting the *natural order* of things. That is to say, matters rushed directly to a state of fait accompli without passing through the most important step, namely the marriage contract, which of course was understood to precede love. A very violent and deplorable custom, which the king demanded to see repressed by the only actors who could realistically hope to hamper the phenomenon. That is to say, the usual families. Like those of Porto, who appear according to the usual hierarchical scheme, led by the Griffi, who drag along with them Marcuccio Issalla, Giacomo Fiorentino, Cataldo Macedonio, Pandolfo Manco, and Giovanni Ferrillo.

For that matter—and this is a curiosity that likewise has at least something to do with the widespread climate of impunity—the city was being troubled by another social phenomenon that was spreading, much to the discomfort of good citizens. A new fad had recently reached Naples: the custom of serenades and music in the streets. "The common folk greatly enjoyed playing music for anyone to hear with flute and mandolin, accompanying their love songs in the street, or perhaps ballads, or bawdy rhymes and doggerel of their own composition." This fashion had previously been dear to the heart of King Manfred, "who often went out at night through the streets of Barletta, singing doggerel and songs and enjoying the cool night air, and with him went two Sicilian musicians." This passion of the king had finally made its way to Naples. In abhorrence of the new fad, many exasperated upright citizens railed against it, glimpsing in this music not only a stratagem of the devil but also a means of undermining tradition and connubial bliss. This was, for instance, the case of the *miles* Nicola Piscopo, who in 1335 brought a complaint against the notary Jacobello Fusco for coming to the street outside his house night and day to sing something approaching a *stornello*, a short Italian serenade with a simple rhyme scheme, that used "dirty words," "a vulgar vocabulary," and smoothly lyrical *cantilene*. These songs were designed to seduce his wife, the noblewoman Giovannella de Gennaro, who, at least according to testimony offered, experienced these serenades as upsetting experiences, because they filled her with *opprobrium*. Once again, in this case, the sovereign weighed in, inasmuch as this was viewed as a fashion imported from elsewhere that threatened the traditional—and at least apparently blissful—conjugal life of a local couple. Indeed, the woman was widely viewed as a *modest* and *upright* wife, "one of the city's matrons"; here let us underscore repeatedly the word *matrona*, which says all we need to know, for its specific meaning, in contrast with *mulier*. And the king issued sanctions, not so much against the fad itself but the fact that the singing notary had allegedly troubled the "virtue of the sacrament of marriage." That said, the notary got off easy, because even though he'd been found guilty of the offense, he was able to benefit from the amnesty extended to Neapolitan citizens against being arrested and hauled before the Curia.[33]

Episodes of deplorable behavior that, at first glance, might have been allowed to run unchecked. But in point of fact, they were quite significant. Because I believe they represent the tip of the iceberg of something much larger, which in the meantime was smoldering away, beneath the ashes, an ember in the heart of a society on a slow boil, within which very sensitive opposites co-existed. On the one hand, it seemed as if everything was falling apart. At the same time, there were those launching themselves into the future, endowed with a fresh new outlook. With an adaptability to new circumstances expressed perfectly by nothing less than the behavior of certain family clans. Which, for instance, accentuate certain forms of prestige. Or which amplify their own spaces of power, no longer driven by the age-old need to defend the city, but instead by the necessity of redefining the methods of their control over the territory, which remained the fundamental element of power within their own zone of affiliation.

One of the most innovative elements was the construction of imposing houses, or *hospitia*, a marker not only of a renewed status, but also a crucial element in the restoration of the clan's rootedness in its piazza, or quarter. An undertaking that was anything but easy to accomplish in a city that was crowded and even then practically impossible to get around in. Where, if it proved too difficult to find already cleared land, it became necessary to undertake time-consuming and laborious transactions involving the purchase of lands and the inclusion of adjoining structures, with the appropriation of not only private lots but also public spaces.[34] This resulted in an unmistakable disruption of the original urban fabric, where not only was the configuration of property thrown into disarray but also many of those social bonds that underlay the development of the pre-Angevin system of the *seggi*. This was a development that began in the fourteenth century, only to attain its maximum extent over the course of the following century, with the dismemberment of ancient units of property and the expansion of new and more-compact family houses.

A nobility, in other words, that refined itself, modifying itself as it altered certain distinguishing features. At the same time, this nobility reached out for new markers of distinction and prestige, such as burial vaults and sepulchres, with the construction of family chapels in many of the leading churches, with special regard for the churches of the mendicant orders, by virtue of their enormous capacity for attraction and engagement. This followed in the wake of the royal family's devotion to those orders, with special attachment to the Franciscans. Another feature was the further proliferation of the intertwining by marriage of family lineages, which increased disproportionately (as in the case of the Brancaccio and the Caracciolo): at the same time a symptom of a spread of the clan over a more extensive territory, thanks to a proliferation of branches that required homes of their own; but also, over the long term, of a loosening of ties, with family groups, which gradually broke free of the principal branch of the family tree, giving rise to new core groups and new clans.

A municipal nobility that now found itself face-to-face with major issues: to start with, there was the increasingly tight alliance between Capuana and Nido against all the other *seggi*, on a chessboard where interfamily ties and networks were diversifying and taking on different connotations from their traditional meanings. The counterpart to the bonds between Capuana and Nido was the growing preponderance of certain groups over others; and while some groups swelled in numbers and power, others, which might be older and more venerable, were gradually weakening, faltering, and ultimately being snuffed out, lacking the wherewithal in terms of marriages and alliances to make the climb up the social ladder. And then what should we say about the determination to rise displayed by new components of the chessboard, not necessarily members of the nobility but springing instead from the multifarious universe of the marketplace, offices, the corps of notaries, who were likewise strengthened by their circuits of solidarity and ability to wield more than mere economic power, and who expected to be consulted and heard in the course of municipal decision-making? Or the common folk, the city's lumpen populace, who were tired of feeling bound and restricted but who, in point of fact, had to be kept under tight control? What then was to be done, at a time when the ancient ties and traditional bonds were starting to fray with a corresponding rise in the difficulties triggered by famine and ever-higher costs of living, and when the recourse to violence seemed to be the most habitual tool employed to settle any and all arguments?

So now what was to be done?

Reinforce the network of clientelism? Strengthen the internal hierarchies of the *seggi*? Become more homogeneous? Close ranks? Or break ranks, allowing new interlocutors inside the tent? And with the king, his court, the government of both city and Kingdom as we describe it, in this logic where the acquisition of power in the city had an immediate repercussion on the dynamics of state control?

Clans at War

These were troubled dialectics, with a vast array of practicable alternatives. The alternatives of a society in turmoil. Alternatives that had another, clearly visible and concrete, effect: in the city, from the first decade of the fourteenth century on, violence increased exponentially. As if, in a world that had been for so long repressed, the cork had suddenly popped out. Bringing forth hereditary quarrels and hatreds, the mirror of a world that was brutal by nature, inclined to bloodshed. A violence that had its further dimension, even more worrisome, in the growing spread of criminal activity, with a proliferation of reports of street muggers, rapists, and organized groups of shakedown artists who troubled municipal life in their vast numbers. So much so that the king himself complained to the captain of Naples, in one of his *Lettere arbitrarie* (Arbitrary letters), about the robberies and violence that were swelling out of control, bellwethers of the gravity of a concerning situation in terms of deteriorating public order. With a decline that not only affected Naples but also its hinterland and the Phlegraean Fields:

> We are hearing with increasing frequency reports and requests
> for intervention because in the city of Naples and the district
> of Pozzuoli, thieves, highwaymen, arsonists, rapists, and other
> perpetrators of despicable acts are proliferating.

What clearly echoes throughout the words of the chroniclers is the warning issued by Petrarch, and later by Boccaccio in his novella of Andreuccio of Perugia in the *Decameron*, namely that it was not an advisable activity to go out for a walk at night: "Because there the number of highwaymen and criminals has grown disproportionately, where they find in the dark of night a favorable occasion to hide from the sight of justice their roguery and their misdeeds"; where at any crossroads you might run into an armed robber; while it was customary, as Fabio Giordano wrote, for "murderers, who worked by night, to toss corpses down wells, thus concealing them." Indeed, so common did this method of disposing of bodies become that, at a certain point, in desperation, extreme measures led to the closing of certain wells...

The highest-impact solution produced by Robert's court, in a situation where criminals were progressively becoming more and more powerful with every day that passed, was the order to institute a curfew. He issued an edict, stating "that all the city's residents must promptly withdraw to their homes every evening at the sound of three peals of the bells of the churches of San Giovanni Maggiore, San Paolo Maggiore, San Giorgio Maggiore, and Santa Maria a Cappella." After the bells chimed for the third time, "no one has the right to walk in the city."[35]

This widespread turn to illegal activity is, of course, the result of a situation that had become critical for the population, with living conditions that were becoming increasingly challenging; this is what we saw in the very first chapter. All the same, we must not forget that it is also the result of a larger failure bound up with the substantial absence of political power and planning. In fact, the state, which under Charles I had displayed itself to the entire Kingdom with an iron fist, now presented itself with a far weaker King Robert, so weak in fact that he wasn't even capable of ensuring basic law and order in the capital city from dusk to dawn, at least not without turning to a curfew or the assistance of families and clans.

Even then, not even the most venerable old clans seemed able to exercise the same dominance as they once had. Ever since the war, they'd been in a state of crisis, in a society where too many of the cards on the table were being reshuffled, and where it was impossible to identify the center of gravity. The families seemed to dwindle in importance, with a loosening of that spiderweb of controls that from time to time people attempted to restore, such as with the popular request to repress the youthful phenomenon of kidnapping women. But their control remained unsteady and seemed to be distributed on a patchwork basis across the territory, with areas where family dominion seemed to hold fast, and others where the family rule was clearly struggling to face up to the challenges of an increasingly harsh everyday life, with growing difficulties.

And then, something even worse occurred: for the first time, war broke out between certain clans...

Among the clans, there was always the risk of quarrels or brawls, a constant concern to which I've previously made reference. Now, however, things seemed to have gone too far. Especially in those families where the use of violence seemed to form part of an inveterate habit, as was the case with the Caputo and the Griffi clans. In those families, close relatives—stepsons, brothers-in-law, sisters, et cetera—would beat each other silly, and we're not speaking figuratively. By and large these beatings took place over issues that involved money. For instance, Caterina d'Abenabolo fought with her stepson Federico Caputo "no less over the payment of alimony than for the restitution of her dowry," and brought a lawsuit against him for having alienated the affections of her children. Lorenzo Caputo and his brother-in-law basically waged war against each other for thirty long years over the ownership of half of the Castle of Pietre (Castello delle Pietre) in Terra di Lavoro. Lancellotto and Balangardo, the sons of Arrigo Caputo, fought physically because Balangardo was responsible for dumping *spurcitias in curtim commune* ("filth in their shared courtyard"). Now let us move on to the Griffi clan: Rinaldello began a fight with Landulfo Proculo over the repayment of a sum of 45 *oncias*. In 1305, Armandello quarreled with Brissoro and other members of the de Loffredo clan over a matter having to do with properties in Pozzuoli. Margherita de Griffo, the widow of Filippo de Ligorio, began a dispute with her brother-in-law Venuto de Ligorio. For ten years a dispute dragged on between the Fellapane and the Arcamone families and Fenicia Griffi over their grandmother's dowry. Another Margherita was involved in a fierce dispute with the Issalla family, her in-laws, over a matter having to do with the payment for the knightly girdle bestowed upon her husband. Catella Griffi, the widow of the *miles* Cecco Domnobono, who had remarried with Goffredo di Costanzo, fought with her three sons from her first marriage...And on it went, in a sequence that seemed never to end.[36] Those aren't the only matters of this ilk that we can list: for instance, the case of Carlo d'Aprano, the son of the *miles* Francesco, who did everything he could think of to have his father declared mentally incapable, because he was squandering the family fortune. Or what should we say about Alessandra Caldora, the wife of the *miles* Marco Gulioso, who brought a complaint against Petrillo Scriniario "for calling her a whore and punching her in the nose"? The chain of disputes and quarrels culminates with the chamberlain Niccolò de Baucis's murder of his own mother: a crime that takes the atmosphere of bickering and fighting just a little further beyond the limits of decency...

While all this seems to concern lifestyle more than anything else, what happened from 1305 on took on a different value. Never before in Naples had there been such a powerful surge in the number of brawls, clashes, and fights. A clear symptom that something wasn't right about the factors of control of the clans, lacerated as they were by the new lines of business coming to the fore, clearly bound up with the shortage of foodstuffs, provisions, and wheat, with the "gabelle of the new taxes on goods being sold." There was plenty of money to be made, of course, at the same time: from the processing of payments, distribution for the various uses, the interest that could be earned. And those who were in charge of this network knew that they had further elements of power to be weighed in the balance, power to share with their friends, power to deny their enemies. And it is no accident that among those privileged in the assignment of roles in the management of this new gabelle, in 1306, we find not only Enrico de Aprano, Bartolomeo de Arco, Leone Marogano, Gentile Moccia, and Filippo Carmignano—but also one last name belonging to one of the protagonists of the great clash that would unfold just two years later: Judge Ligorio Griffi.[37]

Naples, in short order, became a theater of war where it was hard to distinguish between where a social and political motive began and a merely criminal motive left off. These were behaviors in which private and public interests mingled promiscuously, ranging from the control of a city quarter to the city government, which entailed the fiscal administration of one of the principal cities in all of Europe, and that meant taxes, which in turn meant a veritable raging river of cash to be managed. And whenever the clans had a problem to solve, as was their habit, they would turn to the one and only instrument they knew to restore equilibrium and to guarantee a proper sharing-out of the revenues: namely, plain old violence.

From the year 1305 onward, the city was swept by a string of blood feuds, murders, and clashes of unaccustomed ferocity. And there seemed to be a general abolition, in all circumstances, of solutions based on compromise, dialogue, or promised agreements. What prevailed was military might. Tactical organization. The number of members of the clan, which expanded to take in affiliates, *clientes*, and hired soldiers. Soldiers who tended to use tactics far more cowardly than the old-fashioned ambush. Now it was many against one. Often using short swords and daggers. Waiting for one's victim at the corner of an alleyway. Attacking them in front of their house, in their quarter, at the *seggio*, where one could expect to feel less threatened, safer. Without the slightest hesitation when it came to carrying out a murder even inside a church courtyard. With an objective that was unmistakable to one and all. Making it clear who was going to prevail. Who was going to command. Who was going to run the government of the quarter, the piazza, and the city.

The first clash took place in 1305 in the area of the *seggi* of Porto and Portanova. There was talk of a *grande briga* (great to-do) as well as a *sanguinosa contesa* (bloody fight to the death). There were clashes in the streets of Portanova between the clans of the Caputo and the Griffi. The triggering issue: *private antagonisms*, the umpteenth personal matters of neighbors feuding over property, considering that, frequently among the causes, there was talk of "troubled possession of property." *Turbamento* that could easily take place given the fact that houses were cheek by jowl when not actually in direct contact. One more reason that adds to the muddle of unresolved issues, more complicated and more recent, that had to do with supremacy over the entire area contained between the city walls and the port: an area in the process of development, where economic interests grew steadily from one moment to the next.

In short, there were two coteries facing off, among the oldest and most turbulent in the city, and they both understood only one thing: if they were going to settle this matter, force was going to be required. In just a few days, the attacks were underway, with a string of assaults and brawls that grew in intensity with a series of clashes so violent that they qualified, "for the great number of combatants, to be considered as a civil war." A number of families of the *seggio* of Portanova made alliance with the Caputo, among them the Fellapane, the Ligorio, the Moccia, and the Bonifacio, while there was none of the traditional support expected by the Gambitella, who allied themselves with the opposing clan.

The uprisings were put down only through repression imposed by the state, in a royal intervention. The state adopted as their final tool either arrest or exile. A fate that was visited on everyone who could be shown to have actively "disturbed the municipal peace and the safety of the open roads." Among those who were sent into exile, we should mention the clan chief Arrigo Caputo, with his blood relatives Giacomo, Filippo, Rinaldo, and Ligorio. They were accompanied by several of the Griffi and the Ligorio, by the brothers Niccolò and Riccardo Gambitella, and by Filippo Fellapane. The prison doors also swung open to welcome two foot soldiers: Rinaldo Ferola and Biscardo Sclavo, perhaps two of the most ferocious and bloodthirsty members of the clan. The split between the two clans was only settled later, thanks to a series of marriages that restored strong ties between the families: "A double knot of kinship, since the Griffi married Francesca of this surname to Herrico Caputo and Gisolda Gambitella to Lancellotto Caputo, Herrico's son."[38]

Three years went by, and then things started all over again. It was the winter of 1308. A conspiracy was afoot. The masterminds and leaders were Pietro and Bartolomeo Alopa, of the Porto *seggio*. They wanted to strike the man who was acquiring ever-greater power in the quarter and in the management of the municipal tax stream. This man was called Ligorio Griffi. Against him, fifty-seven conspirators were arrayed. Let me say it again: fifty-seven! Eight from the Castagnola clan, five from the Alopa clan, five from the Aquari clan, eight from the Quaranta clan, four from the Domnobono clan, three from the Ferrillo clan, four from the Scillato clan, three from the Mazzone clan, three from the Manco clan, four from the Paniczato clan, two from the de Gennaro clan, two from the Issalla clan, and a great many more from the Budano, Zanzale, Sparella, and other families. It was a coup d'état. Made up of two separate parts. On the one hand, a great many families from the piazza of Porto, who had one single objective: to out-flank, we might say nowadays, the old boss and his consolidated mass of power, which was entirely arrayed around the single-family *seggio*. On the other hand, there were the Griffi, who were unmanageable, seditious, born brawlers. And powerful. In short, we are looking at a full-fledged power struggle to change the terms of who would be in charge within the precincts of the quarter. We have no real idea of how things turned out, not at any level of detail. The conspiracy may very well have succeeded. But the clashes that ensued "did a great deal to disturb the city's public peace." So much so that the Duke of Calabria, the Kingdom's vicar-general, ordered the captain of Naples to submit a report on events and to weigh in in response. The clash was put down, though we do not know with what results, whether those were arrests or exile. But it certainly opened up a laceration whose aftereffects would be felt for a while. With a bloody feud that would reach its height of intensity in 1331.

Indeed, the vendettas never stopped. And neither did the episodes of violence. As was the case in 1313. Camera reports:

> In the Angevin ledgers of this year we find repeated instances of violence and attacks committed in homes, on the streets, in the *seggi*, and even in the churches; among other things we read that Pietro Dentice and Matteo Babuzio, *milites*, that is to say, Neapolitan knights, had been questioned "about the unrest created against Gerardo di Sant'Elpidio, a *miles* and captain of Naples, and Pozzuoli on account of the brawl *seu briga* that took place in the church of San Giovanni Maggiore."

He goes on with a list of woundings and murders that echoed through the years. Pietro Piczatella levels accusations of having been stabbed repeatedly by Giovanni and Nicola, the sons of the *miles* Ligorio Scriniario, while he was taking part in an assembly at the *seggio* of Portanova. In the same location, at the corner of the *seggio*, in 1322, Pandolfo d'Anna stabbed Bartolomeo Scriniario, killing him. Zolino Lanzalonga was at the *seggio* of Somma Piazza when he was beaten by Giovanni Ravignano, also known as Barone, *in oculo cum pugno* (punched in the eye). Bartolomeo de Rahone was accused of murdering the *miles* Pietro Ferrario. In 1333 two Alopa were killed, Giovanni and Goffredo, sons of the abbott (!) Martuccio Scannasorice. Meanwhile in 1335, Pietro de Tauro implored the king to do justice, because the *milites* Niccolò Boccapianola, Giannotto Caracciolo, and Riccardo Aldomoresco, in a brawl, had murdered his son. And that's not even counting an episode that caused great outrage and alarm: the murder of the cleric, royal counselor, and doctor of canon law Giovanni Mottola, "horribly slaughtered near the place known as Arco, or also Capo de Trio, by Giovanni Brancaccio, *miles*, also known as Fontanola, Tommaso Brancaccio, and Giovanni de Acerris." An episode that truly rang alarm bells with its savagery and cruelty.[39]

This, then, is the *barbarica feritas*, the barbaric ferocity, of the Neapolitans, to borrow Petrarch's expression. With an even more ferocious collision: the continuation of the feud that began in 1308 between the Griffi and the people of Porto. The target was one of the largest clans, the clan of the Castagnola, fierce enemies of the Griffi. The Griffi had waited twenty-three years. Now their time had come. Everything was organized. It was August 1, 1331. Lorenzo Castagnola passed by on the Via de Media. The Griffi had already tried to eliminate him back in 1324, but they'd been unsuccessful. And Lorenzo had been so terrified by that experience that his father, Paolo, had launched a plea at court. What was he pleading for? Protection, bodyguards, or something of the sort for his children, Sergio and Rinaldo. Urgently, because the Griffi "were very powerful," with protections in high places, and equipped with a noteworthy military potential. Rinaldo had practically fallen into an ambush shortly thereafter. But he'd put up a fight, and he must have really meant it, because "when he fought with the Griffi, it would appear that they'd come off the worse for it."

This time, on August 1, Lorenzo was alone. With no one to help him. He didn't think he needed anyone. He was near home, in his own quarter. On a street he knew well. We must imagine that he was quite contented: he had just been assigned by the Regia Curia to travel to Provence. The Griffi were waiting for him. They attacked him. There were nine of them against just him. The clan chief, Carmayno; and Alessandro; Nicola, also known as Quinzo; Masello; Guzzulo and his brother Marinello; Petruzzo, also known as Storto; and his brother Paolo; and Guiglielmuzzo. Fathers, sons, grandsons, nephews, cousins? We can't say. Surely blood relatives. With bonds of kinship and affiliation. By house and surname. Bound together by their hatred for the opposing clan. For the people of Porto. For the Castagnola clan.

Lorenzo dropped to the ground. And the Griffi knew exactly what to do next. They had an escape route all figured out. They hid in the house of a relative of theirs, Paganello Griffi. News soon flew by word of mouth. The Griffi had gone too far this time. They'd hit a target much higher than they should have. The populace took to the streets, demanding in one loud voice that the authorities show a response. They screamed for vendetta. And that vendetta was forthcoming, this time with an unexpected rapidity: Queen Sancia, Robert's wife, ordered the authorities to have the family *seggio* demolished, the last one standing in the city. More than a symbol, it was the core of the Griffi's roots in their quarter, the fortification that had protected their power for centuries. Along with the *seggio*, the home of the mastermind behind this murder, Carmayno, was also leveled. A building, just to be clear, that had been erected right next to the home of one of their bitterest enemies. A Castagnola: Matteo Castagnola.[40]

Seven years went by. And Carmayno, along with his brothers Andreotto and Alessandro, had his rights restored by a royal pardon, in recognition of the services he had performed in the past for the court. But by now, his clan had lost its impetus. The events that followed the murder, with the destruction of their founding nucleus, the *seggio*, had proved a staggering blow, and the Griffi had been unable to come back from it. Of course, it wasn't as if the clan vanished the next day. Still, there was no mistaking the signs of decline. Along with that decline, there was a general weakening of the power of the *seggi* of Portanova and Porto and the definitive rise of the noblemen of the *seggi* that had been protagonists of the night of 1343, namely Capuana and Nido. A rise that had been made possible by a new clan war that would ultimately lead to the destabilization of the axis of municipal power, within which the greatest political heft had already been acquired, de facto and de jure, by none other than those two *seggi*.

This new war was structurally different from the feuds we've just described. There was no longer a struggle for power in a specific quarter or a specific zone. No: now the clash was meant to establish just who was in command throughout the entire city, and even beyond. It was 1338. Clashes broke out from one end of Naples to the other. On the one side were the *nobiliores* of Capuana and Nido, and on the other side were the three other *seggi*, plus the representatives of the common folk. At the center of the clash were "supremacy and the question of who was to decide, organize, negotiate, and govern the affairs of the city." So it was nothing minor: it meant establishing shares in the participation in the offices, the splits in the public contracts, and control over tax farming. To be clear, not just in Naples...

Nido and Capuana expected and demanded to be considered above all others. And they had arguments to support their claims: we're the oldest, our nobility dates back to time out of mind. Meanwhile, they showed off the fact that their men walked around the city, from one end to the other, fully armed. A veritable army, vast and numerous. Word was, they had so many men that all the other *seggi* put together wouldn't have as many. One need only count them. Forty-seven clans. United. Where the major clans of the Caracciolo, the Brancaccio, and the Capece, with their many branching subsets, formed enormous and distinct core groups of power within a structure that was already massive and ferocious. They were bound together by a pact, a *consortium* or a *società*, that had already been active going back to before the fourteenth century. With people who were continually trying to worm their way into this consortium, seeking a way to climb the ladder, what was often referred to as the *ritirata*. People who wanted to fit into this context: the most elite organization in the city.

Two *seggi*: which would form together, increasingly stoutly bound, into an association with intertwining ties that braided identities of interest, intent, origin, kinship, brotherhood, and sharing. An association that grew and demanded to grow even further. Taking all power away from the rest of the city.

This idea wasn't popular. No one liked it, or at least no one
else liked it. Soon there was warfare. Open warfare. Things began
in the public assemblies. On the one hand, there were the super-
noblemen of Capuana and Nido. They were starting to mock the
others. Make fun of them. Saying that they weren't really noble,
no, just average, filthy scum who were trying to climb above their
station. They would say it to other people's faces: You're from the
port, you're *puzarachi*, stinking dockworkers… and now what, you
want to come mingle with *us*? The people from Portanova, Porto,
and Montagna-Forcella had prompt retorts: You stink worse than
we ever did, because you include in your ranks people who've arrived here directly from the markets, and whose blood is anything
but pure and ruby red. You're full of families from Amalfi. From
Scala. From Ravello. And in any case not from Naples. People
who are in lines of work that have nothing to do with the status of
nobleman. Nothing to do with chivalry. Vile families. Made up of
grubby social climbers. Shopkeepers. Tradesfolk…

Words flew. And with those words, insults. Tempers grew hot.
Men hurried over, belonging to one party or the other, and started
jostling and shoving. The first punches were landed. Fighting ensued. And out came the knives. This was a battle. And dead men
and wounded men were carried off. Trailing after them, long se-
gues of vendettas, ambushes, quarrels, lasting rancor, and blazing
hatred. "And there came a great deal of killing in the aftermath."

Whereupon King Robert weighed in, with the decree I've already mentioned above, acknowledging the preeminence of Nido
and Capuana. The chapters of this decree were read aloud publicly
in the palace on June 29, 1339. They ended with an injunction: it
is forbidden to bear arms in the city, followed by specific criminal
penalties. An injunction that, as usual, was honored more in the
breach than the letter.

The decree met with the approval of the nobles of Nido and
Capuana, among whom were the leaders of the 1343 hijacking operation. But it created a profound rift of resentment in municipal
society, seeing that the three other *seggi* considered the sentence

"iniquitous, deplorable, not in keeping with the documentation, with the evidence adduced, but perhaps only in keeping with the contingent utility of the moment, and in any case null and void by rights and law." In other words, they were criticizing the king for having made a decision that was, no doubt, driven by the chaotic situation of the moment, the pressure of feelings on the street, the violence that was breaking loose, but also conditioned by the forceful pressure exerted by the *nobiliores* of the two principal *seggi*. So much so that it was pointed out to him that the chancellery had failed to properly read the papers, thus failing to note what had been *fully proven*, namely that many of the noblemen of Capuana and Nido came of less-than-illustrious family. While, in contrast, there were a great many true nobles who had not been deemed such. This led to a tidal wave of appeals, objections, and lengthy declamations concerning matters that might strike us as beside the point but which actually were addressed to genuine issues, matters of management and control of the administration and municipal life. Issues that led the way to new clashes, new quarrels, and new bloodshed.[41]

I would like to introduce at this point a brief parenthesis. Throughout the history that I've recounted here, what's really missing is women. Or, if they do make an appearance, it's only to be insulted, mistreated, or raped. So let me now offer a profile of a clan woman discovered by an extraordinary eyewitness, Petrarch. A woman who was the protagonist of a longtime feud, seeing that she "carried on an age-old war with her neighbors, a war in which a great many had already been killed." But why? Because she was a warrior woman, the only one in this whole entire history of ours. It was the end of 1343, practically simultaneous with the events of the night of November. Petrarch was in Pozzuoli. He wrote a letter about it to his usual friend Giovanni Colonna. This woman was called Maria. She had remained a virgin, an enormous Amazon with whom nobody ventured to trifle, fearful as they were of her potential reactions. Here is how the poet describes her:

She had the body of a knight more than that of a maiden, a stout vigor that would be perfect for any knight, a rare and uncommon dexterity, a youthfulness...she worked not with cloth but with arrows; not with needles and mirrors but rather with longbows and swords; she dreamed not of caresses but wounds and scars. Her chief interest had to do with weapons. Her soul scoffed at steel, she held her own life at little price. She carried on an age-old war with her neighbors, a war in which a great many had already been killed. Sometimes alone, other times accompanied by a few chosen allies, she fought the enemy hand to hand. She was always the first to launch into the fray. And the last to stagger away. She attacked her enemies with great courage, and with incredible patience she would tolerate hunger, thirst, the cold, the heat, lack of sleep, exhaustion. Sleeping outdoors, armed, on the bare earth, using her sword as her pillow, was the reason why, in short order, her beauty had been much eroded.

The description goes on with a rundown of the woman's gifts, truly exceptional. And so a group of knights, their curiosity aroused by the renown of this Maria, decided to test her strength. The young woman accepted their challenge, lifting a large boulder and a metal beam, and invited the knights to do as she had done. The knights did their best, trying one after the other. Nonetheless, none of them succeeded. And that renewed Petrarch's astonishment, because the poet laureate had been present at the contest. This experience persuaded him that perhaps Amazons really had existed. As had the virgins led by Camilla.[42]

A State of Renunciation

But let's get back to our story: the clashes between the Neapolitan clans for dominance in the city were a warning light pointing to a larger deterioration of state power, and it had important ramifications concerning much of the Kingdom. In many towns and villages, it was possible to witness a comparable phenomenon to the clash among factions who were, here as well, in search of new balances and tradeoffs when it came to the management of local power. With the same approach that we find at Naples: which is, let me repeat, the use of violence as a method for resolving disagreements. What makes things even worse, this was frequently done independent of the action of the central government, which not only showed no sign of being able to repress that violence, but in fact found only palliatives that after a while allowed the plague to remanifest. A phenomenon so widespread that chroniclers could hardly help but call them *guerre civili*, or civil wars. Let's examine a few.

In Gaeta, there was a clash between the Aliotto and the Papa families, "enemies to the death and tirelessly scheming to rub each other out, however possible," with daily brawls and clashes and murders on the street. In Nocera, in a rustic duel, the *milites* Riso de Riso, Cervo de Raimondo, and Riccardo de Alberado, as well as the judge Francesco Ungaro, all faced off: "first they came to furious discord among themselves and then, what with their weapons, they compromised the public peace." Relatives and friends came hurrying to help, and an individual clash was soon turned into a hellish free-for-all, with a number of dead men. In Sulmona, the Merolini and de' Quatrari families faced off, with a reprisal that lasted for years and involved both Lanciano and Ortona. In Tropea the Ferrucci and de' Nomicisi families faced off, in a feud that began with the stabbing of the *miles* Pietro Ferrucci by Bartolomeo de Rahone, a partisan of the de' Nomicisi family. The Pipino family bloodied the cities of Apulia. In Salerno, there was a feud between the Santomango and the de Ajello families caused by a terrible outrage perpetrated by the de Ajello family:

> The seed of the rage of the Santomango was the following. Landolfo Santomango had just married the young maiden Bianca de la Porta in 1334, a maiden of extreme beauty and illustrious birth, when Riccardo de Ajello, a *miles*, already filled

with fiery passion for her, violently kidnapped her from her husband and then proceeded to consummate marriage with her and, in order to escape the rigors of the law that had been leveled against him, vanished, along with his hapless prey. This act resulted in a long civil war between the two families, involving nearly all the nobles linked by blood ties.

The king weighed in, but to no avail. The thirst for vendetta was too powerful. With the usual frenzy of alliances, blood ties, and impulses of solidarity driving both sides, in order to repair the outrage suffered or, on the other side, in order to defend their own kith and kin, guilty though he may have been, driven by the need to support any member of the clan and therefore impervious to any considerations of justice and convinced that only the perpetrator had the right to judge his own actions: "Whereupon the leading figures of the town and a great number of citizens, joined by family ties or bonds of friendship to one or the other of the two families, split into two formidable opposing parties and took up arms." With 334 partisans supporting the de Ajello side and 350 supporting the Santomango side, if we can trust the recorded figures. A number that was in any case enormous for a city as small as Salerno was at the time, and which fueled a war that had dire effects on the daily lives of the citizens and in particular on its economic life, "as its flourishing domestic and external trade economy was for years afterward unhinged and decapitated."

Not only did the system of municipal control plunge into crisis. It would seem that everywhere in the Kingdom, in villages just as in small towns, in castles just as in villages and farming communities, on a truly diffuse basis, the level of alarm rose sharply. There was a general increase in the level of social tensions that resulted in outbursts of violence that were frequently indiscriminate. These acts of violence were most often committed by feudal lords, members of the nobility, figures in the administration (whether they came from Naples or not), who launched into a series of abuses and misdeeds, taking for themselves the badge of authority that was rightly bestowed upon them only by the state and the king. They manipulated their authority, using it arbitrarily, recklessly, and for entirely personal ends. There really were a great many episodes, and they are all eloquent instances of a southern Italy inflamed by illegality. October 1310: in Pontelandolfo, in the Benevento area, by night, a horde of armed men, on foot or on horseback, under the command of the chamberlain of the noble-man Simone de Martiaco, entered the town, turning down the deserted streets and bursting into the houses, leaving a great many dead and wounded men on the ground behind them. September 1315: the prosecutors of Cosenza reported that the seigneur of Amantea, Goffredo Schiavello, wishing to throw the fear of God into the citizenry, locked a poor farmer into his house and then set it on fire. December 1317: in Policastro, the Neapolitan *miles* Giacomo Capano evicted by force all the administrators of the customhouse, refusing to allow them to collect the money for the tariffs on incoming and outgoing goods because he insisted that it all belonged by rights to him. January 1318: the people of Castroprignano sent a pleading letter to the king, begging him to do something against the seigneur of the town, because for ten years now he had been extorting from them not only the taxes that they were obligated to pay to the state but also ten *oncias* of gold annu-ally, as well as subjecting then to a series of terrible impositions, among them stealing their seed for next year, something that made it impossible to farm, thereby forcing them to leave their homes and seek refuge elsewhere. September 1318: in Abruzzo Ultra, Branca Furcapetula and her son Giovanni, having assembled a number of armed men, attacked the people of Rocca di Fondi and not only killed a great many of them but also burned a large num-ber of houses; three children died among the flames. June 1319: in Loreto, near Sulmona, the local seigneur, a member of the del Balzo family of the French nobility who had moved to Naples, im-posed a continuous series of extortionate levies upon the popu-lace, thereby preventing them from living their daily lives; anyone who failed to pay was tortured and imprisoned or else intimidated and threatened—he said that anyone who talked, "he'd rip the eyes right out of their head." September 1319: the seigneurs of Limosano, not far from Campobasso, showed up with the usual platoon of armed men before the *casale* of Pesculo and burned all the crops. July 1320: Isabella di Alneto (Isabelle d'Aulnay), the widow of Ludovico di Savoia (Louis of Savoy), sent her men "to kill and wound her enemies among the common folk, to burn and level their houses, and to assault their women." September 1333: the *milites* Borracio and Barrazzello de Balneis gathered a thousand or so brigands and then proceeded to go to Frosolone and put the town to the sword and the torch. October 1333: in Foggia, a certain Palmerio de Gregorio, accompanied by a mob of hoodlums, knocked down a poor woman's front door, the widow Framunda, who lived with her seven-year-old daughter; he ravished the woman and barbarically mutilated the little girl's foot. December 1335: the people of Capriglia, not far from Salerno, lodged a complaint that their seigneur, Giacomo de Molinis, had been caning women (and two of them died under his blows), torturing farmers, imposing taxes on a whim, raping the younger women, and above all creating feudal lords arbitrarily, without any royal mandate. October 1340: the *miles* Corrado Ruffo, accompanied by a troop of knights and a broad array of his followers, roughly a thousand people, sacked and plundered the district of Catanzaro, with a continuous reign of murders, rapes, and thefts perpetrated against merchants, both foreign and local...[43]

These are just a few of the daily episodes. What image are we left with? An image of widespread anarchy, a state that lacks genuine leadership and a central government that had proved incapable of restoring peace or a steady administration. A Kingdom that was already being troubled by another scourge, brigandage:

> One of the terrible afflictions that caused the government at this time serious apprehension and left the populace in consternation was brigandage, for the most part fomented and protected by certain troublesome barons, who never blushed

at the idea of exploiting the services of highwaymen. Back then, murders, arson, demands of large ransom, and extortion were still common at the time, deeds indulged in by brigands and murderers with great temerity and absolutely no fear of meeting with punishment. This chronic and benighted evil, deeprooted back then in a number of provinces, and never fully combated and uprooted, still demanded the paternal care of King Robert; by now, he was sad and wearied at the thought that it was dangerous and unreliable to use the public roads, and that trade relations between towns and the city had been broken off, resulting in increased misery, while the lives of peaceful citizens were frequently exposed to raiding and the daggers of the brigands.[44]

Brigandage was already a subject of discussion in the early days of the Kingdom under Charles II, but the phenomenon grew in virulence at the end of Robert's rule over the Kingdom and the beginning of the reign of Joanna I, when social disarray was rising to its dramatic peak. The territories of Nocera, Gragnano, Lettere, Agerola, and Pimonte were infested with brigands who had set out to accomplish a very specific program: "to subvert the entire region and reduce it entirely to their mercy." In 1316 Gherardo di Sant'Elpidio wrote that in the province he was in charge of, bandits were streaming in from the surrounding areas, and that it had therefore become impossible to ensure the safety of either the citizens or the state. The following year, the Count of Squillace reported that in his lands of Principato Citra all control had been lost and the roads were swarming with *turme* and *coorti* of thieves and murderers. And things got even worse. While traveling in the Valle del Fortore, the Count of Sant'Angelo Niccolò de Jamville, King Robert's own chamberlain, was killed by a large band of brigands. One of the ladies-in-waiting of Queen Sancia (or Sancha), Ilaria di Lauria, complained of the constant aggressions carried out by bandits on her lands in Corneto. In 1321, in Principato Citra, a *società di banditi* (*societas bannitorum*) was formed under the command of a certain Ispamà, who wandered the region, committing robberies and extortions. In Pontecorvo, the local bandit army was led by a certain Cicco de Esculo. In Pescopagano, certain merchants from Perugia, on their way from Barletta and heading for Salerno, were robbed on the public road...

So many episodes that allow us to gauge the scope of a widespread phenomenon that involved more than merely shepherds, farmers, and the rootless, a larger expression of the malaise of southern society. But members of the low- and mid-level aristocracy found in their gangs a propitious terrain for revenge, a phenomenon not dissimilar from the German *Raubrittertum* (robber barons, or bandits), and which was broadly emulated in France, England, Scandinavia, and Poland. A form of banditry that in southern Italy seized on the opportunities that derived from the incandescent political climate but that were frequently sufficient unto themselves, until under their own momentum they grew to amount to a full-fledged private war. The phenomenon also drew in members of the clergy, and not merely priests and pastors, if the bishop of Vico—who, according to the account of the plaintiff, the small-shopkeeper Stefano di Rusiaco—had his unfortunate victim torn out of his family's arms and literally stripped naked, despoiling with his own hands the pitifully miserable things that the plaintiff traded in: three *centenaria* of needles, a cross made of cypress wood, a pear, two bags full of bread, his donkey, and a wooden keg full of wine.[45]

The brigands were certainly estimable opponents. They were capable of great leaps of organizational and military quality, able both to organize assaults in great style on towns that were of substantial size, such as Salerno, Avellino, Eboli, and Aversa, and to exert steady pressure on Naples. Around Mount Vesuvius, in the forest known as the Selva Mala, for at least a good fifty years, between 1330 and 1380, brigand bands were in complete control. An extensive phenomenon of considerable social impact, powerful in part because, while on the one hand there was no lack of complicity from within even the highest nobility, on the other hand, there was little if any ability to unleash armed repression on the part of the established powers. It frequently happened that even local administrators, the very same people who ought by rights to ensure the public peace and civil order, the *baiuli*, were actually in close contact with the bandits, in terribly grim situations of corruption and malfeasance. Word of just such a debacle was conveyed directly to the Duke of Calabria in November 1320 by the communities of Andria, Corato, Ruvo, Gravina, Terlizzi, Casamassima, and Acquaviva. Their words confirmed that the *baiuli* were actually rooting more enthusiastically for the brigands than for the king. Whereupon the duke ordered his chamberlains in that zone to have the *baiuli* arrested and to usher them immediately into his presence. The upshot of that order, unfortunately, remains unknown to us.

What does not remain unknown, however, is the general outcome of the state's response to this kind of lurking, subterranean civil war, which saw the proliferation of episodes of violence, plunder, and abuses of every kind. The answer is obvious: there was the passing of bucks of all sorts, in terms of responsibilities and jurisdictions. The operating principle was that old refrain: since the central state had proved unable to solve the problem, let the local governments and the settlements on the outskirts be left to take care of it. And let them pay the consequences as well, with the responsibility for murders on their territories falling on their shoulders... That, for instance, was the decision made on May 3, 1330, by King Robert. Incapable of responding to the vast number of murders left unpunished, he declared that "from this day forth, if the evildoers are left at large and untroubled by the forces of the law, the cities in whose territory those murders turn out to have been committed without the arrest of a perpetrator will be held responsible for the damage done to persons and things."[46] A defeat born of increasingly difficult times, when the weakening of the direct surveillance of the central power was transformed into an increasingly acute series of cases of malfeasance, corruption, and abuse committed by none other than the staff of the royal administration. The abuses of the *giustizieri*, or justiciars, and those below them in the hierarchic scale, could be counted in the dozens, and were inflicted upon farmers, opposing noblemen, and ecclesiastics. This took place with a vast array of crimes, ranging from the transgression of state norms all the way to extortion and corruption. There were even genuine instances of racketeering to the detriment of the state, as noted by Robert himself in 1332:

> It often happens that all the functionaries of the gabelles, when a load of silk or other goods of relatively modest worth is unloaded on the shores subject to their jurisdiction, allow the modest prey to slip by untaxed, to the detriment of the public purse. But when it comes time to reckon up accounts, they demand that the Curia should exempt them for the sums that they ought to have collected but failed to, either through negligence or else because they fraudulently conspired to thus deceive the state tax office. [47]

The conclusion to be drawn from this whole array of situations is as follows: in a great many cases, the administrators became the worst enemies of those administrated. They tormented them with illegitimate impositions; they hindered their commerce; they failed to protect them, in short, as far as their collective interests were concerned. Agents provocateurs, Caggese crudely describes them. "They are responsible for at least half the ills that afflict the state."

There is one last episode that really says it all about the state of corruption in the administration, a problem that struck at all levels. This episode concerns an outsider who commanded very high respect, the Venetian consul to Apulia, Giovanni Marino Zorzi. The time was June 1317. The consul wrote a letter to his doge, Giovanni Soranzo, with an attachment, a copy of a letter he had sent to King Robert. A letter that lodged his gravest complaints and protests against royal officials who were unwilling to pay 10,000 *oncias* that were rightfully due to Venice. An affair that had bogged down, extremely difficult to resolve, in an overall situation that had long since deteriorated. This was the official *denunzia*, or complaint. But Zorzi, in a pragmatic aside, informed his doge that the affair could certainly be straightened out and come to a satisfactory conclusion if he were only allowed to lavishly oil the right wheels, let us say the most important ones. Namely, he wished to oil the wheels of Tommaso di San Giorgio; Giovanni de Laido, tax commissioner; Giovanni Grillo; and also the archbishop of Capua: all of them advisers to the king. Thus we can see that corruption was a well-known phenomenon, a practice that even pigs and dogs were sure to wallow in, but first and foremost, those renowned and leading financiers of the Neapolitan court, the Florentines.[48]

A story that leaves a bitter taste. Experienced in a climate of disorders, clashes between factions, personal resentments, brawls between clans in the capital, murders, violence, brigandage, starvation, and poverty. In a wave of chaos that made it impossible for the state to see to a regular unfolding of everyday life, the conduct of farming and trade. Measures of a crisis that by this point no longer concerned only Naples, but instead traumatically affected the entire Kingdom. Where violence and abuses were catastrophes that piled up atop other catastrophes, with a devastating and depressive effect. Thus leading to that "age of anguish," to borrow Jean Delumeau's magnificent expression to clearly summarize the level of crisis experienced in southern Italy in this phase of the fourteenth century. A setting where it becomes difficult to establish, with a unitary effort, a policy that might solve the overwhelming problems plaguing southern Italy.

And yet, there had been very different hopes at the outset. The beginning was with Charles I. With the idea of a new, centralized state, but that idea gradually seemed to shipwreck, even though Robert supplied the image of a great sovereign, the expression of one of the most magnificent courts in Europe. This court, however, wallowed in debt, sums that were owed to the Florentine banks, which were constantly at the monarch's heels, eager to claim their due; the court seemed incapable of taking any actions that might be, let me not say definitive, but at least capable of moderating the Kingdom's difficulties. What is more, with a capital city likewise in many ways ungovernable, where the old, traditional clans, the backbone of both city and nation, were also in the midst of vast transformations. A difficult, complicated process that involved pressures from so many directions, involving a generalized fear of the new and where violence was always the first tool that came to hand.

King Robert died in the midst of a critical phase for the King-dom. Basically the time of "great projects" had ended, though it had driven much of the experience of that sovereign. The forces of the state were already in and of themselves inadequate to the ambitions of any hegemonic role in Italy he may have had at the beginning of his rule. So much the worse, now that everything seemed to collapse in on itself like a house of cards. And in his final years, alongside the problems that were already gripping life in southern Italy, new problems came to bear. Such as the ex-tremely important matter of succession. This would be the first time that the Kingdom would fall *in man di femmina*, as people put it at the time—into the hands of a female, namely his grand-daughter Joanna (Giovanna). There was, it must be said, no cause for contesting her succession, in view of the fact that even the act of pontifical investiture allowed for female succession.

In any case, on January 16, 1343, ten months before the raid, after thirty-four years of ruling the Kingdom, at age sixty-five, Robert made his last will and testament. There were no major surprises in that document. Joanna was proclaimed his sole and universal heir. Her husband, Andrew of Hungary, the Duke of Calabria, was excluded from the line of succession, but was given the title of Prince of Salerno. A regency was established, given the fact that Joanna was still a minor, and the head of that regency was the queen mother, Sancia of Majorca. After which, Robert knew that his end was nigh. There was little left for him to do or say. His death agony ended after just three days, in the palace of

Castel Nuovo. And he was buried, in accordance with his wishes, in the mausoleum of the Anjou, the new church dedicated to Saint Clare, for the construction of which he had lavished a veritable river of money: some spoke fancifully of a million florins, a sum that alone would have been sufficient to feed the entire Kingdom for a year. The funeral service was sumptuous, with the general participation of the citizenry at large. Similarly, the sovereign's memory was celebrated throughout the Kingdom, in Provence, and in the allied power of Florence.

With his death, the sun set on an era. There are those who've written that as long as Robert lived, the Kingdom was magnificent, but that after his death, under Joanna, things went to hell. That's not my view. The situation in the Kingdom and the capital, Naples, was as I've described it. Very serious. And that was the situation that Joanna inherited. Full stop. So let me move on to Naples and its setting. The two worlds that had met there at the beginning of the Angevin adventure had traveled together, sharing projects, outlooks, and common political objectives. The main one had been to make Naples the capital. The monarchs had not only succeeded in that but they had done even more: first and foremost, they had turned it into a capital not only from a juridical point of view but in point of fact, by investing resources and cash, transforming it at the root. Right up to the very end, up to the construction of the church of Santa Chiara. Then they had proceeded to encourage the creation of an executive class befitting that capital, with a nobility no longer holed up in the narrow and traditional piazzas of the old municipal power structure. No, they were now transformed into an elite, administrators of the state, feudal lords. Men who through their control of the capital could dream of dominating the entire south of Italy. And could even fantasize about a realm extending over a Mediterranean-wide dimension.

That dream, however, had crashed and burned, with the twenty-year War of Vespers. And that propulsive force had broken off. Dynamism had been replaced by weariness. The weakening of structures and functions. Hence the deterioration and decline. The state was giving way, step by step, allowing the worst realities to surface again. Corruption, feuds between families, indiscriminate violence, all playing out while the central power failed to take any decisive action. In Naples, too, the dynamism of a bygone era now seemed only a memory. After the war, so many things seemed to have changed. Fashion, customs. The traditional ways of life.

Meanwhile, the crisis was growing worse. The city was growing, creating new needs and demands. With people coming in from the outside, knocking at the door and seeking some of the same privileges and opportunities that gave city functionaries and administrators such a comfortable life. People who wanted a better life for themselves. And at the same time, a growing number of mouths to feed. Naples was narrow, small. There was no space. Hunger was everywhere. And there seemed to be no way of fixing anything. For instance, the challenge of worsening crime. Not even the clans seemed able to put a stop to the crime wave, and they were caught in the same abyss of anguish. This desire to recover an identity, to find different spaces in which to maneuver. And as they did, they stepped on plenty of toes. Hence quarrels, brawls, wars, feuds, and clashes.

And their issues became separate from those of the crown. Ever so slightly, but it did happen. What had united the world of the clans with the world of the state was no longer enough. The kings were still the same kings as ever. The monarchy was still the Angevin monarchy. But the connective tissue linking the two worlds was starting to fail, because the underlying project had vanished. And in that deterioration, there were several families who wanted ever-greater influence and power, creating a distinction within their world and establishing who among them enjoyed preeminence. For now, that distinction belonged to those who held the *seggi* of Capuana and Nido, those who hadn't limited themselves to obtaining supremacy but had instead torn it out of the king's hands, in 1339, by presenting him with the threat that they would be willing to undermine the system.

The nobility of Capuana and Nido, who really were vast in their numbers, a city within the city, a world within the world. They really did think about taking care of Naples, seeing that there was no one else to do that at this moment. Well aware of the fact, they claimed that prerogative. Even at this crucial instant. On this night of November in 1343.

Certainly, it is difficult for me to believe that everyone at that moment was thinking about things in those terms, because most of them were driven by hunger, by need, or by a blind, ironbound sense of obedience to their superiors. But can we not rule out the idea that they, the leaders of this adventure that played out entirely in just a few hours, might not have been well aware that their exploit served, yes, to ameliorate a hunger and a famine that had by now become truly intolerable, but likewise to underscore something else? That "something else" emerges clearly, even as the oars slice into the water amid the fear that even the slightest noise might spoil everything. A very specific idea: that whatever the problem may have been, whatever the malaise, whatever the need, in Naples, in the absence of a powerful state, there was still someone who was thinking about these matters. Someone who could take care of things. Someone who could provide bread and survival for the city's quarters, its *rioni*, its outskirts, its squares, the populace of the *seggi*. And that someone was them. The men of the clans. The clans of Nido and Capuana. Who in all their long history had always bound their fate to the destiny of Naples. The only ones who, in all this confusion, continued to think first of the population's survival. Independently, without any need for orders, laws, norms, or regulations. They were enough to take care of matters: with their families and their "clientele." Weapons in hand, their sense of identity and honor, filled with a power that sprang from violence and a spirit of self-defense that had been handed down over the centuries.

Men who, once again, as was customary, behaved as if they were the sole masters of this city. Capable of a test of strength that in the final analysis humiliated the state.

V

VICTIMS (AND EXECUTIONERS)

The Two Horizons

This is how it went: shadows flitted around the ship. They arrived in silence, without even the slightest sound. The men standing guard only noticed them when it was already too late. In the blink of an eye, they found themselves bound and gagged. In the meantime, however, the other members of the crew had woken up. They sounded the alarm. The captain arrived. A brawl broke out. Furious, but soon over. Just one death. The captain: his throat slit. His head practically dangling, so powerful had the blow been. A clean cut. Lying on the ground was the one victim of this night's violence…

Or else…

This is how it went: the boats approached. There was no resistance. The only one to get upset was him: the captain. He shouted and he inveighed. He was determined to be left alone. He didn't like having all those hands on him. Those hands, gripping him, restraining him, dragging and hurting him. He loudly proclaimed that he was from Genoa. And that his masters would make them regret their actions. He refused to surrender his cargo. He insulted the boarding crew. He spat. And eventually his men, too, began to be inflamed by his example. The chief of the Neapolitans, or the elder, or the one who was sick and tired of the noise, or just the single most reckless member of the boarding party, ran out of patience and simply cut the captain's head off, at a single, sharp blow. The situation calmed down. At last, there was silence. And on the deck lay the one victim of this night's violence…

Or else…

You can let your imagination run where it will. The same is true of the written word. Reconstructing this history of November 1343 to suit ourselves, moving tiles and adding details to the small canvas that lies at the basis of this account. Still, however you turn it, whatever angle you look at it, one detail is incontrovertible: in the end, a man is going to be killed. And we know virtually nothing about him. Nothing except for the fact that he's Genoese, and that by trade he is a sea captain, and he sails the seas. From one end of the Mediterranean to another, like so many others who came before him and after him. A man who fell victim, but all the same, a little bit of a killer himself. For a split second, he is one. But why? Because he belongs to an aggressive approach to economics, something that had sprung up in the previous two centuries, and which completely modified the way people understood and practiced trade. A way that, perhaps, we can define as capitalistic. An approach that links the path of his city, Genoa, to that of his city's sister cities upon the water, both of them with different histories and identities, Pisa and Venice, two cities that over the course of the Middle Ages spent more time at war, fighting to claim supremacy over the Mediterranean, than they did simply living in peace with each other. And that links them to the other great center of economic development, a city that had no port but whose ideas spanned and crossed any sea or other geographic border: ideas made of paper, techniques, and numbers. A city that was the *fifth element of the world*, Florence.

If we want to be romantic, I could say that with this one shameful act, with this murder, the *miles* of the clan not only murdered a single man but also the vision that he embodied, which had progressed so notably in the Kingdom, to the point of virtually monopolizing its economy. An idea that revolutionized the existing structures, the city's state of equilibrium, modifying them to their very roots, in an unbalanced relationship between North and South. How that happened can be glimpsed, in transparency, in this chapter, where, however, my chief interest is to examine Naples and its society from another point of view: that of its commercial life and the relations between that life and the world of international capital, of which in some small way the Genoese captain is also an expression. The man who was, at the same time, both victim and, in spite of himself—the last thing he would ever have been able to imagine—executioner.

Let's go back to him now, on the ship's deck. His throat just cut, his head practically severed. It's a snapshot: him, lying sprawled on the wooden deck. And the *miles* who's just overpowered him. He's standing above him, looking down. They're united together: murderer and victim. Two men. Two horizons of sensibility. Let's focus upon them for a moment. The executioner is the Neapolitan *miles*. How do we imagine him? Sneering and arrogant. Violent. Insolent. Sheathed in a diving bell made up of prejudices, rituals, and mental and psychological training that make him what he is: a prominent member of an elite that right here and right now confidently dictates terms throughout this city, with his clan and with the men of the *seggi* to which he belongs, every bit as powerful as the queen, if not more so. Capable of making decisions like the one he just took upon himself, uncertain as to what aftermath it may bring upon him, because attacking a foreign ship is an illegal act. An act of piracy. Obviously, the punishments can be quite severe. But he is indifferent to that, and to make that clear, he uses no words. He places forefinger and middle finger together, like a gun, and flicks them carelessly under his chin.[1] It's an age-old Italian gesture indicating scorn, indifference. He can afford that figurative shrug. He feels special, above the law. In Naples now we'd call him a *mammasantissima*. A man of utter power: he knows he has it and he knows how to use it. And a man of tradition: which runs in his veins like a surge of honor, loyalty, and might, with an unquestioned charisma and influence over his men, his quarter of the city, and in the mental conception he has developed of himself.

On the other hand, we have the victim. A man of the sea. Genoese. He comes from a city that has necessarily been forced over time to reach out and live its life on the salt water. Nature imposed that choice on the city. A harsh topography whose steep slopes left nothing but a narrow strip of land to cultivate. Devoid of any potential, devoid of all resources. So what remains is the sea. The instrument of a civilization that had been waiting for nothing so much as to plunge out into those waters. Because that was where the future lay. That is where potential could be found, with a chance to redraw the borders, which consisted entirely of sky, water, and mountains.

And so the Genoese launched themselves onto the sea. In search of resources—and land—that they lacked back home. And they established a route to follow: trade. It's important to listen to proverbs. Especially the proverb that travels by word of mouth across the Mediterranean: "Is there a Genoese? Then there's a merchant!" But that's not all. And that's not the only way things went. According to one of Italy's greatest medievalists of the twentieth century, Roberto Sabatino Lopez, in fact, matters were far more complex. How else can we explain that in the thirteenth century, every Genoese merchant wanted to become a knight? And what is the reason that, as Benedetto Cotrugli insisted in the fifteenth century, anyone that suffered business setbacks invariably launched into the profession of piracy? Between the two extremes, there is the utterly ordinary. The dull routine of plying the seas. Carrying cargos. Haggling and bargaining. Cautiously hugging the coast. Reaching the easiest, least interesting ports. But then also the farthest, most difficult ports to reach. Daring, challenging. Questing after markets ignored and unexploited by others.

These were people of extreme audacity, in many cases. Ingenious. Imaginative. Such as Guglielmo Embriaco, also known as Testadimaglio, who during the First Crusade helped Godfrey of

Bouillon build siege wagons, the same siege wagons that in the end managed to broach the walls of Jerusalem. Or the brothers Ugolino and Vadino Vivaldi, who, two hundred years before another Genoese navigator, Christopher Columbus, planned and executed (sadly, failing utterly, and dying in the process...) the project of finding an Atlantic route to the Indies. Or the greatest of them all: Benedetto Zaccaria, admiral to Philip the Fair of France, Lord of Phocaea, who'd been awarded a monopoly over the valuable alum mines of that region. He was a pirate, a great merchant, and the first to use the route that led from the east, through the Pillars of Hercules, to England.

Men of the market, men of *commenda*—that typical commercial instrument that allowed everyone to take part, whether rich or poor, old or young, in the ventures of trade—men of the sea and men of faith, but never fundamentalists about it, to use a modern-day term. Never really mystical, hardheaded, with an extra dose of skepticism and tolerance, if you stop to consider that there was never an episode of persecution in the city of Genoa against the Jews. Or, for that matter, against the Albigenses, who were welcomed to Genoa with a generous hospitality.

The Genoese: always ready to find compromises, even with men of the opposite faith, such as the Muslims. For that matter, was it not true that a notorious Venetian slander claimed that you simply couldn't trust the Genoese, all of them the children begotten from a Muslim raid that took place during the tenth century? Therefore Levantines by blood, by race, always ready to make deals with the most alien enemies, by civilization and religion.

Genoa was a city that distinguished itself by a boundless individualism and an indifference to the privileges offered by birth, ready to welcome anyone who came along and proved willing and able to get rich through the amassing of capital and good luck in business. A city with trade guilds that kept their front door wide open. An environment where the only bona fides had to do with trade and the marketplace. A universe that centered around business, which came before politics, inasmuch as "war is war and business is business." And Genoa took commerce as the central pillar of its identity. With a state conceived from day one as a good deal, thanks to the utter and complete identification of its people as a merchant class. A vision that "transformed the Lincolnian principle of government of the people, by the people, for the people into a government *of the merchants, by the merchants, for the merchants.*"² Avaricious? Perhaps that's overstated, even though Boccaccio, who knew a thing or two when it came to people, chose as a good example of a sordidly moneygrubbing human being the Genoese Erminio de' Grimaldi, who "far overpassed in wealth of lands and moneys the riches of whatsoever other richest citizen was then known in Italy; and like as he excelled all other Italians in wealth, even so in avarice and sordidness he outwent beyond compare every other miser and curmudgeon in the world."³

It was also a bellicose world. Where piracy, when needed, took the place of commerce. In a seesawing back and forth where it was easy to go from one condition to the other because, "in a Genoese apprenticeship, there is no difference between market and war."⁴ With a city likewise divided between family clans, who split up the city space appropriately: into *alberghi*. With high towers that dominated zones, separating them from each other, separating one space from another. An old tradition previously emphasized by Benjamin of Tudela, who wrote in 1172: "Everyone has a house with a tower, and when a war breaks out, the terraces of the towers become battlefields." Worse even than Naples. With a political life that swerved regularly between anarchy and dictatorship. Where individual passions were never capable of folding the five fingers of the hand into a single compact fist. Just like in Naples. Everyone always thought for themselves and thought *of* themselves. With actual situations of pure madness, where the crew of a single ship would go to war with itself, massacring itself because its crew members belonged to different factions. Or to the verge of the paradoxical, with Genoese colonies that at times asked the Turks to help them against their homeland, Genoa...

They were individualists. Excellent at trade. Good at selling, good at negotiating. But also, when needed, skillful at piracy. These were the Genoese aboard that ship on the night of 1343. People suited to *galera*, the Italian word for prison but also for galley. From the Greek word *galaia*: not a prison, but rather the ship that dominated Mediterranean trade, "just as well suited for war and for trade, driven either by sails or by oars...the most flexible, sturdy, and rapid ship of all those that carried freight during the trade revolution of the late Middle Ages." The galley: made up of a crew of free men, "a school of individualistic and egalitarian democracy," Lopez writes,[5] but one where there was certainly a difference between the captain and the crew. But the rabble of the crew were equal in every way, in the face of the hardships and dangers that they faced, shoulder to shoulder, side by side, on the deck of their ship...

And so, on that night in 1343, two different horizons were facing off. Two different ways of understanding life and the world. Each of the two characters who incarnated them—the victim and his executioner—felt they were at the center of their own community, which they directed and ruled. With a very similar idea, in many ways, of what the hierarchy was, bound up with family and the clan they belonged to, where violence was understood as a tool for the resolution of disagreements. Men who, however, in this specific context, found themselves at odds, caught in a mortal game that culminated in a brutal murder.

The Neapolitan Hub

Between these two men, in the middle lay Naples, along with her relations with foreigners and her history as a seafaring city. It often seems as if medievalists forget that Naples has very solid roots in the seafaring profession. Already, prior to the Norman age, it had a very busy port. Much busier than people seem to think. In fact, we need to debunk the impression of an immobile world; commercially immobile, I mean to say. No: the city's port did not play by any means a secondary function. The accounts we have before and after the year 1000 speak of a universe of *nauclerii* (plural of *nauclerius*, Latin for helmsman or master of a ship, Italian *nocchieri*), so, sailors, working away in allied industries, hemp workers busily making rope, carpenters building ships. There were people who ran the customhouse for the duke (as we've seen), keeping an eye on the flow of goods coming in and going out, and these were people you'd do anything to avoid interacting with, the forefathers of the nobility of Capuana and Nido: the group of the Atalarico, ready to brawl and fight with anyone, even with the monks of the monastery of Saints Sergius and Bacchus (Santi Sergio e Bacco). Monks who, for that matter, were the owners of a fleet of boats that went all the way to Rome to trade, and who could count on their own products as trade goods, crops cultivated in the area of the Phlegraean Fields and transported, again, by sea, all the way to Naples, and from there, up through the Tyrrhenian Sea.[6]

From that port, aside from the slave trade, what was loaded and shipped was prevalently three types of products: wine, foodstuffs, and linen fabrics. And possibly, I can't rule this out, weapons for the Muslim markets. Slaves were a type of merchandise that was dealt in with a certain regularity: as we know for certain, since the ninth century they had been raided and rounded up in the surrounding Langobard territory by the *milites* of the time and then sold, either directly to Muslim merchants or else through the middlemen of Amalfi. The other category of municipal exports were agricultural products: fruit (apples, figs, almonds, pomegranates, et cetera), chestnuts, hazelnuts. Various types of cereals, *Triticum aestivum* (common wheat, or bread wheat), barley, *germano*, that is, rye. Onions, which were also used in the preservation of eggs and wheat. Beans, *fasoli rubei* (red beans), fava beans, chickpeas, squash, and cabbage. Olive oil and olives. And of course wine, which in time became the leading export product. Already there were a few recognized varieties: aged wine, the *saccapanna*; *musto* or *musto mundo* wine; the *vino latino*, or red wine; and the elite product, *vino greco*, or white wine. Wines that were transported from the hinterland to the city and then exported in barrels, wine jars, or amphorae.

Last of all, it is no legend that Naples was, for those who came from the Mediterranean's southern coasts, Nabl-el-Kattan, the *city of linen fabrics*, according to the description from the 970s by Ibn Hawqal. These textiles were by and large made in small domestic workshops or else in ateliers of varying sizes, such as the one owned by the nobleman Sergio Inferno. The impression remains, in any case, that there existed a rather widespread family manufacturing network, with its looms, its tanks, its degreasing basins mixed in with the already rather chaotic residential grid, with endless quarrels caused by the custom of dumping *spurcitias*, that is, toxic substances deriving from the processing of flax into linen, in the city streets.

So if that's how things went with exports, then what was the situation with imports? The luxury market was doing exceedingly well. In Naples, there were people who could afford to splurge, to buy more than was strictly needed, to buy prized objects, thanks to the profits they'd made in the marketplace. Suffice it to take a look at the dowry that the *miles* Sergio Amalfitano, whom we've encountered previously, gave to his daughter, whose name, somewhat unsettlingly, was Blatta (Cockroach). A dowry that opens up to us a world of tastes, fashions, luxuries, and goods that is totally unimaginable, on the boundary between East and West, made up of silk fabrics, objects and jewelry from the south of France, Spain, and Greece. But Blatta was far from alone in having such a dowry. No, there were other women with similar dowries, belonging to the same social context: not a few of whom actively pursued the business of moneylending, such as Maria Salvacossa, to name just one...

But it was the religious community that poured the greatest flow of its income into the purchase of precious fabrics, decorated draperies, embroidered cloth imported from Byzantium, Tyre, and Alexandria; the Roman Catholic church of Naples also purchased the vases, sacred furnishings, and decorative accessories that adorn the city's churches and monasteries. Many of them were made by specialized Sicilian or Middle Eastern craftsmen, who might have come from Morea and Negroponte (Euboea).[7] There is a great variety of merchandise, amply documented from as far back as the eighth century, with a vast series of objects, abounding in motifs and decorations, all referencing the worship of Christ, the saints, and the stories of the New Testament.

The port's strongest feature, however, its greatest attraction, had nothing to do with the Neapolitans. Even then, it was the people who came from outside. The *foranei*, the outsiders. That is a crucial piece of information: the sea and the port were the mediums that made Naples more or less welcoming to anyone who came from elsewhere. Many people settled in Naples. In the ninth century, Muslims arrived as well. They were the ones carrying out rapid-fire incursions and attacks on the coast, in an era when the jihad was a presence in Italy. Then there were other foreigners. There were neighboring nations, close geographically and often in terms of mindset. People from Gaeta and Sorrento, first and foremost. Langobards from the principality of Capua. Greeks escaping from the territories of the south that had been ravaged by Saracen attacks and who found in Naples the welcome they'd been searching for. And then there were the people of Amalfi, certainly the most active component of Naples's community of outsiders. They were already prominent in the tenth century, thanks to the age-old alliances and relationships that bound together the two cities, allowing a steady osmosis between the two groups of leaders and executives, with methods that speak to the great proximity existing at the highest levels between the ruling classes of Amalfi and Naples.

The Amalfitans began to stand out in a line of business in which they were not destined to be the best in absolute terms, but certainly the first to be successful, in this western Mediterranean that was just beginning to open up to trade and commerce. We should in any case begin with a preamble, without which it may prove impossible to understand future developments. The

constellation of Tyrrhenian cities, among them Naples, at this particular moment formed part of a full-fledged world economy that
had little in common with Europe. A pyramid that had its peak
elsewhere, in an orbit that ran from Baghdad to Al Fustat/Cairo
to the cities of North Africa, Palermo, and Granada. An economy
of cities, wide open, through which all manner of things passed,
from gold in the form of minted coins or in bags of dust to the finest silk fabrics to eunuch slaves, in a circulation that extended all
the way to the Indian Ocean, source of other luxury products, and
more besides. This is where Arab merchants and groups of Jewish
traders moved with comfort and ease, some of whom could already boast networks of enormous depth, ranging from one shore
of the Mediterranean to the other, from Egypt to Sicily and Spain.

The Amalfitans managed to find their way into this circuit,
and they brought with them for the first time the production of
southern Italy and Naples. They took charge of selling Neapolitan
linen, in their ships, along a very extensive route, which notably
expanded the geographic boundaries of the Neapolitan commercial horizons. These were trajectories of trade that brought Naples,
through the Amalfitans, into contact with Calabria, into the ports
of Sicily, to Constantinople, to the harbors of Syria and Palestine,
and all the way to Egypt.[8] Neapolitan linen cloth fetched up at
Alexandria, even though there were major manufactories there,
between the tenth and the eleventh centuries. From Tinnis came
cloth of extremely high quality. In spite of all that, there was still
demand, probably because Neapolitan cloth was more affordable.

Along with the linen, the Amalfitans also exported foodstuffs,
wine, weapons, wood, and Calabrian silk, as well as importing
other Greek, Spanish, and even Frankish processed fabrics (such
as the *adrisca* fabrics), spices, prized objects that they distributed
in Naples as well as the rest of southern Italy. Relations with the
Middle East, Egypt, and North Africa offered the Amalfitans an
opportunity to strengthen their business and prosper through
considerable but, at the time, largely overlooked entrepreneurial ability, the result of the existence of capital to invest and the

extensive scale of their family structures, which entailed stable connections with their place of origin and elsewhere. Included in that network was, of course, the Neapolitan hub.

So what exactly is a hub? It's a transit structure that also serves to marshal commercial traffic, dispatching it in various directions, both incoming and outgoing. A port, for instance, is a hub. The port of Naples in the early Middle Ages, mutatis mutandis, was a hub, which served the function of a marshaling yard: a territory's goods and products arrived there and were then directed and transported onward; and, of course, vice versa. An import-export business that linked the city to another series of ports and urban centers around the Mediterranean.

The importance of this hub does not depend on the number of boats and ships that pass through here—few or many—managed directly by Neapolitans, be they secular or religious. Who would think nowadays of claiming that the port of Rotterdam isn't much to write home about just because it's mostly Chinese ships going through there, and very few Dutch ones? The power of a small hub, as Naples was between the tenth and the twelfth centuries, lay in its ability to serve as a linkage between its hinterlands and the rest of the Mediterranean. There was no need for there to be specifically Neapolitans in charge of it, if there existed another community in the city, perfectly integrated or in search of integration, capable of creating this connection between municipal production and the larger Mediterranean marketplace. And that community, in this specific case, was made up of Amalfitans.

The Amalfitan amalgamation with the Neapolitan environment was a very close one. The men of the coast, so to speak, were willing to be wedded with the lifestyles, myths, traditions, and customs of Naples, thereby becoming an active part of the city, its leading integrated component, with a considerable contribution that consisted of more than just money and investments. And indeed, they were transformed into members of the militia, they appear as judges, they fit into the ecclesiastic world and the city's monasteries. They established close ties with the ducal power, in part through ties of kith and kin. They were not few in number. We have already encountered some of them over the course of this book: the Comite Maurone, the Comite Urso, the Comite Bonito, the de Balneo, the Spina, the Pantaleone, the Coppola, the Frezza, the Augustariccio, and the Amalfitano.

The climate of political solidity and social stability that emerged from the Norman conquest entailed the reinforcement of the Amalfitan colony. This took place with a progressive, parallel integration of the noble families from the entire coastline (especially the towns of Ravello and Scala) into the Neapolitan elite, in the city's businesses, and into its administrative life. This commonality of intents was endorsed in 1190 by the Privilegium Libertatis accorded by King Tancred to the Neapolitan citizenry and to the Amalfitans residing in the city: a document that ratified the partnership between the *nobiliores* and the traditionally most active community present in Naples.

The people of the coast settled in the central portion of the cove of the port of Naples. More or less located between the age-old circuit of walls and the more recently built breastworks. They had a wharf of their own that would long bear the name of the Molo degli Amalfitani e dei Sorrentini, clearly the people of Amalfi and Sorrento, and around the little church of Santa Maria della Scala, they went on to found a quarter all their own that would later take the name of Scalesia.[9] A very particular place: as if a chunk of the coastline had moved there, with its own traditions, its own cults, its own usages and customs, its own family ties and memory turned backward—all the way back to the fifteenth century!—to the original places of their affiliation. An area that was one of the city's most important commercial marshaling yards, where money circulated: the tool par excellence employed by the families of Amalfi to worm their way into the larger Neapolitan context, as we have had the opportunity to observe in the case of the monastery of San Gregorio.

Going back to the Kingdom of Roger II, the traditional local economic system was being transformed. With new protagonists

entering the game. Looking out into the limelight, not only bringing new technical skills and know-how to the marketplace, but
also with a notable degree of aggression, ready as they were to
sweep aside any adversary who might dare to get in their way.
One example: the repeated Pisan attacks on Amalfi, in 1135 and
again in 1137, that destroyed most of the city's maritime capacity.
New powers that allowed for the gradual inclusion of the South's
agricultural production into a system of trade that encompassed
much more extensive geographic territory, as well as allowing
Naples to achieve a notable qualitative commercial leap, "as a
major agricultural producer, the target of intense interest on the
part of merchants and businessmen from more advanced and dynamic areas"; while the city's agricultural hinterland became one
of the epicenters of the productive development of the southern
countryside, something that came about "at the behest of the international market."[10] A sense of Naples's rise can be seen in the
Mediterranean commercial ports that the Genoese considered
important. In the beginning of the 1180s, they considered Amalfi
and Salerno the only significant southern trading stops. Just a few
scant years later, Naples had supplanted them.

Gradually ships hailing from the ports of north-central Italy
took the place of local merchant marines and shipping operators.
The geographic outlook was turned on its head: if the economic
center of gravity had been the Middle East and North Africa, now
it shifted toward north-central Italy. Likewise, attention moved
away from the Middle Eastern marketplace and toward relations
between the Mediterranean and northern Europe, especially
France and Flanders. New merchants arrived, and they enjoyed
extensive support from the Norman crown at first, and later the
Swabian crown, something that marginalized the local merchants
who'd already been working in that marketplace. Starting with
that phase, for southern economic history, nothing would remain
as it had been: it was an unequal trade, with a deficit in the balance
of payments and a decline in the role of entrepreneurs in the Kingdom's economy becoming two decisive factors in an arena that

was by now condemned to an unfavorable economic condition. Did that moment in time mark the beginning of the yawning gap between North and South? The start of underdevelopment? Absolutely not. Let's not get ahead of ourselves here. Perhaps it would be more appropriate to talk, as David Abulafia does, of an *alternative development*, with a new outlook that also brings certain benefits of its own: a reinforcement in the intensity of maritime traffic, a new function for southern ports, and the gradual inclusion of agricultural production of the South into a circuit of trade that incorporates forms and spaces that had hitherto been unforeseeable. An economic universe that, to borrow a lovely image first evoked by Giuseppe Galasso, we could describe as *dependent but not passive*.[11]

But that was the case for the South as a general rule. Not for Naples. Because the city was growing rapidly. And unlike other southern cities, it improved its chances thanks to an array of important conditions: its strategic position, a growing population, its special and privileged relations with political power and, last, the possibility of drawing considerable earnings from the import-export sector, from agricultural production and the capital surplus that it generated, as well as thanks to the municipal harbor structure, a capacious hub for the loading and landing of foodstuffs from all over the Campania region. All things that helped to make the wealth of the Neapolitans, as well as making them increasingly aware of their territory's fundamental, precious, and basic role in any subsequent evolution. This, then, was a crucial part of the Neapolitan *patria*, or homeland, a central element to the network of its economic life, which demanded that they defend it in a massive and unalloyed fashion, with the greatest internal consensus, if the need should arise. As was the case with the episode of Cuma in 1207.

And so the city gradually became the center of commercial exchanges for two Italian maritime powers: Pisa and Genoa. Pisa first started paying attention to Naples. This took place during the course of the siege conducted by Sergius VII against King Roger.

It turned out that the city was strategic to Pisan commercial interests. It was no accident that their vessels bound for Alexandria, in Egypt, or North Africa, Sicily, and points east tended to make land, rather than in Gaeta and Salerno, nowhere else but Naples. And it was here that they established their first foothold, purchasing houses and workshops *in platea Portus* from the monasteries of San Salvatore *in insula maris* and San Pietro a Castello.

This was only the beginning. In the area of the *castellione novo*, to the west of the inlet of the port, where the old arsenal stood, in an area known as *pertuso*, on account of a breach carved into the wall there, as the name suggested, there came into being a full-fledged Pisan colony. At the beginning of the thirteenth century we find the earliest mentions of a loggia belonging to them in that quarter, with an adjoining *fondaco*, or trading post. And then, in 1238, the little church, the *chiesetta*, of San Pietro, located right on the coastline, was handed over to the Pisan consul Oddone Gualdulio and renamed San Giacomo *degli Italiani*. Since then the stretch of waterfront before it took the name of Porto Pisano (Pisan port): an anchorage and basin that, furnished with already existing defensive and harbor structures, possessed an appearance not entirely unlike the moorings that the merchants of Amalfi had established on the eastern end of the port. An exurban area that took on a markedly mercantile configuration and came to be, little by little, absorbed into the urban setting, thereafter undergoing a rapid and chaotic spurt of growth. It came to be known as *la giunta nuova di porto dove si dice a pertuso*, the new section of the port where there is said to be a breach. It was also better known, in the Angevin period, as the ill-reputed quarter of Malpertugio, dangerous and inaccessible, as we shall see.

The Genoese arrived later, but their presence immediately became fundamental, so much so that by the 1180s, Naples "appeared to be the principal destination for 5.52 percent of the total number of contracts stipulated in the Ligurian city, and for investments of a considerable bulk."[12] That was because the Genoese were much more skillful than the Pisans at taking advantage of the commercial opportunities they enjoyed in southern Italy. In 1156 and 1174, the Norman kings William I and William II had already made sure of this by offering the Genoese an opportunity to expand fully throughout southern Italy, so much so that they settled, quite rapidly, just about everywhere, from Naples to Amalfi, Gaeta, Reggio Calabria, Trani, Palermo, and Siracusa. Meanwhile, in Naples, their loggia rose in the heart of the market area that had been built at the behest of the new Norman monarchs, in the Barbacane zone, not far from the Dogana Regia, or royal customhouse, near the so-called Pietra del Pesce. So the whole area around the loggia began to become increasingly commercial, from the mid-thirteenth century onward, eventually becoming the absolute municipal mercantile center, through which ran the *ruga magna Cambiorum*, the "exchange road," Via dei Cambi, where the money changers kept their tables. This was the place where, in the course of the first part of the fourteenth century, the *banchi* (the "benches," or banks) of the powerful banking families, the Bardi and the Frescobaldi and other Tuscan and Roman lenders, were located, as well as many of the shops of the *nobiliores*.[13]

You will surely understand that the southern area of Naples, so sharply characterized by its port, was now undergoing a transformation that would give rise to a second residential nucleus, which eventually grew and developed along the water, driven by shared commercial requirements. A market dynamic, designed for merchants, noteworthy among them the outsiders. For now, in these early years of the thirteenth century, they were almost entirely Pisans and Genoese. It wasn't really a very good idea to force them to live too close. Practically side by side...

War Among Foreigners

There existed disagreements and old grudges between the two communities, matters that had nothing to do with Naples but everything to do with their homelands. Hard feelings between nations; grudges that often broke out into ferocious public violence.

The problem was no joke: both powers were expanding rapidly into the Tyrrhenian and the larger Mediterranean, in parallel, with growing influence. Neck and neck, shoulder to shoulder. For a while, despite the vastness of the market, there hadn't been any clashes. However, starting in 1119, problems began to appear. With long, dragged-out wars, stubborn, bloody, and, even worse, uninterrupted. And even where there wasn't a war, there was always lurking tension, with endless quarrels, exchanges of accusations, long-distance defamations, denunciations, sniping, guerrilla warfare, arson and wreckage of each other's warehouses, pirate attacks, raids, sudden stormy battles. In a word, a general state of disaster. Which could only have come to an end on the day that one of the rival sides dropped dead. Exhausted and dispirited from the clash.

Even in the larger conflicts that involved the empire, such as that which pitted Guelphs against Ghibellines, all that one of the cities needed to do was choose a side and it could be sure that another city would go over to the opposing side. To understand this dynamic, we need only describe what happened when the Genoese decided to start helping Frederick II to win back his empire. The year was 1220. The emperor had succeeded and now he was in Modena. The Genoese expected, given their fervent support, to be granted new privileges. Or at least to continue along the path that had previously been blazed by Frederick's father, Henry VI, who was very well disposed toward them. But that's not the way things went: the emperor had other intentions. He withdrew all the concessions he'd made. The Genoese were deprived of the exemptions they'd been granted on all tariffs for the previous ten years; they were likewise evicted from the Palazzo di Margarito in Messina, which they'd been given in concession. To make matters worse, the two Genoese who'd been appointed to the highest offices in the Kingdom, Alamanno da Costa, Count of Siracusa, and Guglielmo Porco, grand admiral, were relieved of their posts. Genoa had lost all the territory it had so laboriously acquired in the south of Italy, in terms of political space and economic influence. And word had it that the Swabians had extended to the people of Genoa "open hands, full of nothing but wind." In other words, a con job ... once the Genoese were out, who was there to take their place? The Pisans, ready and eager to move in on the new opportunity created by this unexpected vacuum. And on November 24 of that same year, 1220, Frederick, in order to block the overweening power of the Genoese in the South, brought the Pisans up to the same rank as the Ligurians, with a new privilege. Indeed, more than a privilege: a smack in the face, an outright insult to the Genoese. Who took it pretty hard, but to all appearances showed no sign of intending to retaliate. They went on supplying Frederick with their aid, in an effort at collaboration that in any case was clearly necessary if they were to continue conducting business.

Why have I tarried at such length in the twists and turns of this story? Because an event of this nature could hardly help but poison the already-terrible relations between Pisans and Genoese, as if there were any need for that. Especially so in the cities and the harbors, where the central power structure was at its weakest and therefore could offer no significant impediment to the tensions that could explode at any moment between the two nations. It is no accident that a terrible brawl broke out overseas in 1222, in Acre, a city where the merchants of the maritime cities called the shots. A clash that reached extreme levels of violence, with such huge blazes that the grand municipal tower and a vast area that belonged to the Genoese were completely destroyed.

Four years passed. And tensions exploded in another arena. Namely in the city of Naples, where an incident occurred that was every bit as serious as what happened in Acre. The story is recounted in the documents of an exceptional judicial inquest that remains, perhaps, the only piece of documentary testimony from the period that allows us to hear the actual voices of several Neapolitan *milites* who were eyewitnesses to the beginning of the clashes and who, to a certain extent, took part in them, in an attempt to quiet things down. It was a winter Thursday. To be precise, February 24, 1226. The *miles* Bartolomeo Turnopardo, listed as a witness, offered this statement:

> I was out walking with the *milites* Guglielmo Melia; Bartolo-
> meo Bonifacio; Adinolfo Appaia; Pietro Apocefalo, the son of
> Sergio; Giovanni Apocefalo, the son of Pietro; and Riccardo
> Moccia along the harbor beach. Suddenly I saw two men play-
> ing by the water, a Genoese and a Pisan. They were joined by
> another Pisan [*here there is a gap in the document*]. After which,
> a group of Pisans arrived, and they tried to throw the Genoese
> into the water by main force, but amid all the shouting he tried
> to put up a fight. There was nothing to be done: the Pisans tossed
> him into the sea and as soon as the Genoese emerged from the
> water, they started stabbing him. He took to his heels, and the
> Pisans followed in hot pursuit, all of them with their knives un-
> sheathed, soon joined by others, who shouted to go get weapons
> and launch an attack on the homes of the Genoese.[14]

So a group of Neapolitans were walking on the beach. Then, all at once, they see two young men. They seem to be playing, close to the water's edge. Other men show up. Many against one. Knives are pulled out. A brawl ensues. What happened? Had an injudicious word too many escaped the two young men who were playing next to the water, as a witness tried to suggest? Or had the Genoese indulged in some sort of provocative behavior that tested the tempers of the Pisans? Or was the whole thing unleashed by the young Pisans, who just happened to cross paths with the Genoese and decided this was a good opportunity to start a fight? To challenge him? And then to attack him and throw him in the water, on a chilly February day? We know nothing with any con-fidence. Only that things rapidly amped up. First fists flew. Then stabbings ensued. The Genoese, wounded, ran away. He sought refuge. And he ran home as fast as he could.

In the meantime, the group of Pisans grew. And it began to move quickly through the streets, inciting the other Pisans to declare war. To attack the homes of the Genoese. With the whole city involved, with children running through the narrow streets, screaming "Help, help, the Pisans are fighting with the Genoese" (that's not a phrase of my own invention, I'm quoting the actual words of the witness Marino Sparella); women shutting themselves up in their homes for safety; men busy with their work trying to figure out just what's going on, down there by the port. And who stare in disbelief at what actually is happening. Until just a moment ago, everything was calm as could be, everything was going fine here at the *seggio* of Porto: there were people playing *ad tabulas*, as we learn from a genuine man of the clan, a member of a family that we know well by now, Giovanni Castagnola, who was spending some time with Filippo de Griso. There are others sitting around talking, such as the *miles* Roger Quaranta, who was keeping company with other *probiviri*.

But now what? Now all hell had broken loose. With the Pisans by this point crowding in front of the Genoese *fondaco*, or trading post, the property of Albizzo Manzo. The place was full of people— merchants, couriers, workers, passersby, and customers—all of them blithely unaware of what was about to happen. And sure enough, a Pisan whirlwind crashed against the place. They barely had time to lock the doors and fasten the shutters in an attempt to transform the *fondaco* into a fortress before the attack was unleashed in full force. Because this was definitely a military-style assault, and in fact the Pisans hardly seem ill prepared. They were equipped with a full-fledged arsenal consisting of longbows, crossbows, *quadrelle*, weapons that we have a hard time understanding just where they came from, considering that their possession was prohibited in the city. In all likelihood they had lain well concealed in the Pisan warehouses; the promptness with which they were extracted leads me to think, and I wouldn't want to make an unfounded assumption, but it seems that there might have been a certain degree of premeditation behind this attack…

Combat broke out, fierce and ferocious. From outside, the Pisans, with their various ballistic weapons. And from inside the

house, the Genoese, who were responding with anything they
could lay their hands on, throwing rocks, swinging clubs and
poles and anything else that came to hand. The Neapolitans, at
this point seeing the grim course matters seemed to be taking,
with a brawl rapidly deteriorating into a battle that might soon
drag in the entire quarter of the harbor, dazed at the idea that the
situation might be slipping entirely out of their control, quickly
got organized. Most of those present in the *seggio* took off running. They plunged into the fray, working to separate the warring
parties. But in the meantime the Pisans were taking to their heels.
And it was no easy matter to stop them. They had taken over the
port. The Neapolitans feared that they might be about to try to
set fire to the ships. But that wasn't what they had in mind. No, it
was much worse: in their vast numbers, they boarded the Genoese
ships: they tore away rudders, helms, sails, and weapons. By so
doing, they rendered the ships useless, unnavigable. Reduced to
mere wooden hulks, riding helplessly at anchor. In cruel mockery,
one of the Pisans climbed aboard the largest ship there. He shim-
mied his way up the mast. He tore down the Genoese banner. And
he hoisted up, in its place, the pennant of Pisa. The worst imaginable affront.

Evening fell. For a while, due to a combination of exhaustion
and the repressive intervention of the *milites*, the tension subsided.
As soon as they felt a little less cowed by terror, the Genoese sent
an envoy to the Neapolitan Curia, in the church of San Giorgio
Maggiore. To lay out the facts, to lodge a complaint about what
had happened. To invite the municipal authorities to take a stand.
But the Pisans were not about to admit that the Neapolitan authorities had any right to sit in judgment over them. They started
spreading rumors. They started taking offense. Eventually they
resigned themselves to the situation. And under the pressure of
the municipal representatives, they handed back rudders and sails,
but not to the Genoese. To the Neapolitans.

The Curia immediately began an investigation, without so
much as a moment's hesitation. The very next day, the debate was

underway. Among the investigating magistrates, the *comestabuli*, we find the usual well-known names: a Caracciolo, a Landulfo, two Guindazzo, a Scriniario. Before them come representatives from the two nations. Of course, the findings were all to the detriment of the Pisans, who began to raise objections, hanging their hopes on questions of jurisdiction. Privileges accorded them by the emperor. Safeguarding the liberties acquired and their acknowledged independence. The Curia found a compromise, with banns of peace and for the transgressors the payment of a fine, and a substantial one. Two thousand *oncias*. That's more than thirty kilograms (and nearly seventy pounds) of gold.

So do you think it was over now? Don't be ridiculous. For two days, the truce was kept. Then came Sunday. And the festive leisure of that day encouraged another brawl, this one worse than the previous one. Most Neapolitans, we might say, were at the stadium. Actually, not technically at the stadium. They were really out watching a tournament. In front of the plaza, or Slargo del Carbonetum, just outside the city walls. It was a common occurrence to hold a tournament there. These tournaments were enthusiastically attended. In this particular kind of tournament, there weren't a lot of horses. No, but there was plenty, and I mean *plenty*, of violence. Like in a gladiatorial game. And *gladiatorius ludus* is exactly the term Petrarch used when he witnessed one in the fourteenth century, being shocked to actually behold a young man, there to fight, having his throat cut. So shocked that he immediately left both the plaza and the tournament, filled with repulsion and disgust. That was the occasion when he spoke of the "barbaric ferocity" to which I have previously referred.

All right, then. Let's come back to our protagonists. The tournament was underway. The plaza was packed. *Milites* with their wives. Common folk. The middle class. And lots and lots of outsiders, among them nearly the entire Genoese community, who had left their homes, blithely unconcerned. Was it not true, after all, that they had made peace with their former rivals? That being the case, what danger could there possibly be? But in fact this tournament was the exact opportunity the Pisans had been looking for, and they took advantage of the absence of the overwhelming number of the Genoese. Since they knew the Genoese had left their houses empty and by and large unguarded behind them, they attacked. And to do so, they used the very same weapons that they had used in the previous battles, weapons that had absolutely not been confiscated and must have been lying at the ready in their loggia. The attacking Pisans were numerous indeed. The defending Genoese few and far between. Also, unarmed and caught off guard. They tried to fight back, but the Pisans were out of control, well armed, and highly organized. They immediately got the better of their foes: they killed one Genoese, they wounded many others, and they hurried down to the port once again to attack the Ligurian ships.

New cries of dismay. New complaints being lodged. New disappointment on the part of the Genoese colony. Who then assembled en masse the following day at the church of San Giovanni Maggiore, where the Curia meets. Practically none of the Pisans showed up, in contrast. Except for the consul, with two *scolari* and two escorts. Invited to present a justification for showing up alone like that, the consul shrugged and explained that all the others had stayed home to protect their Pisan property. Because if they had dared to go out, the Genoese would surely have attacked them. Were they being less than straightforward? Oh, certainly. They were clearly trying to make themselves, as the aggressors, look more like hapless and frightened victims of some aggression. But the Genoese, who were all present, had come with no intention whatsoever of doing anyone any harm. They had, after all, shown up empty-handed, unarmed, there to come to an understanding, certainly not to unleash new clashes. Otherwise, instead of going to the Curia, they would have gotten busy organizing an attack on the Pisan homes.

The Curia decided in any case to carry out an inspection among the *fondaci*, or trading posts, of the two communities, in an attempt to reconstruct the actual facts and try to determine whether there was any likelihood of a new eruption of the conflict. And they found the Pisans, by no means intimidated, armed to the teeth and barricaded in their houses, ready to start up again with their attacks and violence. Instead, there were truly very few Genoese. Barely fifteen of them, and more dead than alive, including several of the wounded from the day before, huddling in fright in their homes. And so they went back to headquarters, to San Giovanni. The Curia once again invited the Pisans to come in, unarmed. The consul replied that that would be impossible because the hall was full of armed men and was therefore dangerous. The decision was made to search those present. None of them were armed. And the back-and-forth continued. The consul pulled out documents, deeds, privileges. The arguments seemed to drag out endlessly. In the end, the *milites* grew impatient. So they got to the verdict rapidly. And to the end of this story. They decided that the Pisans had failed to comply to the terms of the compromise and had, in fact, openly violated it. And that if they continued to fail to respect the order, the Neapolitans would confiscate their ships and their goods until Frederick II issued his opinion.

We don't know how matters proceeded from there. Whether Frederick weighed in with a big fat amnesty canceling all potential liability. Or whether in the end, their backs against the wall, the Pisans put up their money and paid for the damage they'd done. In any case, I find this piece of history lovely and very particular. It serves to measure the intrusion of outsiders into the Neapolitan social space, a presence that in the case in question was something more than merely invasive... the outsiders who by the very nature of their status live a life apart, entirely shut up within the hive of their own colony, which in time becomes like a piece of home in an enclave elsewhere. This becomes a place where outsiders can rediscover the pace and style of a daily life that feels familiar. The city they're living in may be very different, but that insistence on having a piece of home in the middle of Naples meant that they were not only experiencing all the habits and customs of home but also all the tensions and hatreds and obsessions as well, and meant that among those hatreds and tensions were the feuds between Genoese and Pisans. The official filter for relations with the outside world, when it came to juridical and criminal matters, passed through the community's representatives, the consuls, whose word was the word of the community.

A separation, however, that we shouldn't take as a form of isolation, inasmuch as foreigners not only took part in the commercial life but necessarily the general everyday pursuits of a city like Naples, which appears *open*: suffice it to consider how the Genoese mingled with the crowd of Neapolitan people, on a Sunday, at the moment of the tournament, and just how they participated in this collective event in exactly the same manner as the Neapolitans.

For that matter, the episode also explains one other thing. Specifically, I should add, not limited to Naples: the close proximity, indeed, I ought to say the contiguity, between the people of the city and the outsiders. Between the people who had come by sea and the Neapolitans. So close that eyewitnesses, practically looking out from the walls of the *seggio* of Porto, between a chat and a game of cards, were surprised to notice the sudden outburst of violence that was unfolding just a few steps away from them. A brawl that developed out of chance motives, but which was fueled by substantial and abiding grudges and rancor. *Milites* who weighed in to put down the brawl and judge the perpetrators, and this observation takes us back to our general overarching story: one further piece in the puzzle, if there had been any need for it, in order to understand the Neapolitan social situation and capacity for control that the clan exercised, among other things, in matters whose nature was not narrowly limited to the milieu of their own quarter.

In the Hands of Capital

The arrival of the House of Anjou shook the presence of foreign colonies in Naples like an earthquake (and a powerful one). Here, too, in fact, the transformation was quite radical. Genoese and

Pisans by this point were hardly alone anymore. New people had arrived. Among them the Provençals and the Marseillais. The monarchy immediately offered them certain advantages. For instance, they were afforded the use of a particular wharf, called the Molo dei Provenzali, between the Castel dell'Ovo and Castel Nuovo, in the area currently known as Santa Lucia. What's more, their privileged situation showed no sign of changing under Charles I. These were favors that the Marseillais repaid with a rock-solid loyalty and the offer of their ships and their men in the course of the Angevin expeditions and the War of the Vespers. The Catalans also settled in the city under the new dynasty. And they grew in number in the entourage of Robert of Anjou's wife, Queen Sancia. They settled in a quarter that is exactly midway between the old city and the freer and more open part of the city that extends around Castel Nuovo, in the area of the Malpertugio; and in that quarter they set up their *fondaci*, or trading posts, and they organized their banks along the Rua Catalana, which still exists today, at the mouth of the extremely central Via Depretis. And it should be noted that their consulate was entrusted to Neapolitan notables, with an assignment that for seventy years became the appanage of the di Costanzo clan.[15]

But it was the nations originating from Tuscany that with their impact profoundly revolutionized the economic life of both the city and the Kingdom, with a history that is doubly bound to the history of the Anjou. In fact, it was they who, at papal behest, financed the southern enterprise, supported it at every turn, and adopted its objectives as their own. They did that with credit on an international scale, based on the exceedingly important fairs of Champagne, what could truly be called the pumping heart of the European economy, which is where they obtained the capital that they later loaned the pope, money that was crucial in funding Charles's activities. Loans that were repaid with the tithes of the church, collected throughout Europe by the very same banking houses. A flow of Tuscan finance capital that never faltered, upon which Charles drew on a continual basis, even after the conquest of the Kingdom. On occasion he would hand over as collateral portions of his personal treasure, such as his golden crown studded with precious stones. This he handed over to the Sienese merchant Nicola Orlandini, on September 28, 1268, in exchange for 1,040 golden *oncias*.

The Angevin enterprise, therefore, should be somewhat reconsidered. Without a doubt this was a major military enterprise. But this was also an undertaking of vast economic scope. It was based on the idea of capital as an engine driving political decisions and activity, which constituted a locus toward which the interests of a great many stakeholders converged: the pope, Charles, and this new universe of merchants and bankers, who understood the potential for the biggest business opportunity they could possibly imagine: getting their hands on one of the principal markets in Europe and transforming it into a great commercial and economic opportunity.

And so, in the aftermath of the conquest, just what was the result? What happened was that these individuals who lived off banking and the markets, loans and money changing, found themselves gazing out at a limitless space in which to implement their ambitions. At first they came from a great many different cities. So in Naples there began to be a great circulation of Sienese, Pistoians, and Lucchese. But there was one group that took greater advantage of the situation than anyone else did. Who were better at this than anyone else. And these were the Florentines, who used their alliance with the House of Anjou to lay the foundations for a great future project. They just loaned and loaned money to the crown. And what exactly did they ask for in exchange? Letters of safe conduct, privileges, concessions, permits, and monopolies. With an approach that, let it be clear, continued over time, rather than being cut off immediately. They insisted on it being protracted in order to allow for their growing presence throughout the Kingdom. The first to begin this were the Frescobaldi, in 1265. Then came the privileges in favor of Lotaringo Bandini, Coppo di

Scaldo, Marchetto de Florencia, which were all approved between October and December 1266.

From that point on, the Florentines proliferated. They established themselves in both Naples, as was only to be expected, and in the largest and most important towns in the Kingdom, in its cities, in its ports. They took control of the vital pinch points of the Kingdom's economy. They took over the mint. They put together a piece of financial machinery that spewed out rivers of cash thanks to a scheme of cloth for foodstuffs: fabrics were imported (fine cloth as well as textiles of middling quality) in exchange for oil, wine, fava beans, and everything else that southern Italy had to offer. In particular they were looking for wheat, essential to life in a metropolis like Florence, which was in the throes of expansion. Their presence seemed to transform itself into an invasion, or a process of colonization, that functioned on the basis of these people's skill at circulating cash, on their financial genius, the accounting techniques that they employed, the networks of relationships that by this point extended from one end of Europe, with multiple businesses scattered across the continent but coordinated by a single mastermind.

And the relationship between Naples and Florence became necessary. Indispensable. "Florence appears," as David Abulafia put it, "when the House of Anjou appears."[16] That sentence does an excellent job of summarizing a de facto state of affairs, namely the way that Florence's initial wave of success was closely bound up with the enterprise conducted under the leadership of Charles. A reciprocal air that became a vicious cycle where Florence, in order to survive, absolutely required the support of Angevin force of arms. Though of course said arms were very unlikely to succeed without the inflow of Florentine money... An ongoing swap that enveloped both cities' universes and made them consubstantial. An Angevin-Florentine system, in other words, that gradually grew, attaining its apogee under Robert's rule of the Kingdom. In a combination that was clear to one and all: alongside the political and military crutch, the royal power required a second crutch to be able to stand upright: a financial one. That was essential for every single movement, action, intervention, or operation imaginable.

The situation was unmistakable: the Angevin state possessed only extremely limited capital. And the tax revenues would constantly melt away like snow in bright sunlight, as we've seen. So who was it that was constantly busy putting a patch on this landslide of debt? Them. The Florentines. Who were clearly in the pole position with respect to all the other Tuscan nations. And they were soon transformed into the privileged interlocutors of the monarchy, the Kingdom's financial and economic load-bearing pier. Rising above all the others was the great joint venture of three families: Peruzzi-Bardi-Acciaiuoli. That troika formed in 1316, and was later joined around 1330 by the Buonaccorsi. Together they created an almost symbiotic relationship with the crown, with a condition of *familiaritas* that was not only fomented by economic factors but also by a joint subscription to shared ideals and projects. This was an element that knit together even more intimately the already-solid relationship between monarchy and bankers.

And the Florentine joint venture invested a lot of money. In the first place, for the king, his family, and, more in general, for the operation of the state, in all its components. An unlimited pool of credit, for any and every type of operation, from the most trivial to the grandest and most overarching. A practice that evolved from a passing phenomenon to a customary one. The Tuscans, though, did not limit their interests to the king; they focused on everyone who surrounded him. The people of the court, the administrators, the feudal lords, the counts, and the barons. And why not? Also the *nobiliores* of the city, motivated by the opportunity to get rich quick, the profit that seemed to fly through the air on fluttering pieces of paper, on trades, on interest. After all, if the court was doing it, if the sovereign himself trusted them, these mighty columns of European finance, and was smart enough to take advantage tirelessly of this steady flow of cash, why shouldn't they dip into the same river themselves? Whereupon the noblest denizens of the *seggi*, the functionaries, the bidders on public contracts hurled themselves into this new adventure. An escapade that for now seemed to promise only the happiest of outcomes. Good news for everyone. What could be better than to scoop up money without even breaking a sweat?

In exchange, the Florentine presence became pervasive. A full-fledged state within the state. They received tax exemptions and immunities. They were encouraged and they were lured in. They were given assistance from above in their civil lawsuits, when it came to their interactions with customs, and in their dealings with other businessmen (of the Kingdom and otherwise), who gradually practically vanished from the marketplace, holding on to nothing but marginal and subalternate roles. In time, they actually became the de facto managers of the entire Kingdom's finances, providing the services of safekeeping, coordination of revenues, and, of course, being in charge of money. For the Florentines, Naples was a paradise whose economy they managed without so much as a cross word, with the sovereign's full and complacent trust. This was the apogee, the high point, and it lasted for more than twenty years, but its truly golden age extended from 1315 to 1325, both for the really big companies and for all the other commercial operators, such as the Scali, the Visdomini, the Alberti, the Coppi, and others, whose territories extended from Gaeta to Tropea, and from Salerno to Barletta. They built manufactories, they managed iron mines, they formed substantial communities in Capua, Nola, Benevento, Venosa, Rapolla, Lucera, and Crotone...In other words, there wasn't a single city that didn't have one of them. There was no exchange, business operation, or manufacturing concern that didn't involve them as protagonists.

But it was necessary to pay the Florentines. And in order to pay them, the state ran up more debt. At a reckless pace. In something approaching a frenzy. And what did the state do to settle its debts? It sold off its assets, some of its most prized possessions.

The bankers of Florence proceeded by degrees, little by little, eating away at the state's room to maneuver, its tax revenues, in what
clearly must have been an attempt to outflank the Kingdom's ad-
ministrations, both the central ones and the local ones. They took
charge of the tax farming, the transport of cash, the payment of
salaries to the functionaries, the provisioning and the salaries of
the troops, and so on. They literally absorbed the state. They became the state.

It was on these foundations that the Florentine monopoly
developed and sank its roots, with a sort of spiraling movement,
like a dog chasing its tail. Indeed, the more they exploited these
privileges, the more numerous they became. And with them they
also increased their capital and the possibility of acquiring ever-
larger market shares, pushing the local businessmen into a corner.
The locals found themselves playing strictly bit parts, becoming
little more than middlemen. In the face of this Florentine power,
any other rivals simply vanished into thin air. The Florentines had
won the trade war for the economic control of the Kingdom.

A truly terrifying monopoly, because it gave no quarter. The
reason? Very simple: the activity of the Florentine merchants was
enriching Florence, and how. But it was all to the detriment of Naples. And Tuscany's sudden great good fortune coincided with the
unquestionable impoverishment of southern Italy. Which in its
turn had an immediate fallout, in the form of an economic crisis,
social tensions, violence that broke out unexpectedly, brigandage,
and famine. And this is not some mechanism of cause and effect
that I'm dreaming up here myself. All you need to do is consider
the facts, one by one: what happened in the harbor of Barletta,
which I described in the first chapter, with the citizenry in an uproar at the sight of the Tuscans carrying off their wheat, leaving
the population in a state of utter panic at the growing, spreading
hunger, with no alternative but open revolt.

In any case, that's the way things were going. Along this track,
driven by the continual demands of the court. Where King Robert
asked and the Florentines responded, with a continuous infusion

of capital: for the construction of churches, for the creation of art-works, for the maintenance of the capital and the palace, for the court's outlays, for the tithes to be paid to the pope, to finance the politics of marriages, for diplomatic negotiations, to maintain unaltered Angevin military influence over the Mediterranean and in the peninsula, for extraordinary expenses, for the sovereign's travel, and so on and so forth. In short, the machinery of the King-dom wouldn't budge unless it was well and thoroughly oiled by Florentine money. The only problem was that the whole mecha-nism was turning into a Ponzi scheme, doomed to collapse: be-cause the king, unable to pay off the debts he'd contracted, simply ran up new debts, which piled up, one atop the other, in a never-ending spiral. Loans, therefore, stopped being a temporary expe-dient and turned into a habitual financial procedure. The royal loan became the heart of the Angevin-Florentine financial system. A twisted game in which both participants were burning their end of the candle. Both utterly incapable of getting out of it. Until, at last, came the collapse.[17]

For the Pisans, in this setting, faced with these commercial superpowers, there was no room for maneuvers. Their presence in Naples dwindled and shrank, until they finally vanished entirely. Just think, they had been some of the first to guess the opportuni-ties available in southern Italy. This marginalization was partly the work of Charles I, who was irritated with the Pisan attitude, and so he made up his mind to eject them from the Kingdom entirely, in March 1267. One factor in his decision, we must believe, was the umpteenth brawl that they had unleashed in the city against the Genoese and the Provençals. A decision that was withdrawn in 1280 with the payment of the usual fine of 2,000 golden *oncias* for the damage caused by the Pisan pirates. But then things went downhill fast under King Robert. Pisa embraced the Ghibelline party. The city's corsairs sailed their vessels up and down the Tyr-rhenian coast, infesting them and attacking into the Angevin sea-ways. They attacked the coastline, they plundered the cargos, and they bullied the merchants.

Then Henry VII's invasion offered the Pisans one last opportunity to make a comeback. The city became the emperor's general headquarters. Then came the Battle of Meloria, and the Pisans came dangerously close to losing their entire fleet. They came to an agreement with Naples in 1317. Relations remained tense, however, and there was no clear solution in sight. And none of that was good for the merchants' business: every time that there was a break between Naples and Pisa, affairs suffered, with the ever-present threat of expulsion, which would have put an end to their business interests there. In any case, there were those who continued to trade with the capital. Unusual exceptions. But they proved the rule, operating basically in solitude, without the old political and financial support their forefathers had enjoyed. Also without the support of a powerful and bellicose colony. Looming high over all the others was the de Barba family, with Sigiero, an intimate of the king; the Gambacorta; and the Gallico. But the business volume of the Pisan loggia seemed to be dwindling away, ever smaller. Until it finally died out entirely in the 1340s.[18]

The fate of the Genoese is a more controversial matter. We are no longer talking about a linear path, a steady ascent, with a progressive trendline of growth and a slow but inexorable conquest of the Kingdom, as was the case with the Tuscan and Florentine capital. What we're looking at here is something terribly undulating, subject to leaps forward and sudden, unpredictable slides backward, due to the particular, chaotic, and frequently out of control internal Genoese policies, which seemed to move in no direction in a stable fashion, with continual changes of position, invariably subject to internal oscillations due to clashes between factions and family clans, devoid of any single government authority and control. Marked by the city's perennial individualism, its implacable grudges and feuds, the running battles between *alberghi* and parties, the revolutions that seemed to come about in Genoese political life practically every other year.

A condition that would have driven a Venetian crazy. Venice, where the state was everything: the pride and the fulcrum of identity and affiliation; where the populace identified completely with the well-being of the state. That certainly wasn't the case in Genoa, the place where the state "was an enemy to deceive or a prey to capture and conquer," according to the suggestive image conjured up by Roberto Lopez. A state that was constantly wallowing in a condition of shortened means because the citizenry was so averse to paying taxes, because they refused to believe in their government. And because they found that state to be distant and hostile. They stubbornly refused in the most categorical way to acknowledge that the need for tax revenue might change with the general requirements of the republic. And for that reason, the Ligurian city lacked the resources to build its own state-owned and -operated fleet. Instead it remained in thrall to a constellation of private associations, family run and owned, that replaced the state, had their own ships, and faced up to the risks, as well as pocketing the profits. Because Genoa isn't a state at all, and it lacks a permanent character and an authority that transcends mere individuals. No: Genoa is still a *commune*, an assembly of diverse people, not aggregated, founded on "a temporary compact for the protection of private interests." It is clear that for the Angevins, dealing with such a complex entity inevitably created frustrations, short circuits, and reactions that could be violent in relation to the continuous pinwheels, sudden changes of course and political conduct. Let's take a closer look at what happened.

The treaty of August 2, 1269, between Charles I and Genoa did nothing to undermine the city's trade interests in the Kingdom. A great deal proceeded exactly as it had in the past: guarantees on people and goods, discounts on the taxes, the right for the Genoese to occupy their quarter of Naples and to continue to possess a loggia in that quarter. But—and there was a but—they were going to have to lose something in terms of rights, so that they could be considered on a sort of parole, free on condition of good behavior. In concrete terms, this meant that the consuls lost their jurisdiction over crimes committed by people of their own nation, which had traditionally enjoyed very special treatment.

Responsibility for the prosecution of this category of crimes was now handed over to the Angevin state. And now Charles imposed another condition: the privileges conceded might very well now expire, in the case that the Genoese decided to abandon the alliance with the papacy and with Charles himself. In that way, all of Genoa's commercial activity was poised on a razor's edge, with a sword of Damocles dangling over Genoa's domestic political decisions. It's easy to imagine the dismay experienced by this breed of hardy nonconformists who so often operated in perfect freedom from their homeland—a homeland whose decisions and plans for the future they so frequently disregarded. It must have come as quite a shock. But that was that: what the king says goes.

And the Genoese realized it immediately, when in 1272, sparks began to fly between their city and the Kingdom. The harassment began to be ramped up. All the merchants present in southern Italy were arrested, and the Curia ordered the confiscation of fabrics, goods, and cargos ready to be shipped out. Economically speaking, it was a disaster. Because this broke a larger circuit, one that transcended the mere interests of Genoa. Because in the Kingdom the Genoese imported fabrics from Lombardy, Milan, Bergamo, and Brescia, or else from southern France, such as from Narbonne. Once one relay had been interrupted, the whole circuit lay in disarray. With a heavy and generalized fallout, considering the southern market's intake capacity.

The response came immediately. Because Genoa wasn't some small city. It was a great power. Especially on the sea. That's where it dominated. And sure enough, Genoa reacted with a vengeance, with the tools of piracy. Ligurian corsairs set sail to devastate the coastline; they began to intercept shipping between southern Italy and northern Italy; they attacked Neapolitan ships. What they were especially trying to do was to harrow the principal network of economic exchange from and to the Kingdom, namely the Florentine trade. They waylaid the Florentine ships and confiscated their cargos. And so, a disaster caused by the Angevins was now accompanied by another disaster for the southern port cities caused by the Genoese. Three years of war. After which, since it was impossible to go on like that, there were further negotiations. Another understanding, but one that was unfavorable to the Genoese: the Neapolitans returned the ships they'd captured and the cargo they'd confiscated, and they ensured the survival of their loggias and colonies, but nevertheless they eliminated all existing commercial privileges. No more special tax breaks. No more special cuts in tariffs. Basically, the line of commercial policy that called for an open attitude toward the Ligurians was now being abandoned.

A few years went by, and peace returned between Genoa and Naples. A restoration of equilibrium prompted by the new necessities that had emerged as a result of the War of the Vespers. The ships and the money of the Genoese bankers were making the Angevins greedy. And a great many Genoese decided it would be a good idea to show their loyalty to the southern monarchy and enter into its service. A flow of allegiance encouraged by the favorable political climate that had been established in Genoa, where a great many families now openly supported the Angevins. And while the Doria, Grimaldi, Fieschi, Spinola, and Lomellini families, as well as many others, were guiding the city's direction, many of their kin came south to serve Charles II. Genoa itself, though, continued to change its stance with some considerable fickleness. First it was in, and then it was out. And the alliance with the Kingdom might become, from one moment to the next, unpleasantly *sticky*.

And in fact what happened in 1295 was that the Ghibelline clans ejected the Guelphs from Genoa, and their leaders took refuge in Munich. And the complicated structure of the alliances, which had always rested on foundations of the most fragile equilibriums, collapsed instantaneously. Charles II weighed in: there were new clashes, new wars, new prisoners, and new problems interfering with commercial shipping. The corsairs once more began to infest the Tyrrhenian coasts, badly hurting not only the merchants but also royal officials themselves, such as Filippo d'Alatri and Egidio di Falloso, the Baron of Cellino, who was captured while sailing *ad servicia Curiae*, only to be liberated after payment of a nice fat ransom: 300 florins.

And now we come to the umpteenth truce, which opened all the ports of southern Italy to the Genoese, allowing Ligurian merchants freedom of movement throughout the Kingdom, permitting them to buy wheat and to export up to 10,000 *salme* of it every year, as well as freedom from arbitrary expenses piled on top of the import and export tariffs on it. In exchange, there were two sole conditions: no aid to the king of Sicily; and no more aid to the pirates, who were to be promptly eliminated. The year was 1306.

Privateering warfare. This, of course, was a real sore spot, and it deserves a few more words. For the Genoese, but not for them alone, it was often preferred to traditional warfare. And it was more convenient. Better a skirmish than a major battle. At the same time, it was a fundamental way of enriching oneself, and fast. A method underlying the initial capitalistic fortunes of Genoa and Pisa and their *primary accumulation* (suffice it to think back to the taking of Mahdia in 1087 ...), as well as the fortunes of individual families or even single persons. In Genoa, the galleys underwritten by the family clans, such as the Doria, adhered for many a long year to the tradition of piracy as a tool of conquest and wealth. So now they were using it against the Angevins. For that matter, it was no novelty to the Ligurians. They had first tasted privateering warfare with their mother's milk. It was a part of their tradition. Their great-grandfathers and their grandfathers had all practiced it, in much the same way that the clans in Naples exercised violence to control the street, the marketplace, the *seggio*, and the quarter. They were fully cognizant that iron-bottomed men like Benedetto Zaccaria, though rich in lands, mines, capital, and feudal landholdings due to the sums they'd invested in trade, the masters of unimaginable fortunes, at times when things hadn't been going especially well, had shown no shame in engaging in piracy as an alternative form of business. Showing a willingness to combine capitalism and violence, in a medley that could certainly bring substantial benefits.

The people of Genoa knew even better that the Mediterranean rivalries with Pisa or with the Aragonese fleets or with Venice were first and foremost corsair battles. It was not, however, merely a matter of the Genoese. The Catalonians were doing the same thing. And for that matter, an Angevin document enumerated the individual articles that made up the cargo of several Neapolitan ships that they had attacked between 1330 and 1334 along the Barbary Coast and even within the confines of the port of Tunis. This list of goods ranged from wheat to barley, oil, Greek and Latin wine, fruit, fabrics, and so on, including even peacock feathers and enslaved people.

Likewise, the Kingdom's nobility ventured into this line of business in times when they couldn't afford not to. We are reminded of this fact by Giovanni Boccaccio, who reproduced the state of mind of the merchant-pirate in his portrayal of Landolfo Ruffolo of Ravello, "who yet, not content with his wealth, but desiring to double it, came nigh to lose it all and his own life to boot": "mortified beyond measure to find himself thus reduced in a short space of time from opulence to something like poverty, he was at his wits' end, and rather than go home poor, having left home rich, he was minded to retrieve his losses by piracy or die in the attempt."[19] Among these pirates there were certainly also a number of *milites*: one thing that allows us to imagine that was the skill and confidence of the boarding of the ship in November 1343, which makes it clear that deep down they must have had some experience with fighting on the sea, at least how to move in silence, coasting stealthily all the way to Baiae. After all, there were plenty of pirate-merchants in the Bay of Naples itself. As well as on the island of Ischia. They were so experienced and successful that they managed to sail as far as the African coasts, all the way to Gabès, all the way to Djerba, both in modern-day Tunisia.

Indomitable, defiant of peril in their quest for profit, the chronicles say in their treatment of piracy. Courage and capitalist spirit were what drove these men, as well as a cool acceptance of danger and risk. They had a vision of the world in which there existed no other God but profit. It was an abuse that Charles II strove mightily to put an end to. An abuse that he had to stamp out, but was roundly unable to. Because in Genoa, as all agreed, it was the best method available for enriching oneself. Georges Yver is stinging but clear: "In Genoa, though they might diverge on any other issue, the Guelphs and the Ghibellines were in perfect agreement, without the slightest problem, on continuing the corsair war." In any case, the dialogue on this topic was open and underway between the Kingdom and Genoa. And two years later, in 1308, a treaty was drawn up with the Republic of Genoa, negotiated by Philip, the Prince of Taranto.

Eventually there came a moment of supreme understanding between the two coteries. This happened during the period of the utmost influence of the Guelphs in Genoa with a massive plot twist: King Robert was assigned lordship over the city for ten years. It was 1318. That concession was renewed for six more years in 1324. This was the highest point of success that the sovereign could aspire to, in the context of an expansion of his power over northern Italy, pushing west toward Piedmont and Lombardy. A triumph that grew even greater in 1331, when the king drained wheat and other foodstuffs from the South and sent them to Genoa, which was in the throes of famine; yet another instance of that transfer of resources from one end of the peninsula to another that had been the cause, as mentioned, of the serious upset experienced in the southern regions. In 1333, the seigniory was extended for another five years. It seemed as if the plan had worked. The beginning of a long journey, side by side with Genoa. With that kind of exorbitant sea power, they might even start dreaming of the conquest of Sicily again.

Unfortunately, those calculations turned out to be much mistaken. Because once again the king had failed to take into account the spirit of the city. Its sheer bellicosity. Its factions. Its endless imbalances. Its well-organized anarchy. So what happened was

that the Ghibellines came back into power. Whereupon they expelled their adversaries, friends of the king of Naples. Who veered
from triumph to the precipice. This entailed a thousand problems
for the commune itself, inasmuch as "this change badly undermined the good state of Genoa itself and its trading," as Villani
tells us.[20] Soon enough, matters were back to a state of guerrilla
warfare. Piracy and naval blockades. With the Guelphs in Munich and the supporters of King Robert blockading the city. And
with the Ghibellines sailing off to engage in piracy, the length and
breadth of the Tyrrhenian Sea. Aided by ships that came from as
far off as the Genoese colonies on the Black Sea, who had always
been loyal to the imperial cause, thus even more greatly height-
ening the confusion and danger. So much so that some of them
sailed to the waters off Naples, forcing the Duke of Calabria to
intervene to ensure the safety of the coasts and islands of the Bay
of Naples. With incessant skirmishes that wound up dragging in
even those who had nothing to do with this purely Genoese civil
war, such as several Venetian ships that were attacked by Robert's
Ligurian followers. And that created significant diplomatic problems and an unending succession of reprisals…

But the Genoese went on trading in Naples, in spite of the war
and reprisals. The lure of money, as we can well imagine, was immense. And in fact the possibilities of profit were enormous. Business was like a wheel that must needs continue turning, and which
nothing can be allowed to hinder. And so the Genoese proceeded,
practically undisturbed, with their trade. According to eyewitness
accounts, they were very numerous. Lots of immigrants who took
up residence in the capital. Men who came not only from Genoa itself but also from Genoa's colonies, as was the case with the Musso
clan, who came from Famagusta. And the private shipbuilders all
put themselves at Robert's service to create lines of cargo ship-
ments that focused on Naples as the hub of all of their movements.

This was a period in which the capital's role on the sea grew
in intensity: already Naples was a fundamental component of the
trade between the western and the eastern Mediterranean. Naples

became, thanks to the intermediation of cities like Genoa, a market that sold provisions to a number of European countries, as we learn from, among others, a French historian of the period, Jean Froissart. Greek and Latin wine, raw Calabrian silk, cotton, slaves, fruit, wheat, dyes, fabrics, objects both precious and otherwise, crude and processed iron, lead, alum, gallnuts, and spices: these were just a few of the goods mentioned that flowed in or out of the Neapolitan market, as recalled by the Florentine merchant Francesco Balducci Pegolotti in his book, *Pratica della mercatura*.

The Genoese were also operating in other settings. Certainly not with the same entrepreneurial spirit as the Florentines. Nor with the same number of people employed in their companies or in their dealings. Still, they did employ a very high level of employees, capable of operating with great ability when it came to the Kingdom's maritime pursuits, the preparation of ships, the construction of the arsenal. Roberto Passano was a *magister protontinus* in charge of shipbuilding. Niccolò de Braida, with Tino de Camaino, was in charge of the construction of the arsenal of Moricino. Some were skilled goldsmiths, such as Franceschino de Janua. Others devoted themselves to lending cash, alongside the Acciaiuoli and the Peruzzi, among them Giorgio Spinola, the brothers Pietro and Manuele Vinzali, and Giovanni Buonaventura. Others still went into the ranks of the administration or became functionaries, attaining dizzying heights. We find them in the ranks of the *giustizieri*, the *familiares*, and the chamberlains, the jurists and judges of the high court, the *maestri razionali*, and the university professors. And a great many more were *capitani di città*, in Naples, Salerno, Sulmona, L'Aquila, Capua, Lucera, and Gaeta.

And a great many of them took advantage of their special relationship with the court to win benefices and pensions. Carlo Fieschi, the Count of Lavagna, received an annual pension from the king of eighty golden *oncias*, while his wife, Teodora, acquired an appanage of one hundred *oncias* on the revenues from salt in the customhouses of Manfredonia, Salpi, and Cannes. The Spinola family was among those that received the richest gratifications,

starting with Odoardo Spinola, the grand admiral of the Kingdom, who, with his son Corrado, was awarded enormous rents
amounting to as much as three hundred *oncias*. But the whole clan
seemed to become an integral part of the universe surrounding
the sovereign: Palamede became chamberlain; Berengario became *camerario* (chamberlain); Barnabo and Riccardo enjoyed
pensions that went well beyond a hundred *oncias* each. Ingetto
had a pension of sixty *oncias*; his son Niccolò had one of forty.
It went much the same for other family groups, who lucked into
golden opportunities in Naples. In particular, the Doria family,
with Antonio and Castino, armed as a knight by the king. Or the
Grimaldi family: Antonio and Percivalle, the sons of Gaspare, received a pension of fifty *oncias*; Annichino was an official at the
royal stables; Gabriele was named giustiziere, or justiciar, in the
Capitanata; Carlo and Vinciguerra, sons of Ranieri, became royal
advisers.

Some of them later settled in the country. They didn't entirely
turn their backs on the sea, which certainly had created immense
but unpredictable fortunes. After all, a single tempest might be
enough to cause their ruin. So they went in search of something
more solid. Something that could serve as a solid foundation.
Something that didn't pitch, yaw, and roll the way a ship does.
Something compact. Solid. Land: the finest way of entering the
aristocracy. Something that embodied the desire felt by so many
Genoese to find a form of stability, once and for all. The Grimaldi
family owned lands near Maratea, the barony of San Demetrio
di Monteleone and the city of Policastro, received by the brothers Gabriele, Antonio, Percivalle, and Luciano as a fief from King
Robert. Of the Spinola family, Galasso became the baron of Greci
and of Savignano in the Capitanata. Charles II assigned Babilano
Doria the castle of Rocca Mondragone, later inherited by his sons
Niccolò and Federico.[21]

The unfortunate captain of November 1343 didn't seem to
belong to this universe. It was a universe of the elite, the *grands
commis d'État*, light-years distant from this humble foot soldier

whose horizon seems to have been limited to charting the ship's course and looking after the cargo. In any case, I'm not willing to see him relegated to a limited and squalid dimension consisting of nothing but cargo, sails, hawsers, and harbors. I can picture him as someone who saw himself, during all his years, as a part of something larger called Genoa that ranged from the lantern all the way to the shores of the Black Sea. A whole that often fell victim to the forces of anarchy but that played a fundamental role in the birth of the European market and capitalism.

Traps for Merchants

I sense another question about this man, one that of course will never be answered: Did he land at Naples? Did he stroll along the harbor front? Did he ever stand there, his vessel tied up at wharfside, tossed only by a very faint pitch and roll, looking up at the line of the coast, rising upward from the *fondaci*, or trading posts, from the arsenals on the beach, higher and higher to the great cathedrals? Again: we will never know. And if he ever did stroll through the streets and lanes of this city, at least once, it probably wasn't with the spirit of a tourist. No, it was with the attitude of someone there to work. A single individual element of a larger economic system that had its control tower not in Naples but far, far away: back in the homeland. In Genoa. As I said, if he ever did stroll through the city, he did so as a foot soldier. We might imagine that he could have been drawn by the zone of power, by Castel Nuovo, by the beauty of its gardens. But that certainly was no place for someone like him. It might be the right place for the owners of his cargo, who had illustrious names and plenty of money to spend, Bartolomeo Squarciafico and Bonifacio Cattaneo. Or else for the gilded youth of the city, the offspring of the clan nobility, Neopolitanized Frenchmen, the court milieu, scions of the highest Florentine financiers, among them Giovanni Boccaccio.

No. I can better imagine the captain among the reeks and odors of the port. Amid a succession of wharfs, markets, workshops, and *fondaci*, many among them the property of Neapolitan *milites*; and the businesses of the artisans: saddlers, goldsmiths, *chiodaroli* (nailsmiths), glass makers, *ferrari* (blacksmiths), *zabattari* (cobblers), armorers, and so on. Where sailors, longshoremen, porters, merchants, and money changers all worked side by side and gathered to socialize. Here were the fishermen, with their processions of fishing boats moored along the shore, their nets stretched out to dry. This was where animals were butchered, at the Buczaria. Here you could find taverns, stalls where you could grab a bite to eat, hotels where outsiders could rent a room. A setting that was in many ways befouled, contaminated, infected by the miasmas rising from the waters that pooled and grew murky in the port, where all manner of detritus was tossed and animal carcasses were piled up, blocking the drainage of the sewer system.[22]

A dank, dense quarter, where the air was often unbreathable, as noted by Boccaccio's contemporaries. A place composed of a succession of "storehouses, narrow alleys, foul taverns, filthy but even worse…alleys, passageways, cramped workshops, the abodes of the lowest paupers," connected by that single street built at the behest of Charles II, running up from the spaces of the ducal port to the moorings of the Pisan port. A place given over to prostitution, which had been driven out of the highest reaches of the city into the lower depths. In fact, we read that:

> In Naples, King Robert issued an order that all the prostitutes living there in the Piazza di San Gennaro *a Diaconia* [the Piazza di San Gennaro at the Elm Tree] were to be evicted immediately from that location, out of respect for the proximity of said church and the Monastery of San Severino. He therefore commanded the Neapolitan nobleman Filippo de Pando to take action "against these intemperate women who were enriching themselves with the deplorable practice of prostitution, which brings such indecent scandal to the residents of the *platea* of San Gennaro in Diaconia, not far away from the Monastery of San Severino Maggiore."[23]

Groups of women who very plausibly joined the numbers of those working girls in the neighborhoods of Porto and Portanova, if we believe Camera, again, who claimed that the public administration gave no thought to the possibility that "by changing location, the women quite simply went on to pervert and deprave the residents of other quarters." But these mass evictions must have been regular events, designed to protect the collective morality. We can rely for instance on the official complaint filed by the notary Bernardo Serviente, who had taken legal action against a certain Tommasa Saperta, madam of various bordellos in the San Paolo area, to ensure that the *mulieres meretrices* should be evicted from there and sent to live in a different part of town.

In Portanova, the prostitutes did their streetwalking along a portico known familiarly as Assumaceli. Even though every effort was made to send them away, they unfailingly returned, no doubt because of the powerful market demand. While there was another market for prostitution adjoining the Piazza delle Corregge, between the harbor area and the royal palace, which is to say in the piazza where the horse market was held: a particularly popular location where, as we shall see shortly, Andreuccio da Perugia first met that lovely temptress Madonna Fiordaliso.

A tariff that was levied on prostitution served a threefold function: to restrict the liberty of the prostitutes, to prevent them from mingling with honest women, and to concentrate them in *postribuli publici* so that it would be easier to carry out the weekly *ricolta*, or collection of money: "the tax collector demanded from every prostitute a certain payment on a weekly basis, and he had to make sure that all the prostitutes live in the *postribuli publici*, or bordellos assigned to them." A story that continues down over the ages, unchanging. As Croce wrote:

> These dens of iniquity remained there during the centuries that followed. In a sanction dated 1577 we read that "from the residence of dishonest women and prostitutes in the street of Rua Catalana and its *fondaci* and locations, there develop countless

brawls and disorders every day, noise, arguments, murders, robberies, and every sort of evils and scandals due to the fact that in the middle of said street by night and by day there are congregations and assemblies of said dishonest women and prostitutes, outsiders, jailbirds, vagabonds, and other similar sorts of people."[24]

And if you ever talk with an elderly Neapolitan who can still remember where the bordellos were located before the Second World War or in the immediate postwar era, up to and including the 1950s, they will point out the exact same locations to you, especially down on the Rua Catalana...

That was more or less the *rione*, or district, of Malpertugio, teeming with life, business, and corruption.[25] A reference that directs us immediately to two things: Boccaccio's novella of Andreuccio of Perugia in the *Decameron*, and one of the finest pieces of Neapolitan history ever written, by Benedetto Croce, about the three adventures Andreuccio experienced.[26] I'll refrain, then, from saying too much, because both of these works of the finest literature are well known. All the same, the story should be summarized, for those who might not ever have read it. And also because, aside from the details of the episode, it refers us inevitably back to this sordid, foul-smelling, dangerous city, with its thousand faces and its troubled coexistences.

Andreuccio came from Perugia. He was a merchant, trading in horses. Naples was the ideal marketplace for him, both to sell and to buy. He arrived in the capital city, found a hotel, and then inquired as to the location of the market. The following morning, he went straight there. To the Piazza delle Corregge. He began wandering around, ill at ease in this immense metropolis. As Benedetto Croce writes: "He felt like a stranger, and somewhat the object of mistrust in a new city and among new people." Nonetheless, he proceeded. He evaluated the horses that interested him, but good merchant that he was, he chose to bide his time. He remained implacable in the face of the first few offers. He was still hoping to drive a good bargain. Still, eager to make it clear that he was in any case a man of some substance, and a man with considerable resources, he pulled out his purse, which was heavy with gold coins. Five hundred florins. Something that no merchant should ever dream of doing in any market in the world. Especially not now, in Naples, in this part of the city, where there were always a thousand prying eyes, immediately ready to focus on the first likely sucker with a pocketful of cash.

And there were plenty of prying eyes. Among them the eyes of a woman "of loose morals." A young woman. Not Neapolitan, but an outsider, just like Andreuccio. To be exact, in her case, a Sicilian. And what was her name? Madonna Fiordaliso. She was accompanied by a little old lady who was also Sicilian. This little old lady recognized Andreuccio, because she had seen him before at his father's house: both in Sicily, where he had worked as a merchant, and in Perugia. So she approached him. This marked the beginning of a piece of theater, with tears of joy and cries of delight. The young woman, at this point, came to a halt. She waited for the little old lady to finish her performance. And she caught a whiff of a ripe caper: she asked the little old lady to tell her everything about Andreuccio. Everything, every detail about his family. And she made a plan: for that evening, she arranged for the little old lady to be somewhere else. And then she sent a serving woman to Andreuccio's hotel with a message: a gentlewoman wishes to speak with you. Come to her home this evening.

Brimming over with confidence, Andreuccio thought to himself: "How excellent!" A delightful evening, served on a silver platter, with a charming and lovely lady. Without a moment's hesitation, he went with the serving woman. He followed her through alleys and down lanes, straight toward the gentlewoman's home. Into the Malpertugio quarter, where, we should mention, Boccaccio suggested "this was no place to go at night, and especially not for an outsider." Instead, he went there without hesitation. He came to the lady's house. There she stood, atop a handsome staircase. Very young and very beautiful. Dressed and adorned in the most decorous fashion imaginable. And so there was nothing to suggest she might have ill intent or loose morals. She descended three steps and threw herself into Andreuccio's arms. Hugs and kisses and sweet words and a steady refrain of "Oh, my dear Andreuccio, my dear, dear Andreuccio."

The young man entered the home. No two ways about it. Nice furniture. Nice scents and aromas. Deluxe fabrics. "This is a great lady," he thought to himself. Fiordaliso helped him to a seat beside her and told him a fine story woven out of the few pieces of information provided to her by her old serving woman. And she began to tell him a succession of nonsensical tall tales: that she was not just some unknown stranger, but actually Andreuccio's sister, born while her father, Pietro, was in Sicily. He was an ingrate, because he'd abandoned both her and her mother. But now they had supposedly reconciled. Everything was going to be fine, once they got a chance to see each other.

Andreuccio was no fool, and he went along with it. He complied with the story, because he had very different objectives in mind. What he was aiming at was an amorous adventure. At first, he didn't entirely believe her. But Fiordaliso was really quite convincing. She trotted out a succession of well-established details, incontrovertible facts. And the young man fell for it. The woman invited him in, eventually, to stay for dinner with her. And after that, to sleep there, since heading home alone to his hotel in the Naples evening was a highly dangerous prospect, especially for a merchant from elsewhere. Andreuccio agreed. Fiordaliso gave him a room. He began to undress. He stood there, half naked. He needed to move his bowels. He entered into an "adjoining place," writes Croce, a sort of cesspool between buildings, and the outcome was less than ideal for him. The wooden plank he was walking on broke, and Andreuccio fell down, into the depths of the cesspool.

At that point, Andreuccio was in deep shit, literally. What about his clothing? It's all in the room. With his purse and all his money. He's been had. He starts to yell. Then, filthy from head to toe, he manages to get out. He knocks at the door of the first building he comes to. He knocks again, louder this time. Then he starts to pound on the door. He makes a hellish amount of noise. People look out the windows and some tell him to go to hell. Others surmise he must be drunk. Others tell him to pipe down. Still Others threaten to come down and beat him soundly... and a few explain to him the way things are: he needs to cut it out, once and for all, of his own accord, or else there was someone who would shut him up, like it or not: the Scarabone Buttafuoco, the boss of all the bosses, the *mammasantissima* of the neighborhood, who ruled the roost in the streets of Malpertugio, the pimp who looked after Lady Fiordaliso, "who terrified the neighbors and demanded either their submission or their complicity," and who, Croce comments, "seemed like a present-day high dignitary of the Camorra."[27] One of the bosses of those more or less disciplined hordes of *latrocinatores* and lawbreakers who would go out, as a group, by night, assaulting homes and buildings, consisting of large numbers (*magno numero*) of noblemen who'd fallen on hard times, vagabonds, deserters, former jailbirds who terrorized the city: the children of that very same environment, in their mindset and their psychology, that had produced the men of the system of the *seggi*, with the same idea of controlling the territory and government of their own share of the quarter. "Gangs of lowlifes who were called *ruffiani* in the fifteenth century and subsequently *compagnoni*, the genuine forefathers of our latter-day *camorristi*," nothing more or less than the poverty-stricken face of an identity built over three hundred years of history.

Andreuccio's adventures continued. He ran away, covered with filth. Half naked and robbed of his money. But it still wasn't over. It was nighttime and he was afraid. In the street, two furtive fellows appeared, carrying a lantern. Fearing the worse, Andreuccio darted into a hovel. But by pure coincidence, the other two men darted into the same hovel. Andreuccio curled up in a corner of the hovel to avoid being spotted. The two men removed the clanky old armor they were wearing. Suddenly they smelled a bad odor. They held up the lantern and looked around. They spied Andreuccio. The two men stood there in astonishment and asked him what he was doing there on the ground in that condition. The young man told his story. The two men smiled. They knew what house he had wound up in. Things could have gone worse. He could easily have died. In fact, no doubt the girl and her pimp would have murdered him.

This was hardly a hugely surprising development in that Naples. It is enough to read this contemporary account of an episode that takes us back to a similar situation that resounds with comparable details, where theft and murder lurked around every corner. This was a story taken from the chronicles of the time that might very well have come to Boccaccio's notice, dating from 1334:

> Benenato de Apenna from Conca dei Marini in the duchy of Amalfi lodged a criminal complaint with the judges that his son Carletto, who had contracted a legitimate marriage with Diamante, the daughter of Giacomo Paolillo, also from Conca, had traveled with his new bride to Naples *to win the indulgence of Saint Clare.* For this purpose, they took a room in the city, but his bride Diamante stealthily fled the room with a certain adulterer, taking with her many objects belonging to her husband. And since it had all happened with the advance knowledge of her relatives, they decided that some vendetta might strike them, and had the unfortunate Carletto murdered.[28]

Once he'd finished his story, Andreuccio heard a proposal. He could come with the two men. And he could help them in an undertaking that would solve his problems, the loss of his clothing and the theft of his purse. What they were going to do was enter the cathedral and break open the vault where the Archbishop Minutolo lay buried, having died just days ago. Child's play: in they'd go. They'd break open the vault, "of marble built and very large," lifting the very heavy (*gravissimo*) lid, but the three of them would manage it without difficulty. One of them would creep inside. And then they'd steal everything: the bishop's vestments and paraments and especially the most valuable item, the archbishop's ring. Andreuccio was up for it.

They set out for the cathedral. Still, it was hardly a short walk. And Andreuccio was putting out a certain stench. The accomplices, tormented by that smell, persuaded him: As soon as we get to a well, we'll help you down into it, you'll be able to rinse off, and we'll be done once and for all with this stench. They came to a well. Andreuccio let them lower him down to the bottom, keeping his eye the whole time on the rope and bucket that he would need to be hauled back up. But then some men from the Curia went by, keepers of the public order. Out of breath and thirsty, they drew near, approaching the well, exhausted from having chased after the latest thief in the night, though without catching him. At the sight of these men, Andreuccio's two accomplices took to their heels. And in so doing, they abandoned the unsuspecting young man at the bottom of the well. Meanwhile, the police officers stopped, tired and overheated. And, after removing their chainmail and putting down their weapons, they started hauling on the rope, convinced that it was tied to nothing but a bucket full of water. They pulled and they hauled and, in the end, instead of the bucket, out popped Andreuccio. An entirely unexpected apparition. The police officers took fright and turned to run. Just then Andreuccio's two accomplices reappeared, and they told him to come with them. This tormented night in the belly of Naples could now continue.

At last the trio arrived at the cathedral. It was around midnight. They got in, as planned, unseen. They made their way to the archbishop's tomb. They used crowbars to lift the heavy lid. And then the question arose: Who's going into the tomb? Andreuccio refused. The two men threatened him. Either get in there or else prepare to meet your maker, as you so richly deserve. The threat frightened him. So he climbed into the vault. On personal terms with the corpse. Andreuccio was afraid, but he wasn't stupid. First of all, he slid the ring off the dead man's hand, but he didn't hand it to his confederates, choosing instead to slip it onto his own finger. He handed them the archbishop's miter, crosier, gloves, et cetera. He insisted that there was nothing else in the tomb. What do you mean, there's nothing else? It's the most valuable item in there. The ring! Where is it? Beats me, came the response. Then look harder, they retorted. Andreuccio pretended to search, and then said it again, No, nothing here. So then what do you think his two accomplices did? Perhaps because they were angry about failing to find the dreamed-of ring, or else to avoid having to split the small trove of treasure that they had found with Andreuccio, they lowered the cover of the tomb and sealed him in. And Andreuccio was trapped inside, buried alive alongside the archbishop's corpse.

He was lost in despair. He knew that he might very well die in there of asphyxiation. Or even worse: he might be discovered, captured, and hanged. But luckily Naples is a place with an overabundance of thieves. There were others who'd come up with the idea of pulling off that robbery and stealing the archbishop's vestments and ring. Soon enough, Andreuccio heard voices around the tomb. A steady mutter. Among them all, the voice of a priest, saying: "Why, what are you afraid of? You're afraid of the corpse? I'll go into the tomb!" Then came the noise of the metal crowbar prying up the marble lid. Two legs descending inside. Andreuccio grabbed hard onto the priest's legs. He hauled down. There came a scream. A scream of utter terror. The archbishop had awakened from the afterlife and wanted to kill them all! The whole band took to their heels. But they'd left the tomb wide open behind them. At last Andreuccio was able to get free. And he ran all the way to the hotel. He packed his bags, and even before day broke, he made his escape back to Perugia. With his five hundred florins invested in a ring instead of in horses.

No account and no document could provide a better description of the Neapolitan underworld during the reign of King Robert and Queen Joanna. A time when Naples, its streets, and its square were transformed after sundown into an enormous hunting ground dominated only by evildoers, thieves, whores, and *compagnoni*, meaning mafiosi. Where the police merely played at hide-and-seek, running lazily after criminals, while teams of burglars learned their trade next to the tomb of a dead archbishop. A city where even the aristocratic clans had given up their rule over the territory. But we know that's not the case. And it's the episode from 1343 that gives us that certainty.

We ought to say something about this magnificent novella. We need to wonder whether, when all is said and done, these characters really existed or whether they were the product of pure fiction. Concerning the female protagonist, a document dated 1341 mentions not a Madonna Fiordaliso but a Sicilian woman named Flora who lived in Malpertugio: a *pensionaria*, a woman living on a pension, who occupied a room with an adjoining loft, who might very well have entertained men by the hour. Concerning Scarabone Buttafuoco, a document from five years earlier speaks of a Francesco Buttafuoco, Sicilian, who had remained loyal to the Angevin cause and who received an annual pension from the royal court of ten *oncias*, to be drawn from the gabelle on salt in the Principato Citra and in Terra di Lavoro: an individual who would seem to be anything but a criminal. As for the tomb of Filippo Minutolo, Croce writes that "you can still see today in the Cathedral of Naples, in the venerable chapel of the Minutolo or Capece Minutolo family, a chapel that is a distinguished monument of history and art"; adding that precisely this chapel "was, to a large extent, in its present form, the work of the Archbishop Filippo Minutolo, under whose supervision the reconstruction and enlargement of the Neapolitan cathedral began," an archbishop who dies on October 24, 1301.[29]

But what about Andreuccio? Recently, the Neapolitan historian Bruno Figliuolo made a captivating discovery that opens new cracks in the wall of history that allow us to understand where Boccaccio found the idea for his story. An official note of protest sent in 1365 to Queen Joanna by the Collegio dei Priori of Florence made a sweeping denunciation of the state of decay that had overtaken the capital, with an increase in criminal activity that

damaged trade and unleashed an endless array of vexing challenges for the Florentine merchants and the members of their
nation, seriously compromising their personal safety. The reason
that had unleashed that letter of complaint had less to do with the
threats and insults that the Neapolitans, to some unspecified extent, regularly directed at the Florentines working in the city of
Naples, but instead a pair of events in the chronicle of misdeeds
that had recently reached the Priori of Florence, that is, the city's
government. What had attracted their notice were reports of lawsuits and accusations. The first report had to do with the *miles*
Paolo Scossidato having taken, unlawfully and by force, a horse
belonging to Giovanni Latinucci. The second report, however, is
so much more intriguing:

> What is worse, the merchant Cenni di Bardella, who had gone
> to the house of a matron to talk with her, had been seduced
> by her and deceitfully locked into a room; and when he had
> tried to make his escape, the woman's son, a nobleman, beat
> him shamefully with a club and wounded him badly. And, as
> he tried to escape, others made their way into the house and
> tried to capture him and rob him of everything he had on his
> person.[30]

Cenni (Bencivenni) di Bardella was a personage of some importance in the business environment then operating in Naples,
connected with the Acciaiuoli company and particularly active
in the wheat trade. Hence the power behind his complaint. An
episode that in a singular fashion reminds us of exactly what happened to Andreuccio, and which Figliuolo imagines might have
had a certain resonance in Florence as well, a city of the saltiest
tastes—a place where a chat in the dark of night, in an ill-famed
part of town on the part of a prominent personage in the milieu of
the international market with a no more clearly identified matron;
and a jealous son who weighs in to safeguard his mother's virtue;
and other random passersby who enter the house, believing that

the unfortunate victim is actually an evildoer who has slipped inside with the worst-possible intentions—these were all elements that could suggest anything other than a simple circumstance or an innocuous conversation. Cenni's misadventure could prompt skepticism, wry wisecracks, insinuating questions, and the shared notion that the man had found himself face-to-face with a contrived situation. Something masterminded. A trap into which Cenni fell head over heels, "foolishly but not entirely unawares."

There are a great many other pieces of supporting evidence offered by the historian that add to the likelihood that Boccaccio's novella might have specifically been inspired from this episode of current events. One thing, though, remains certain: occurrences of this sort fed in Florence, in this very same period, the notion of Naples as *a paradise inhabited by devils.*

The Sunset of a System

To bring this chapter to its fitting conclusion, let me begin with one last story, dating from 1318. A trial was being held in Florence. The party of the first part, the plaintiff, pleading harm, was the Neapolitan *miles* Francesco Caracciolo, while the defendant was one of the largest banks of that time, the Florentine family of the Frescobaldi. That was tantamount to saying that in Naples, the person lodging the complaint was someone who could boast the kind of power that derived from deep roots in the territory, as well as social status and the considerable force of a clan. The defendants, on the other hand, represented a boundless seat of power, spanning borders and large as Europe itself: the power of capital. It just so happened that Francesco had deposited with the bank no fewer than 425 golden *oncias*, equivalent to 2,125 florins, a truly large sum that gives us some sense of the extent to which the power of the clans was also based upon solid economic foundations. But the Frescobaldi had in the meantime gone bankrupt, dragged under by their dealings with the king of England. As a result, Francesco discovered from one day to the next that the money he had deposited with their bank was now gone. It had been swallowed up in the sinkhole of a bank failure that had involved a great many other Neapolitans who all belonged to the same class, among them Tommaso Caracciolo Carafa, Tommaso Vulcano, Landolfo Faiella, Nicola de Marenda, Pietro de Vignale, Marco Talenti, and Serefeo Cafatino.

In Naples, Francesco had no tools with which to recover his money. He had only one solution: head back to Florence, carrying with him letters patent that attested to his authority and perhaps a fair number of *clientes* in his entourage. Just imagine: someone accustomed to being in command, to having everyone standing at attention and listening to what he had to say, who was the king of his own quarter and in his own city. Now, instead, he has to present himself, hat in hand, in a world that he no longer governs, a world that is alien to him, whose mindset and mechanism he cannot grasp, a world that spins at velocities that are absolutely foreign to him.

The only thing to do, then, is to resign oneself. There are no shortcuts, no easy ways of settling the problem with strong-arm tactics, as he might be tempted—or accustomed—to do. So he follows the narrow path. A trial. Which takes a fairly long time, but does eventually come to a conclusion, one that establishes his rights: the *miles* is entitled to get all his money back. Francesco must have been overjoyed to have had his rights restored. But then he realizes (or perhaps someone explains to him) that he's going to have a hard time enforcing the verdict. The other side brings up ten thousand quibbles, the property of the Frescobaldi family is frozen, many members are in flight, and it's going to be hard to get an accounting and access to that money. Francesco isn't sitting still for this. To hell with the money, he may have thought. But at least I want to see them behind bars. And he manages to get one of the partners of the company put in jail. But due to the intercession of the Florentine government, the merchant is soon set free.[31]

We cannot say whether this occurrence dragged any further ramifications in its wake. But this episode alone clearly marks the

vast distance between the Neapolitan mindset and this vast, foreign universe. A distance that would in time actually grow to the
level of rejection toward the Florentine Niccolò Acciaiuoli (the
protagonist of an extraordinary career at the side of Queen Joanna
I, whom he served as *gran siniscalco*, or grand seneschal, something akin to her steward).[32] Someone who could boast membership in the nobility of the *seggi* and who, having recently risen to
fame and honor, came from outside the city and, relying primarily
upon his own financial prowess and might, was now doing his best
to construct a somewhat fabricated status. Something along the
lines of Don Calogero Sedàra in the *Gattopardo* (*The Leopard*),
based upon aristocratic birth alluded to but unproven, based on
novelistic concoctions, narratives of imaginary exploits that had
never taken place.

That said, in spite of the break in relations and the rejection,
a great many members of the Neapolitan clans were very glad indeed to take part in the Florentine financial system in Naples, as
the case of Francesco Caracciolo clearly shows. The chief characteristic of this system was that it supplied not only the fundamental underlying service of economic support to the state, but also
banking services to private citizens. Unfortunately, we no longer
possess the ledger books of the banking companies operating in
the fourteenth century, and we therefore cannot reconstruct the
detailed transactions involved in the deposits, with the names of
who was making them and the exact sums entrusted to the banks,
and not only in Naples but also in the various branch offices scattered throughout the Kingdom. But still, we can form an idea of
what the clientele were like. There were people of all sorts: lofty
prelates, monasteries, and convents; outsiders and foreigners who
wanted to make sure their money was safe in a city and a Kingdom
that were all too often dangerous and scary; major merchants and
other companies operating in the Kingdom; noblemen and members of the bourgeoisie, eager to safeguard their possessions from
the ill will of other men and the tax authorities; barons who, much

like their king, were delighted to be able to avail themselves of the fat coffers of Florentine bankers, always willing to unleash vast rivers of cash; modest merchants and small landowners who went into debt for laughably small sums; and so on. The deposits were made either in cash (*pecunie quantitates*) or, frequently, in the form of jewelry, precious fabrics, pieces of fine luxury craftsmanship, et cetera. It may be, though there is no way we can be sure about it, that the banks took a commission in exchange for the service rendered. Without a doubt, however, they kept a very accurate accounting of the sums, with clear indications of the sum or the object deposited for safekeeping, in exchange for which a receipt was issued that allowed the depositor to withdraw the sum or the property from their account whenever desired. Those deposits, of course, were essential to make the whole mechanism spin: they represented the reserve that the bank could draw on at any time in order to satisfy their need for liquid cash. In a word, then, they were the flywheel that guaranteed the bank's credit and served to drive the conveyor belt of loans, where deposits and loans went hand in hand. For instance, one of the Acciaiuoli's associates, Chiarizo Benticlaro, loaned King Robert three hundred *oncias* in 1339, money that came from a deposit made with the Acciai-uoli bank by a Venetian living in Naples, namely Marino Grioni. Or else there might be even more complicated twists and turns, such as that undertaken by the Bonaccorsi bank. Finding itself in debt in 1341 with the archbishop of Brindisi for two hundred *oncias*, it asked the Count of Celano to cover that sum, promising to put that in their ledger book either as a credit in his name, or else entering it as a credit against the debts the count had already contracted with the bank.[33]

The system continued to spin. But it wasn't perfect. Its re-balancing frequently sacrificed this company or that, as they weakened and not infrequently slid into bankruptcy, drag-ging with them en masse their current account holders. Various families went under—the Bonaccorsi, the Frescobaldi, and the

Scali—until it turned into the largest collapse of the banking system of the medieval Western world: the collapse of the Bardi and Peruzzi banks. It all began in the middle of 1342. And the theater of this disaster was Florence, not Naples. The Tuscan city was going through a painful period of political torment. What happened was that Lucca fell under Pisan control. What was to be done? Florence was in serious difficulties, needed urgent help, and therefore turned to its longtime friends, the pope and King Robert. But given the larger situation, neither the king nor the pope had any interest in responding to that call for help. The crisis had them both in its vise grip. Heading into a new business venture hardly seemed like the best idea. The leading Florentine citizens made a decision, and they had absolutely no idea how freighted with consequences it would prove for their future. They chose to turn their back on the king of Naples and let the chips fall where they may. Instead they began negotiations with the Holy Roman Emperor, Louis IV, "the Bavarian." They were going over to the Ghibelline side: a political move that explicitly shattered the traditional alliance between the Angevins and the Florentines.

As soon as Robert heard the news, he went wild: he couldn't believe that Florence could have betrayed him so coldly, that this marked the end of the union that lay at the very foundation of his Kingdom's inception. News spread rapidly through the capital. Florence was about to change sides. The world as it had been known and understood up until that moment—with Naples and Florence under the same roof, sharing the same objectives—would soon vanish entirely. And what about our money, in their bank—a great many depositors thought—how are we going to get our hands on it again if a war breaks out? What are we going to do if we need our cash? Who can guarantee we'll ever get it back? Panic broke out. In technical terms, a run on the banks ensued. Lots and lots of Neapolitans went running to the cash offices of the Bardi, the Peruzzi, and the Acciaiuoli, demanding their deposits. Bellowing at the top of their lungs. Shoving to the front of the line were barons, noblemen, and prelates. This is Villani's account of what happened:

> King Robert became so jealous that he didn't know what to do, greatly fearing that Florence might take sides with the empire and the Ghibellines. And many of his barons and prelates and wealthy men of the Kingdom, who had deposited their money with the companies and merchants of Florence, for that very reason became suspicious, and they all demanded repayment, and the Florentines lost the trust of their clients everywhere they were doing business.[34]

Diplomatic tensions between King Robert and Florence showed no signs of subsiding. And the Florentine administrators went ahead with their choice. They gave the go-ahead to Ludwig the Bavarian and his men. But at this point, the Florentine representatives realized what a calamitous mistake they'd just made. And they did something even more spectacular: they turned away Ludwig the Bavarian's ambassadors. They simply told them to go back to their master, apologizing for having wasted their time. But it was too late now. Florence was steering straight for a cliff, with consequences that were both political and financial at the same time.

What was happening in Naples (the account holders rushing to the local bank offices, rumors spreading in the marketplaces and down at the port, fear spreading to those who had been waiting before acting, waiting to withdraw their savings, trusting—or hoping—that this would be nothing more than a brief, albeit violent, downpour) was merely a mechanism, a whirlpool in which there were wild gyrations in the price of gold, wars raging, flows of silver from the Far East, market highs and lows amid the crisis, deflation, English and French profits, tithes for the pope, Mongol invaders, but one which was now exploding to devastating effect. And so, after the Neapolitan bank run, the situation spun out of control. The first to fall were the Peruzzi, and as they went, they dragged a great many other companies behind them:

> In such a manner that, shortly thereafter, on that account, both losses of the city government and due to the loss of Lucca, a great many good companies of Florence collapsed, and these were their names: the company of the Peruzzi; that of the Acciaiuoli managed to keep going for a little while longer, staving off collapse for the moment, given their joint power, but did fail shortly thereafter; and the Bardi suffered a great collapse, and failed to pay those they had debts to, followed by their utter collapse; the Bonaccorsi went into bankruptcy, as did the Cocchi, the Antellesi, those from Uzzano, the Corsini, and the Castellani, and Perondoli.[35]

On October 27, 1343, only a few days prior to the raid this book is framed around, the Peruzzi declared themselves willing to submit to the decisions of their creditors, trying to stave off the lodging of a legal complaint, to be followed by the judicial procedure of bankruptcy. After which, a full-fledged panic broke out. The partners fled Florence, first among them Giovanni Villani's brother, Matteo. In June of 1344, it was the Bardi's turn, and they dragged a whole slew of other banks behind them. Most of the red ink that had accumulated consisted of the money loaned to England and the Kingdom of Naples. There was talk of vast sums. Hundreds of thousands of florins. According to Giovanni Villani, the shortfall affecting the Peruzzi and the Bardi amounted to nine hundred thousand florins that had been loaned to the king of England, as well as a hundred thousand florins to the king of Naples. So a total of one million florins...

That was the credit that the two major banks were claiming. Or, perhaps we should say the credit that they might have claimed...because there was no way to collect: not from the English, inasmuch as the loans had been gobbled up by the Hundred Years' War, nor from Naples, given the fact that the state coffers were empty and the crown had absolutely no way to find the money and pay it back.

The money that the two banks were expected to pay out to their account holders, both Florentines and outsiders, was roughly half of the credit: 550,000 florins. An enormous sum. Among that money, there was certainly a fair sum due to people belonging to Neapolitan high society, money that vanished into thin air. Involving situations, we have to imagine, that were very similar to those experienced by our personage Francesco Caracciolo. To make matters worse, certain banks in Naples, before news of the bank collapse had a chance to circulate, fraudulently continued to accept deposits and commit to operations involving the transfer of cash. Indeed, none other than Matteo Villani, for instance, did so. He was a money changer in the capital and was in regular contact with the Buonaccorsi bank in Avignon.

The words used by Caggese, according to whom, following Robert's death and the collapse of the major Florentine banks, one might safely say that "the hegemony of Florentine merchants in southern Italy was dead,"[36] strike me as cursory to a fault. Because it wasn't true: the Florentines continued exerting great economic influence in the Kingdom, first and foremost with the company of Niccolò Acciaiuoli. And they continued to play a fundamental role in the control of the wheat trade, with figures of primary importance—among them Gaspare Bonciani, who had been very active during the realm of Queen Joanna II—with a structural imprint that swept past the French domination in the Kingdom, considering the fact that as late as the height of the fifteenth century, the pivot points of the southern economy still spoke a Florentine dialect and had names like Strozzi and Medici.

But what did in fact decline and vanish once and for all was the Angevin-Florentine system. This marked the end of that lengthy trend, dating back centuries, that had sealed the interactions of Naples and Florence, based on the economic and political alliance between the two partners, with a reciprocal relationship that dated back to the earliest years of the Kingdom's formation.

A model of financial and political relations that became increasingly complex and intrusive, as we have seen, made up of recurrent loans in exchange for tariff exemptions, monopolies, and public works contracts, resulting in the virtually wholesale transfer of all control of the country's tax system to the Bardi-Peruzzi-Acciaiuoli joint venture. In the end, the burden was excessive and a bitter collapse ensued.

After the collapse and over the course of the fourteenth century, accounts of financial operations by Florentine investors, it seems to me, practically vanish, though we could not say that the old system of collecting funds from the largest players in international finance was entirely abandoned. One reason was that as far as the monarchy was concerned, this remained the most reliable system as well as the one offering easiest access to much-needed resources. In that sense, we have some information. Infrequent, but there is some, according to which capital was being sought, not so much in Florence, but to a greater extent in the other economic epicenter of Europe, namely Venice, but in accordance with the same operative methods of the past, with the exchange of money for public contracts and tariff exemptions.[37]

A new phase, in the final analysis, where we wouldn't exactly say that the Tuscan community abandoned the court, indeed, it continued to participate actively in its administration and the formulation of its policies—something that, in particular, the previously mentioned Niccolò Acciaiuoli would do brilliantly, in quite a star turn. But in that attitude we can glimpse the unmistakable signs of the decline of an era, with the genetic mutation of men of finance, active in the world of capital, into *grands commis d'État*, interested by this point in only one aspect, the underlying logic of state power, which was in some ways more profitable and less risky.

And so, as we said, an era was ending. But not only here in Naples. Elsewhere, the same thing was happening. The age of entrepreneurship was drawing to a close, the time of aggressive and creative Pisans and Genoese, the era of the Florentines who created financial colossi (with clay feet), a world where money and credit flowed just as fluidly as oil. Instead, this time marked the dawning of a very different period, a fourteenth century as hard and inflexible as stone, where the spaces and boundaries shrank, where investments and speculations dwindled equally. And the very mindset of outsider merchants closed in to an equal extent, making them warier, more prudent, cautious, and vigilant. In terms of everything they saw, in terms of everything that surrounded them.

Who can say whether our captain was thinking something of the sort as he watched the sun sink rapidly into the west, in the waters off Baiae, in this November of 1343. Perhaps he was thinking that times were truly growing difficult. And that his cargo, which in other years might have presented absolutely no temptation to anyone, would certainly now constitute a fat and tempting capture. For anyone. Useful when the one thought was to sate the hunger of an entire city. A king's ransom…a cargo that, once it arrived in Genoa, he might have been thinking, will make my masters wealthy. And perhaps some of that money might trickle down to me as well.

Or else…

Or else, he might have been thinking about nothing at all. Or else, he might have been thinking about his family. Or that the night was going to be chilly, chillier and danker than usual. And that he didn't feel like sleeping. Tomorrow, after all, the ship would be setting sail at dawn.

VI

BEYOND THE NIGHT

Into the Abyss

Those readers who might have imagined that something spectacular would happen in the aftermath of the raid will probably be bitterly disappointed: basically, nothing happened at all. A ship was towed into port. There were prisoners. There was a dead body. There was wheat that, for a while, alleviated the sufferings of the populace. There were noblemen who, perhaps, for a day or two, were carried around their quarter in triumph and who felt like the absolute kings of the city, for a while, enjoying the sweet taste of success. There were authorities who might as well not even have existed, and who didn't so much as blink an eye. There were shipowners who had lost a cargo, a ship, and a captain and who, up north in Genoa, reckoned up their losses and flew into a rage. And then, that was that. The effects of this commando operation immediately subsided. This event, which might so easily have opened up to the future—giving rise to reactions that one way or another might have churned up the waters, making them seethe with new developments—instead simply vanished from sight just a few days later. Actions that evaporated instantly, swallowed up by a maelstrom. Everything that had happened tumbled into a precipice, whereby the account of the episode, its importance for those who lived through the era, faded away until it became nothing more than a piece of personal memory, devoid of any and all redeeming collective or social value.

It took no longer than a few days' wait—how many days? Perhaps eight, perhaps ten, or more, or less, I couldn't say—and people quickly forgot that in Baiae there had ever even been a ship laden with wheat, and that the nobility of Capuana and Nido, with the assistance of a great many other people (craftsmen, common folk, clan members, all working together as they had previously done, in the past) had once again banded together to defend their city, rescuing it from hunger. People forgot because they had other things to worry about. And they even forgot about hunger, because they were overwhelmed by fear.

Indeed, the day of Santa Caterina arrived, November 25, 1343, Saint Catherine's Day. The day of the tsunami. An enormous wave swept over the coast, and the effects propagated eastward. As Villani tells us: all the way to the port of Pera, in Constantinople. In Naples, the scenario was a genuine nightmare. The beach was inundated by mutilated corpses, slammed against the sharp rocky shoals, and "shattered like so many fragile eggshells," as Petrarch told us, having been an eyewitness to the tidal wave in person. The wave was so violent that it was capable of sweeping away anything and everything. People, livestock, animals, buildings. Even the port structures appeared to have been gravely damaged, swept away with unheard-of force. All that remained of the quarter overlooking the sea were ruins, sucked away by the roaring waves. All around the beach was a desolate landscape, terrifying to behold. Even the queen came to survey all that remained of the coast. She came with her entourage. And she was aghast, just like everybody else. She could do nothing more than to behold what had happened. Please consider this chronicle of events, taken from a fragment of text written at the time:

On the feast day of Saint Catherine who was broken on the Wheel of this present year of 1343, there was a tempest so tremendous that the sea rose up with mountains of water and the wind from the mouths of Capri drove it toward land, and the water mounted halfway up the Monterone, in such a manner that we who were by the Scogliuso [a lane not far from the port] lay face down on the ground, feeling sure that Judgment Day had arrived. All of the houses shook like reeds in the wind, and many collapsed, so that the queen herself went barefoot in tears to the church of San Lorenzo. In the port, not a single boat or ship remained that hadn't been sent straight to the bottom; some eight hours later, the cruel and thieving sea went back to its rightful place, carrying away with it a treasury of things worth more than 200,000 *scudi*, leaving on the ground more than ten feet of sand, so that those who happened to be inside a given house found themselves forced to exit through the windows.[1]

Along the coast of Campania, people reckoned up the damage. Aside from what had happened in Naples, the *mare latrone*, the thieving sea, swallowed up Amalfi "to the extent of one-third of its land" and cruelly tested Pozzuoli, as well as sinking a Genoese flotilla that was offshore, not far from Naples, loaded with victuals and foodstuffs.

But any attack on a Genoese ship meant there was a price to pay, one way or another. And, if you were Genoese, a raging storm was no excuse. The owners of the ship, Bartolomeo Squarciafico and Bonifacio Cattaneo, therefore lodged a complaint with the Royal Curia. But the city of Naples pretended, quite simply, not to hear. Whereupon the two shipowners turned to the doge of Genoa, Simone Boccanegra, urging him to demand formal reparations from Queen Joanna. There ensued a judicial controversy that bounced back and forth, with *andirivieni e indecisioni* (comings and goings and uncertainties), "also a result of the disorders then unfolding in the capital."

That's right: the new Kingdom under Joanna. It had only just begun, and it was in a state of chaos. The situation in the city was alarming. In 1344, public safety was under siege, hemmed in by disorder and violence. The captain of Naples, the Count of Terlizzi, Gasso de Dynisiaco, was asked to bring to a halt the phenomenon of "citizens and outsiders committing brawls, riots, murders, thefts, scuffles, and all manner of things that disturb the peace of the city of Naples," which "so often involved the recourse to weapons." A full-blown pestilence, as it was described, disturbing everyday life, and clearly something that needed to be repressed in the most resolute manner imaginable. This, then, was the text of the decision:

> whereas, if the perpetrators fail to appear before us within two months of the time of the publication of this decree, and therefore find themselves in a state of contempt of this order, we shall therefore proceed with a sentence of *forjudicationis* so that blood relatives, relatives by marriage, kith and kin, relatives in the first and second degree, and even friends shall be placed under arrest, precisely because of the assiduous and uncontrollable multitude of crimes and their excesses that are currently undermining the peaceful condition of the entire city of Naples.[2]

This document ends with striking words, both because of the hope they convey and the good intentions that they express. Words that strike me with the awareness conveyed that, were this criminal behavior to be abolished, the city would surely be a better place. It expressed a powerful wish for the future. Namely that once the wrongdoers had been extirpated, the state itself might get back on its feet: "once this pestilence has been ripped out of the city's heart, the state will be able to rise and find again, with the help of God Almighty, its troubled tranquility."[3]

If the situation with public order was serious, it became critical starting the following year, on account of the assassination of

Andrew of Hungary, the queen's first husband. That murder gave
rise to an extended series of dynastic conflicts, with a succession
of sieges, battles, and invasions by mercenary troops (amplified
by and linked with an array of domestic tensions) following in its
wake, which would strike deeply into the heart of the entire socioeconomic context of Naples and the Kingdom.[4]

So hijacking a ship had not been sufficient to satisfy the needs
of a metropolis the size of Naples, which had a thousand needs
and a thousand necessities. And the city soon plunged back into
famine, this time an even darker outbreak, an even crueler reprise.
With the collapse of 1347, when "the whole world was swept by
the greatest famine and shortage of all those things that are need-
ful for the survival of human beings." And who was farsighted
enough to foresee pestilences? And yet they struck: one, two,
three, four... In 1348, 1363, 1373, 1382... One worse than the
last, foretold, as we read in the *Chronicon Siculum*, by omens, signs
in the sky, comets. Such as, for instance, in 1382, when "there appeared a mercurial comet in the north by west, and immediately
thereafter, the fourth pestilence began."

Meanwhile, brigands were besieging the capital, setting out
at a brisk pace from their lairs on Mount Vesuvius: highwaymen
attacking streets, travelers, carriages, with exploits that from one
year to another became increasingly daring and spectacular: in
1341, they kidnapped Giovanni Barrile as he was on his way to
Rome to witness Petrarch's coronation as poet laureate. In 1343,
"the great number of brigands made it impossible to bring wheat
and victuals into the city." In 1344, they stole Queen Joanna's
household silver, two times in a row. In 1347, the official of the
fish taxes, Giacomo Macedonio, reported that it was impossible
to bring in the city's revenues because brigand raids prevented the
transportation of fish to Naples from the coastal towns of Castellammare, Torre Ottava, and Resina. The brigands' unscrupulous
greed was so great that in 1379 "one could not venture as far as
a bridge known as the Ponte della Maddalena, where men were
sliced open like calabashes and women were gutted cruelly."[5]

The account provided by Archbishop Pierre Ameilh, in a letter to Cardinal Guy de Boulogne dated January 22, 1363, gives us insight into another element: as had been the case in the past, alongside the brigands, *milites* worked likewise to worsen the situation, men who had fallen on hard times, impoverished men, who were simply trying to survive once again by doing violence in a criminal fashion. And the archbishop revealed all his helplessness, in a situation where all of the chapter's economic activity seemed to be hindered, if not blocked entirely. His *familiares* were being intimidated by main force. The merchants who worked with them were terrified. The *greco* wine, the heart and soul of the bishopric's economy, sat unsold. The barrels of wine could not be loaded aboard ships. Production had to be halted. The wine barrels sat in warehouses, going bad. Everything seemed to be sinking, helplessly, in anomie.[6]

And the state, in the face of this constant danger, this reckless impudence, remained practically helpless and inert: it took each blow, showing no sign of retaliation, thus demonstrating, for the umpteenth time, the chronic incompetence of the central power, its inability to exert control. In part because the gangs were well rooted in the territory, enjoying ample protection and complicity. And the problem would not be solved even with the edict *contra malandrenos* issued by the chancellery of King Charles III (also known as Charles the Short, or Charles of Durazzo) in 1382. That edict called for the state to proceed against the brigands by capturing them, taking a scorched-earth policy against their network of protections, with the demolition of their houses and their vineyards, forcing their families into exile outside of the Kingdom. There was another measure, on the other hand, that was more successful, and it directs to the type of intervention adopted on a vast scale by the Angevin state in this phase of the fight against criminal behavior: the co-opting of these gangs into the ranks of the royal army. Indeed, the army legalized them on a de facto basis, restricting the violence to the outskirts of Naples. This period, in fact, marked the interruption of that violence.

The Clans at the Sunset of the Angevin Dynasty

With this government, so *scombujato ed intralciato*, ramshackle and incapable, in a general condition of confusion and general deterioration, at the peak of administrative difficulties, with the destruction of papers and documents—such as, for instance, the difficulties that arose during the course of the civil disorders that ensued following Andrew of Hungary's murder, or during the occupation of Castel Nuovo by the troops of Louis I of Hungary—how can anyone imagine that our Squarciafico and Cattaneo clans could handle such a situation? In point of fact, they could not. So they wound up striking a deal of some sort, in accordance with conditions that, as I explained at the beginning of this book, we cannot reconstruct.

What about the masterminds? The ones who organized the raid in the first place? So what did the clans and the families do in this context, so very turbulent, this political and administrative precipice? Incredible to say, they maintained their control over the city, they ensured that the city remained on a steady course, and it was they who continued to govern Naples, on the same old, traditional, and customary basis. Even in the weltering chaos. Even in a period when public order already seemed to have slipped completely out of control, leaving the authorities flat-footed. They did so at the moment of greatest popular terror, when the populace—out of control—launched an attack on the bread ovens:

> In the year of Our Lord 1374, in the month of August, the Neapolitan people rose up and, bearing banners, broke loose; and they began to run through the city, shouting, "Long live our lady the Queen and long live the people of Naples, and to death with traitors." And amid this tumult, driven by famine, they sacked and plundered many of the houses of the bakers.

The revolt wasn't put down by the civil authorities, who were incapable of taking effective action, as usual. No, it was they who did it. Once again, it was the *milites* of Capuana and Nido who took it upon themselves to repress the tensions, restore calm to the city (*reducent ad concordiam*) and, first and foremost, felt strong enough to make promises concerning the city's future provisioning. And who emphasized, proudly, that they "would never have allowed the people of Naples to starve or the city of Naples to be destroyed."[7]

Capuana and Nido wanted to continue to command all the other clans, the other *seggi*, the city as a whole. All the same, once again, what was lacking was consensus. Their preeminence, originally established by King Robert in 1339—where it would have been appropriate to replace that term with the more concrete terms of *government* and *control of the city*—created tension, much more than concord. And soon the clan war broke out again. With a first phase, dating from 1346. There was a standoff between the men of Capuana and those of Portanova, with a brawl of major dimensions that took place next to the Torre d'Arco, the tower that served as a boundary between the two areas of reciprocal influence. The brawl provoked "disturbance and grave scandal." What ensued, as per routine, was the destruction of the homes of several protagonists, their exile, and the confiscation of a third of their property.

And that was nothing yet. This was the beginning of August 1380. It was a very difficult moment for the fate of both the Kingdom and Queen Joanna. Soon, in Naples, "a tremendous and bloody battle took place between the nobility of the city's piazzas and quarters. The aristocrats of Capuana and Nido claimed the right to take precedence over all the other *seggi*, in accordance with a decree issued by King Robert; but the clans of Portanova, Porto, and Forcella insisted that actually *they* were the better and more venerable knights."[8]

What lit the fuse was an open provocation: a group of young men from the most respected families of Capuana and Nido, followed by their usual entourage of *familiares*, servants, and *fideles*, entered an area that didn't belong to them that was instead controlled by the clans of Portanova. They arrived at the Piazza della Selleria, the saddlers' square. No one can say who started things. Was it these young men, driven by their customary arrogance to seek out an intimidating incursion into the area controlled by their adversaries? Or was it the residents of the other quarter who—and the facts uphold this observation—customarily prevented people from the *seggi* of Capuana and Nido from coming through? The fact remains that insults began to fly. And it took only the blink of an eye, as always, to pass from words to deeds. The men of the clan of Portanova emerged, fully armed, quickly got organized, and attacked the young interlopers. Who in their turn backed off, retreating. Pushing farther on, toward the Torre d'Arco, but still with weapons at the ready. Still ready to fight.

News spread throughout the city. Allies came running from all directions, and not just *milites*. And not just *clientes*. Also *stipendiarii*, low-level labor paid directly by the heads of family, armed and ferocious. People from the hinterland, recruited from the neighboring small towns of Ottaviano, Somma, Scafati, and Marigliano. The clash grew in ferocity. For the *seggio* of Capuana and Nido, among the most bitter battlers we can list two Piscicelli, a Passarello, a de Aversana, a de Loffredo, a Galeota, a de Somma, a Capece Latro, a Dentice, an Imbriaco, a Guindazzo, a Zurlo, and a Caracciolo Russo. For the side that was attacked, there were three di Costanzo, a Gattola, an Agnese, a Scannasorice, and a Mormile. All of these names, in the end, appear as charged with having been responsible for the uproar. And in that uproar, the losses were higher than ever before, greater casualties than in all the previous showdowns. A great many of them died: men of the clan Vulcano, Piscicelli, Cossa, Caracciolo Russo, Bozzuto, and Aiossa clans for the *seggi* of Capuana and Nido; for the other side, members of the Mormile, Cafaro, and Campanella families.

Had it not been for the personal intervention of the queen's husband, Otto, Duke of Brunswick, supported in his stance by a great many barons, members of the court, and high functionaries,

things would surely have gone even worse. His political intervention interrupted the war and restored at last a thin and merely apparent veneer of order, considering the fact that for days on end,
perhaps for a month entire, the two opposing sides had remained
immovable, entrenched in their positions, armed and ready in
their respective jurisdictions. There was no way to go on like this.
From all sides, voices were raised: It's unthinkable that in a civil
metropolis, in the capital of a Kingdom, a person cannot move
freely from one place to another without being instantly singled
out and attacked, inasmuch as a member of an opposing clan. Action must be taken and once and for all these tensions must be
restrained, though they also emphasized that those most badly
harmed were the people of Capuana and Nido, because "it was
also noted that they, when they needed to do business in the lower
districts, found themselves fearful of going there, because those
districts were controlled by their enemies."[9]

A truce was established. The queen invited a sizable delegation
representing the two parties to the war. It was ordered that they
swear an oath and, more important, that they leave their weapons
at home, at least until Otto could return to the city and restore
peace and order. But the debate over who could claim supremacy
went on for a good long while yet. And as soon as Charles III of
Durazzo entered Naples, in July 1381, the problem arose again.
And the first among the most prominent *cives* to step forward
were, once again, the same names: a Caracciolo, a Piscicelli, and
a Guindazzo for Capuana; a Brancaccio, a Carafa, and a Vulcano
for Nido.

A controversy that didn't end here: this issue of supremacy and
the role of certain families over others. It continued throughout
the period of the greatest dominance of the Caracciolo, at the turn
of the fifteenth century, with one notable protagonist, Sergianni,
the favorite of Queen Joanna II. Sergianni Caracciolo, around the
year 1425, not only held the title of *gran siniscalco* (prime minis-
ter), but also the titles of Count of Avellino and of San Giorgio
and Duke of Venosa. He died on August 19, 1432, not far from

the area of his family's greatest influence, in the rooms of Castel
Capuano, murdered by a group of professional hit men in the pay
of the queen herself, who was by now sick and tired of him. Still,
the family preserved its influence. It continued to play a central
role under the last Angevin, René of Anjou, thanks to Ottino Caracciolo, the grand chancellor, a man of war, a distinguished jurist,
who remained faithful to his king until the very end. Indeed, he
even accompanied his king, briefly, into exile.[10]

The history of the lengthy relationship between the Neapolitan family clans and the House of Anjou, which began in the aftermath of the Swabian siege under Conrad IV, had a final and
extraordinary surge. A moment when, once it had become clear
that the crown possessed little if any remaining strength and was
useless at ruling the state, the *nobiliores* attempted the final leap
forward to transform themselves from the Kingdom's ruling class
into actual executives of the official government, with the filter of
the monarchy reduced to little more than a powerless veil. If you
stop to think about it: what an impressive rise, from the limited
prospects, strictly on the scale of their quarter, of the earliest Angevin period, all the way up to the current outcome, wielding full
control of the entire Kingdom...

This happened at the moment of the state's greatest weakness,
just as the last of the Angevins, René, was about to take the throne.
And in February 1435, even before he could arrive in the city, the
nobility offered him a sort of diktat, though it was couched in
terms of absolute diplomacy. This was the substance of their offer:
an architecture of the state that would emanate directly from
them. The masterminds behind this project could hardly help but
be the noble clans of Capuana, the Caracciolo, Minutolo, Latro,
Aprano, and Guindazzo families. A project that called for various
phases. First and foremost, the selection of two representatives for
each *seggio*, in order to establish a council of regency that would
be responsible for appointing local and peripheral administrators
(mayors, prosecutors, *baiuli*), to safeguard both the state and the
capital. It, too, would defend all royal prerogatives. In the second

place, those elected would possess a governing mandate on several levels, which would further involve concentrated diplomatic activity and a condign and complete legislative policy and capacity for intervention, consisting of *acta*, *capitula*, and *mandata*.

An "extraordinary entity," comparable to others established in preceding moments of crisis in the monarchic power (such as that of the Eight of the Good State during the regency of Margaret of Durazzo or the Twenty of the Good State in the years 1418–20), which according to stated intentions would only have lasted for a couple of months, but which instead went on for longer, lasting at least until September, with the certainty that it would be able to constitute a die-hard rump in the governing faction with the Angevin sovereign.[11]

But as the saying goes, weeds never die. Even now that the Angevin universe was rapidly declining, and the troops of Alphonse V of Aragon were practically at the gates, on November 22, 1435, in the presence of Isabella, Duchess of Lorraine, who was regent in her husband René's absence, the Neapolitan nobles found a pretext to quarrel. And that pretext was always the same: preeminence, precedence, and the greater honor of Capuana and Nido with respect to all others... In the regent's presence, the men of Capuana demanded to swear allegiance first, followed by the noblemen of the *seggio* of Nido. Only then, they said, could the representatives of the noble *seggi* have their turn. Not all the noblemen present were in agreement. A quarrel broke out and soon took on increasingly acrimonious tones. The noblemen demanded: Who must first pledge *ligio omagio* (liege homage) to the sovereign queen? And then they continued:

> By Your Majesty's commandment, we have come to pledge our liege homage as may please Your Majesty. Because we, as the children of obedience, are willing to do whatever Your Majesty may command us, in compliance with our honor, our priority, our dignity, and our preeminence. First and foremost, however, we wish to ensure that now and always and in every event our

privileges will remain safe and unharmed and might have perfect stability, as it was in the past, perennially observed, and so there might be to vigorous effect and dignity, and for the future we intend to make use of our reasons.[12]

Behind the formal and ostensible character of a plea directed to the queen, the message that the leading clans of Capuana and Nido were trying to convey was as clear and gleaming as a knife blade. They weren't accustomed to receiving orders, only giving them, especially when interacting with a ruler who appeared to their eyes weak. It was a clear act of extortion. Their traditional prerogatives were not to be touched, and must continue to possess, for the future as well, *vigorosi effetti et dignitate*, which is to say full validity. Otherwise we shall oppose this monarchy in the case that our demands are not accepted (*per l'avvenire intendimo usare nostre ragioni*, for the future we intend to make use of our reasons). This took place in the context of relations between the aristocracy and the sovereign power, where it seems clear to me that there was no mistaking the nature of the request: the existing equilibriums and the aristocracy's role in the municipal context and the larger context of the Kingdom were absolutely not to be trifled with. At the same time, in terms of power relationships among the various family components, it is stunning how extreme the tensions remained between one *seggio* and another, because the stakes remained unchanged: supremacy in the government of both the capital and the Kingdom.

In the presence of Isabella, there was a swirl of centuries-old tensions and impulses that sprang out of the contingent moment, the determination to wrest guarantees for the future. And the representatives of the various *seggi* began to grow heated. Voices were raised and people tried to drown each other out, shout each other down. The voices of the men of Capuana and Nido—Giovanni Cassano, Gabriele de Loffredo, Marino Brancaccio, Nicola d'Alagno—drowned out all the others. The Count of Nola, Raimondo Orsini, the royal chancellor Ottino Caracciolo, Gerardo de Arcucci, the Count of Pulcino ... but there was no way to muddle forward. The presentation ceremony simply couldn't go on. And so it was interrupted.

The funny thing is that it all took place in the queen's presence, and she seemed to be stunned in the face of all that pandemonium. In the end, she left the room, accompanied by the bishop of Chartres, François, who had been summoned to act as referee. And he made a decision that fully accepted the demands of the *seggio* of Capuana: first of all, all privileges and immunities and dignities established by tradition were to be preserved, so as to maintain the integrity of the rights of the noblest clans against any attacks. In the second place, the preeminence of Capuana over all the other *seggi* was to be preserved, with the right to be summoned before anyone else (*primus locus*) in the course of the ceremony of swearing the oath.[13]

All that arguing, all that combat, all that quarreling, all that warfare and then, when all was said and done, everything that King Robert had called for in 1339 was restored, for all intents and purposes.

In the meantime, it was growing late. Saturday, June 2, 1442, was the last day of Angevin Naples. This marked a lengthy historical season that had begun with another siege, almost exactly three hundred years earlier, when Naples was nothing more than a shoal in a Byzantine sea and its *milites* didn't yet know with what sort of soul they would grow up and then grow old. To the cry of *rahona rahona*, a new era was now beginning, with a great Renaissance prince who was going to commemorate the inauguration of his Neapolitan Kingdom with a theatrical triumph. This new prince was Alphonse the Magnanimous: a personage who would rule another commonwealth that would extend from one end to the other of the western Mediterranean. Once again, the Neapolitans were obliged to modify their identity, configuring it to the styles of the new times and the new monarchy. And they did so successfully. But for a great many of them, the bond with the House of Anjou would remain fundamental. Tenacious. Stubborn. In their blood. Like the way people feel about the house they live in. The *seggio* where they go to meet and argue and discuss. One's own quarter, where it is still the families who command.

A Long-Term Phenomenon?

"This journalist is acting all amazed. And yet he's a Neapolitan," my friend says to me, as he's reading the newspaper. "This article of his thinks it's discovering the wheel. The fact that here, in the heart of Naples, in Forcella, there's a war among the families. And that apparently the families here behave as if they were kings. As if everything belonged to them. Where the ones who are coming out on top now are very young *uomini senza onore* (men without honor), men without roots, men without tradition, dressed strangely, wearing their trousers down below their boxer shorts, with an American baseball hat, with a chain around their neck. People who are all *rich and vicious*. They're the children, he writes, 'of a network of identities, affiliations, and hierarchies where the watchword is the control of the territory, the only kind of control that can guarantee nothing happens.' In other words, just listen to this, 'by means of these tools they are able to ensure the uncontrolled management of the drug-dealing market, the shakedown rackets, and loan-sharking.' What a great journalist! He talks the way you talk... He's acting like he's a professor. What did he, just fall to earth from the moon? Does he think he's telling us something new?"

He stops, the way he always does, when he thinks he's about to say something fundamental for the life of the universe itself, and resumes with a sigh: "I can still remember, from when I was a kid, and I lived right around the corner. Right here," and he points to a *vicolo*, an old alley, right next to the ancient Roman forum, behind Piazza San Gaetano. "I must have been sixteen, maybe seventeen, years old, and they'd stop when I was out on my scooter, which I had to ride without a helmet. If you wore a helmet you never knew what the hell could happen. Because the only people who wore helmets were professional hit men. Anyway, they'd stop me and they'd ask, *So listen, huh, who do you belong to?* Who do I belong to? I'd reply. I belong to me. There's no such thing, they'd say. Because you had to belong to someone, to Cicciotto, or else to *'o Muollo* or this other guy or that other guy. The guys who were *i capi*. The gang bosses. In here, in this neighborhood, in this quarter. And if you need something, if you needed help because someone had stolen your car tape deck or your scooter had gone missing, they'd step right up and provide their service. You know what they called that service?"

"I know," I reply, "The return horse. I've used it myself."

He starts up again, talking over my words, as if I'd never talked at all: "And those guys were on top of things, they knew more than the cops, they knew everything, they seemed to have a thousand eyes, and nothing ever happened. In fact, when guys started dealing around here and a couple of kids died with a hypodermic dangling out of their arm," and here he points out another corner of the street, darker, even more sordid, "you know what they did? They came out onto the street with baseball bats and beat them bloody, one by one, the dealers. And they told them: *Nennì,* unhuh, this area belongs to us, our children live here, and you guys belong to the other guys, farther up the hill, this isn't your house. So clear out, and you go tell them what's what… and to think that the guys from here used to go up the hill to deal, right around the corner from Piazza Cavour, and they never had any problems, right? Those guys up the hill? They were completely *sciemi*. Real lunkheads. But if they acted like who-knows-what? If they got ahead of themselves? Then it was baseball bats. And for real. Hand-to-hand combat, just to be clear. No pistols, *comm'è mo'*. The way it is nowadays."

My friend went on with this strange series of recollections. I couldn't tell if he was angry, as if he couldn't put up with that story anymore, with a creeping sense of disgust that had spread right out to the very tip of his hair. Or whether, instead, as is so often the case with everything that has to do with memory, mixing and mingling it all like a cotton candy stand, he isn't just pulling those thoughts out all interconnected, one after another, in a sort of particularly pernicious short circuit. And now the conversation was taking a turn that I couldn't have expected, and which I wasn't liking one little bit. An almost positive turn. As if this were a quarter that, like it or not, for better or worse, was actually working better and seemed to be governed reasonably well in their hands. Organized by them. Under *their* control. The control of the bosses. The clan chiefs.

I shiver briefly. I stop listening to him. I can hear him continuing with his line of thought, mingling stories of old experiences with personal reflections and the words of the newspaper article. As I ponder, an image surfaces inside me. As if it hadn't sprung from my brain, but directly from my viscera. In it, there's a boat. Or actually: more than just a boat. There are men aboard, some commanding and others obeying. And they all speak the same language. That tells me that they're all united by something deeper, something that you might call a bond. A bond of something more than kinship, a bond that grew there. A bond that has consolidated there, amid those alleys, lanes, towers, loggias, porticoes, the voices of children, the cries of the marketplace, the alluring calls of prostitutes, the sounds of knives, the barks of insults and challenges. Challenges to fight, to brawl, to bring it on. With very specific rankings, hierarchies, with the clan chief at the helm, all the others rowing, trustingly. Because he knows what he's doing. Because if he wants to, he can talk to the king, he has plenty of people around him, he's wealthy and powerful. Most important of all, he takes care of other people's problems for them. If you're one of his people and you're hungry, he'll give you some money and you'll become a member of his clientele, you'll become one of his employees. And if a child is left an orphan, or if a woman is widowed, or if an old man is sick, and if the city is troubled by famine, he'll take care of it. Him and others. The men of his clan. Down in the *seggi*.

Which means that my night of November 1343 isn't dead. It hasn't fallen into oblivion. It's still here, still clinging to the most profound life-forms in this city. It's there, in the city's most retrograde mindsets. And it's not really all about money. No. It's the biggest problem there is, what they lightly call, variously, culture, imprinting, DNA, or long-period structures. And I can't help but doing it, as I listen to my friend as he scatters his recollections to the winds. I can't help but put together these two things, the world of yesteryear and the world of now... fitting together the puzzle pieces. Drawing a line, a long straight line, between that past and now. A link with a time seven or eight hundred years ago.

And seeing a bloody damned continuity in it all...

ACKNOWLEDGMENTS

To Rosaria Fiorentino and Alfonso Leone: what little I know about Naples is all thanks to them. To Fedra and Lea, with all my love.

CHRONOLOGICAL LIST OF RULERS

LEADER	BORN	DIED	DATES IN POWER
Duke Sergius VII	Unknown	1137	1122?–1137 (Duke of Naples)
King Roger II of Hauteville	1095	1154	1130–1154 (King of Sicily)
Emperor Lothar II	1075	1137	1133–1137 (Holy Roman Emperor)
William I	May 1120 or 1121	1166	1154–1166 (King of Sicily)
William II	1153	1189	1166–1189 (King of Sicily)
Henry VI	1165	1197	1191–1197 (HRE) 1194–1197 (King of Sicily)
Otto IV of Brunswick	1175	1218	1211–1214 (HRE)
Frederick II	1194	1250	1220–1250 (King of Sicily and HRE)
Conrad IV	1228	1254	1251–1254 (King of Sicily)
Manfred	1232	1266	1258–1266 (King of Sicily)
Charles of Anjou (Charles I)	1226	1285	1266–1285 (new dynasty, King of Sicily)
Charles II of Anjou	1254	1309	1285–1309 (King of Naples)
Frederick III of Aragon	1272	1337	1296–1337 (King of Sicily)
Robert of Anjou	1276	1343	1309–1343 (King of Naples)
Joanna I of Anjou	1325	1382	1343–1382 (Queen of Naples)
Joanna II of Anjou	1371	1435	1414–1435 (Queen of Naples)
René of Anjou (René I)	1409	1480	1435–1442 (last Angevin king of Naples)

GLOSSARY

baiulus: a royal official, a member of the bureaucracy, ranging from governor to judge; related to "bailiff."

cambellanus: chamberlain, a senior royal official in charge of managing a royal household; also an official in charge of finances in other institutions.

cliens (sing.) / **clientes** (pl.) as in *clientelism* or *client politics*, the *clientes* were a feudal lord's political base, the mass of individuals he could rely upon.

comestabulus: the name derives from military district introduced by the Normans, encompassing a vast territory that comprised many fiefdoms. The feudal lord of the city where headquarters was based was the commander of all the troops in the district, and reported to the *comestabulus*.

consiliarius: counselor or adviser

compalazzo: this delegate was sent by the Norman king to command over the city of Naples (from the Latin: *comes palatii*)

compare: a person who accompanies a groom to the altar, a best man, but the bond of companionship is more complex than that. Comparable to a *padrino*, the godfather who provides a blessing or benediction.

curialus: notary

estaurita: a very particular kind of church, unique to Naples. The word comes from the Greek *stauros*, for stake or cross, but it also refers to a solidarity group that adheres to each of these special places of family worship.

fondaco: A type of inn, especially as the residence of a merchant or trader; a trading post, a trading factory, from the Arabic word *funduq*. It was also a place where tariffs were collected.

fondichiere: person in charge of a *fondaco*, understood as a warehouse adjoining the customs house.

giustiziere (sing.) / **giustizieri** (plural): "justiciars," royal officers

miles (sing.) / **milites** (pl.): knight/knights

moggio (sing.) / **moggi** (pl.): a measurement of surface area equivalent to roughly a quarter hectare, between 2,600 and 2,800 square meters, about 2/3 of an acre. Also the amount of grain such a patch of land will produce, obviously subject to wide variations.

nobiliores: the foremost representatives among the city notables.

oncias: an *oncia* was a unit of account, not an actual minted coin until much later. One *oncia* corresponded to 30 *tarì*, 4 golden *carlini,* and 5 Florentine florins.

pendino (sing.) / **pendini** (pl.): steep narrow lanes, running from the city heights down to the water.

platea (sing.) / **platee** (pl.): street, a word derived from Greek.

regiae marescallae magister: the master of the royal stables

res publica/respublica: the commonwealth, or, literally, "public thing," a term taken from Roman tradition, like English "republic": the city's political entity and identity.

rione (sing.) / **rioni** (pl.): a neighborhood or quarter under political control

salma: a volume measurement for grains (1 *salma* is equivalent to 8 *tomoli,* also equivalent to 32 *quarte*), roughly equivalent to 275 modern liters; one *salma* of wine is roughly 154 liters.

staio: a volume measurement for olive oil, roughly equivalent to 20 modern liters.

seggi: the *seggi* were the groups into which the representatives of the various family clans organize to protect and extend their interests. There were roughly thirty of them until the beginning of the Angevin era. They underwent reforms under Charles I of Anjou, who reduced their number to six.

secreto (sing.) / **secreti** (pl.): Beginning with Frederick II (king of Sicily, Italy, and Germany, and Holy Roman Emperor, 1194–1250), the *secreti* were functionaries entrusted with the collection of indirect taxes and tariffs, known as *secretus Siciliae*, as well as the division of the kingdom into four administrative districts (Abruzzo and Campania, Puglia or Apulia, Calabria, Sicily), with provinces managed by *vicesecreti.*

solidus: a Byzantine gold coin, roughly four grams in weight; hence, *soldi,* or money.

tarì: a one-gram gold coin of Muslim derivation, adopted in Naples definitively in the 960s.

NOTES

I. The Night of 1343

1   Shortly after I wrote this book, I happened upon this quote by Javier Cercas (*L'impostore*, Milan, Guanda, September 2015, pp. 264–65, *The Impostor: A True Story*, New York, Vintage, 2019, p. 228):

> A historian is not a judge, but the ways in which they work are similar; like the judge, the historian studies documents, corroborates evidence, connects facts, questions witnesses; like the judge, the historian pronounces a verdict. The verdict isn't definitive—it can be appealed, revised, refused—but it is a verdict.

2   Georgi et Iohannis Stellae, *Annales Genuenses*, edited by Giovanna Petti Balbi, in *Rerum Italicarum Scriptores*, XVII, II, Bologna, Zanichelli, 1975, p. 138. The account was quoted in Giovanni Vincenzo Verzellino, *Delle memorie particolari e specialmente degli uomini illustri della città di Savona*, Savona, Bertolotto & Isotta, 1885, p. 249, where we read, in more concise language, a description by Giovanni Stella: "A galley from Savona was captured by four of King Robert's galleys and taken, with all her men, to Naples."

3   Michelangelo Schipa, *Contese sociali napoletane nel Medio Evo*, Naples, Pierro, 1906, p. 140.

4   See Matteo Camera, *Elucubrazioni storico-diplomatiche su Giovanna I regina di Napoli e Carlo III di Durazzo*, Salerno, Tip. Nazionale, 1889, pp. 12–13.

II. The Motive

1   Suffice it to read the book by Daniel Cohen, *The Prosperity of Vice: A Worried View of Economics*, Cambridge, MA, The MIT Press, 2012 (*La prosperità del*

vizio. Una breve history dell'economia, translated by Giuseppe Maugeri, Milan, Garzanti, 2011).

2   Jean Drèze and Amartya Sen, *Hunger and Public Action*, Oxford, Clarendon Press, 1989, p. 46. See also Amartya Sen, *Poverty and Famines: An Essay on Entitlement and Deprivation*, Oxford, Clarendon Press, 1981, pp. 162–65.

3   Fritz Curschmann, *Hungersnöte im Mittelalter. Ein beitrag zur deutschen Wirtschaftsgeschichte des 8. bis 13. Jahrhunderts*, "Leipziger Studien aus dem Gebiet des Geschichte," VI, 1, Leipzig, Teubner, 1990.

4   "Medieval sources teach us that the very term famine in most cases should be understand in its proper meaning of high food prices, and not in the improper definition of an absence of food": Luciano Palermo, "Il principio dell'entitlement approach di Sen e l'analisi delle carestie medievali," in *"Moia la carestia." La scarsità alimentare in età preindustriale*, edited by Maria Luisa Ferrari e Manuel Vaquero Piñeiro, Bologna, Il Mulino, 2015, p. 29. By the same author, "Di fronte alla crisi: l'economia e il linguaggio della carestia nelle fonti medievali," in *Crisis alimentarias en la Edad Media. Modelos, explicaciones y representaciones*, edited by Pere Benito i Monclús, Lleida, Editorial Milenio, 2013, pp. 47–67.

5   Antoni Furió, "Disettes et famines en temps de croissance. Une revision de la 'crise de 1300': le royaume de Valence dans la première moitié du XIVe siècle," in *Les disettes dans la conjoncture de 1300 en Méditerranée occidentale*, ed. Monique Bourin, John Drendel, François Menant, Rome, École Française de Rome, 2011, pp. 349 ff.

6   Pere Benito i Monclús, "Famines sans frontières en Occident avant la Conjoncture de 1300," in *Les disettes*, p. 81.

7   Wolfgang Behringer, *Storia culturale del clima. Dall'era glaciale al riscaldamento globale*, Turin, Bollati Boringhieri, 2013, p. 133 (*A Cultural History of Climate*, Polity Press, Malden, MA 2010, p. 93–94). Concerning the Little Ice Age, see Jean M. Grove, *The Little Ice Age*, London–New York, Methuen, 1988.

8   Palermo, "Di fronte alla crisi," p. 57.

9   Palermo, "Di fronte alla crisi," p. 61.

10   For the two quotes, see, respectively, Pietro da Ripalta, *Chronica Placentina nella trascrizione di Iacopo Mori* (MS. Pallastrelli, 6), edited by Mario Fillià and Claudia Binello, Piacenza, Tip.Le.Co., 1995, p. 88; and *Annales Placentini Gibelini auctore Muctio de Modoetia, Monumenta Germaniae Historica, Scriptores*, 18, edited by Georg Heinrich Pertz, Hannover, Impensis Biblipolii Aulici Hahniani, 1863, p. 568, l. 38.

11   *Excerpta et compendio chronicorum omnium sec. XIV quod Italice concinnavit Angelus Marius Edoardi Da Erba*, in *Chronica Parmensia a sec. XI ad exitum sec.*

XIV, edited by Luigi Barbieri, Parma, Fiaccadori, 1858 (*Monumenta historica ad provincias Parmensem et Placentinam pertinentiam*, 10), pp. 406–07.

12   Giuliano Pinto, *Il libro del Biadaiolo. Carestie e annona a Firenze dalla metà del '200 al 1348*, Florence, L. S. Olschki, 1978. Concerning Lenzi, see Giuliano Pinto, "Domenico Lenzi o Benzi? A proposito dell'autore del *Libro del Biadaiolo*," in *Studi sulle società e le culture del Medioevo per Girolamo Arnaldi*, edited by Ludovico Gatto and Paola Supino Martini, Florence, All'insegna del Giglio, 2002, pp. 519–29.

13   Charles de La Roncière, *Prix et salaires à Florence au XIVe siècle (1280–1380)*, Rome, École Française de Rome, 1982, p. 717.

14   de La Roncière, pp. 718–19.

15   Pinto, *Il libro del Biadaiolo*, pp. 86–87, 296, 302.

16   Pinto, *Il libro del Biadaiolo*, pp. 322 ff., p. 375.

17   Mathieu Arnoux, *Le temps des laboureurs*, Paris, Albin Michel, 2012, p. 284.

18   These data come from Giovanni Vitolo and Aurelio Musi, *Il Mezzogiorno prima della questione meridionale*, Florence, Le Monnier, 2004, p. 86.

19   You can follow this process in Amedeo Feniello, "Entre la terra i el mercat. Les estructures fundacionals de la capital de Nàpols (segles X-XIII)," in *AFERS*, 80–81 (2015), pp. 2–26.

20   Giuseppe De Blasiis, "La chiesa e la badia di S. Piero ad aram," in *Archivio storico per le province napoletane*, 23 (1898), pp. 216, 219, 241.

21   Romolo Caggese, *Roberto d'Angiò e i suoi tempi*, Florence, Bemporad, 1922, I, p. 494.

22   Caggese, *Roberto d'Angiò*, pp. 495–96.

23   Giovanni Villani, *Nuova cronica*, edited by Giuseppe Porta, Parma, Fondazione Pietro Bembo/Guanda, 1991, vol. II, lib. IX, par. 186.

24   Caggese, *Roberto d'Angiò*, p. 499.

25   Vitolo and Musi, *Il Mezzogiorno*, p. 49.

26   I refer the reader to the book by Pietro Egidi, *La colonia saracena di Lucera e la sua distruzione*, Naples, Pierro, 1912. And, as an example, to the *Codice diplomatico dei Saraceni di Lucera*, edited by Pietro Egidi, Naples, Pierro, 1917, Doc. 491 dated April 6, 1301, where the creditors of the curia of the *dominus* Philip III, Prince of Taranto and son of King Charles II, pawned in Sicily, were paid thanks to the sale of the men and assets of Lucera.

27   See Matteo Camera, *Annali delle Due Sicilie dall'origine e fondazione della monarchia fino a tutto il Regno dell'augusto sovrano Carlo III di Borbone*, Naples, Fibreno, 1860, II, pp. 85 ff.; Camillo Minieri Riccio, *Studi storici fatti sopra 84 registri angioini dell'Archivio di Stato di Napoli*, Naples, Rinaldi and Sellitto, 1876, p. 120.

28 Caggese, *Roberto d'Angiò*, pp. 515–16. Concerning the business dealings of the Bardi, Peruzzi, and Acciaiuoli in the Kingdom of Naples, see Amedeo Feniello, *Dalle lacrime di Sybille. Storia degli uomini che inventarono la banca*, Rome–Bari, Laterza, 2013, pp. 140–49.

III. Masterminds and Perpetrators

1 Now Villaricca.
2 For a description of this event, especially concerning its economic and social upshot, see Amedeo Feniello, *Napoli. Società ed economia (902–1137)*, Rome, Istituto Storico Italiano per il Medioevo, 2011, pp. 237–63.
3 Michele Fuiano, *Napoli nel Medioevo (secoli XI-XIII)*, Naples, Libreria Scientifica Editrice, 1972, p. 82.
4 "Negotia quaedam cum illis de libertate civitatis et utilitate tractavit" (Fuiano, *Napoli nel Medioevo*, p. 94).
5 Amedeo Feniello, "Contributo alla storia della 'Iunctura civitatis' di Napoli (secc. X-XIII)," in *Ricerche sul Medioevo napoletano*, edited by Alfonso Leone, Naples, Athena, 1996, pp. 111–17 and 130–31.
6 See Michelangelo Schipa, *Contese sociali napoletane nel Medio Evo*, Naples, Pierro, 1906, pp. 23–29; Giuliana Vitale, *Élite burocratica e famiglia. Dinamiche nobiliari e processi di costruzione statale nella Napoli angioino-aragonese*, Naples, Liguori, 2003, p. 38.
7 Vitale, *Élite burocratica e famiglia*, pp. 39–40.
8 Camillo Tutini, *Dell'origine e fundazion de' seggi di Napoli*, Naples, at the expense of Raffaele Gessari, 1754, p. 57.
9 Monica Santangelo, "Preminenza aristocratica a Napoli nel tardo medioevo: i tocchi e il problema dell'origine dei sedili," in *Archivio Storico Italiano*, 171 (2013), pp. 273–318.
10 See Tutini, *Dell'origine*, pp. 97 ff.
11 *Catalogo ragionato dei libri registri e scritture esistenti nella sezione antica o prima serie dell'Archivio Municipale di Napoli (1387–1806)*, III, edited by Raffaele Parisi, Naples, Giannini & Figli, 1916, p. 54.
12 Carlo de Lellis, *Discorsi delle famiglie nobili del Regno di Napoli*, Naples, Onofrio Savio, 1663, II, p. 253.
13 Alfonso Leone and Filena Patroni Griffi, *Le origini di Napoli capitale*, Altavilla Silentina, Edizioni Studi Storici Meridionali, 1984, p. 45.
14 See Benedetto Croce, *I seggi di Napoli*, in *Aneddoti di varia letteratura*, I, Bari, Laterza, 1953, p. 297. Summonte, a leading Neapolitan scholar, recalls that "in every piazza, quarrels and disagreements between the members, except when it came to matters of murder, were expected to be discussed and resolved

before the authorities of that same piazza": Giovan Antonio Summonte, *Dell'historia della città e Regno di Napoli*, Naples, at the expense of Giacomo Raillard, 1693, pp. 219–20.

15 Giuseppe Sigismondo, *Descrizione della città di Napoli e suoi borghi*, Naples, Presso i Fratelli Terres, 1788, I, pp. 44 ff.

16 See Giovanni Vitolo, "Culto della Croce e identità cittadina a Napoli," in *Tra Napoli e Salerno. La costruzione dell'identità cittadina nel Mezzogiorno medievale*, Salerno, Carlone Editore, 2001, p. 106.

17 Feniello, *Napoli. Società ed economia*, pp. 55–56.

18 Bartolommeo Capasso, *Topografia della città di Napoli nell'XI secolo*, reprint Sala Bolognese, Forni, 1984, p. 150.

19 Feniello, *Napoli. Società ed economia*, pp. 256–60.

20 The solidus, the Byzantine coin, was used from the mid-tenth century onward strictly as an accounting currency. The coinage employed in actual transactions in Naples was the gold *tarì*, of Muslim origin and equivalent to one-quarter of a solidus. This was supplanted by less-refined coinages, like those produced in Amalfi and Salerno between the eleventh and twelfth centuries. A system that continued to be employed during Norman times. See, among other references, Lucia Travaini, "I tarì di Salerno ed Amalfi," in *Rassegna del Centro di Cultura e Storia Amalfitana*, 10 (1990), pp. 7–72.

21 Romualdo Trifone, "La famiglia napoletana al tempo del Ducato," in *Archivio Storico per le Province Napoletane*, 34 (1909), p. 711.

22 De Lellis, *Discorsi*, II, p. 255.

23 Vitale, *Élite burocratica e famiglia*, pp. 148–51.

24 Roberto Sabatino Lopez, "Risse tra Pisani e Genovesi nella Napoli di Federico II," in Lopez, *Su e giù per la storia di Genova*, pp. 217–229, in particular p. 226.

25 Tutini, *Dell'origine*, p. 83.

26 The will of Sergio Amalfitano can be found in *Monumenta ad Neapolitani ducatus historiam pertinentia*, edited by Bartolommeo Capasso, Naples, ex Regio typographaeo equ. Francisci Giannini, 1881–92, II/1, Doc. 402; and in *Il "Codice Perris." Cartulario amalfitano*, edited by Jole Mazzoleni and Renata Orefice, I/1, Amalfi, Centro di Cultura e Storia Amalfitana, 1985, Doc. 81.

27 Giacomo Todeschini, *Visibilmente crudeli. Malviventi, persone sospette e gente qualunque dal Medioevo all'età moderna*, Bologna, Il Mulino, 2007, p. 30.

28 Max Weber, *Economia e società*, Italian translation, Milan, Edizioni di Comunità, 1968, p. 241 (English edition, *Economy and Society: An Outline of Interpretive Sociology*, Berkeley, University of California Press 1978, p. 938; German edition: *Wirtschaft und Gesellschaft. Grundriß der verstehenden Soziologie*, 1922).

29 Feniello, *Napoli. Società ed economia*, p. 89.

30 *Monumenta ad Neapolitani ducatus*, II/1, Doc. 355.

31 Armando Petrucci and Carlo Romeo, *"Scriptores in urbibus." Alfabetismo e cultura scritta nell'Italia altomedievale*, Bologna, Il Mulino, 1992, pp. 239 and 242.

32 The episode, quite notorious, is recounted in Gennaro Maria Monti, "Riferimenti a S. Gennaro di un napoletano del Milletrecento," in *Nuovi studi angioini*, Trani, Vecchi & C., 1937, pp. 543–48.

33 See *Tancredi, conte di Lecce, re di Sicilia*, Atti del Convegno Internazionale di Studio (Lecce, 19–21 February 1998), edited by Hubert Houben and Benedetto Vetere, Galatina, Congedo, 2004.

34 Tutini, *Dell'origine*, p. 89.

35 Pietro da Eboli, *Liber ad honorem Augusti*, edited by Giovanni Battista Siragusa, Rome, Tip. Forzani & C., 1906, p. 33.

36 "cum gaudio et pompa feliciter ad patriam." See Antonio Vuolo, "I Santi Massimo e Giuliana a Cuma e la loro translatio a Napoli," *Hagiographica*, 17 (2010), pp. 173–85.

37 Quote found in Fuiano, *Napoli nel Medioevo*, p. 187.

38 Fuiano, *Napoli nel Medioevo*, p. 200.

39 Amedeo Feniello, "Federico II di Svevia. Stereotipi intorno ad un mito," in *Mundus*, IV/7–8 (2011), pp. 17–21.

40 Leone and Patroni Griffi, *Le origini di Napoli capitale*, p. 83.

41 Leone and Patroni Griffi, *Le origini di Napoli capitale*, p. 84.

42 Tutini, *Dell'origine*, pp. 135–36.

IV. The Two Worlds

1 Camillo Tutini, *Dell'origine e fundazion de' seggi di Napoli*, Naples, at the expense of Raffaele Gessari, 1754, pp. 132–33.

2 Giovan Antonio Summonte, *Dell'historia della città e Regno di Napoli*, Naples, at the expense of Giacomo Raillard, 1693, p. 250.

3 See Giuliana Vitale, *Nobiltà napoletana della prima età angioina: élite burocratica e famiglia*, in *Ricerche sul Medioevo napoletano*, edited by Alfonso Leone, Naples, Athena, 1996, pp. 187–223. And Gennaro Maria Monti, *Il patto dotale napoletano di Capuana e Nido*, in *Dal Duecento al Settecento. Studi storici giuridici*, Naples, I.T.E.A. Edit. Tip., 1925, pp. 2–33.

4 See Marie Guérin, forthcoming, *Textiles et parures d'une princesse de Morée à la cour de Naples au XIII siècle*.

5 Amedeo Feniello, *Dalle lacrime di Sybille. Storia degli uomini che inventarono la banca*, Rome-Bari, Laterza 2013, pp. 130–37.

6 Giuseppe De Blasiis, *Le case dei principi angioini nella piazza di Castelnuovo*, reprint Sala Bolognese, Forni, 1974, p. 15.

7   Alfonso Leone and Filena Patroni Griffi, *Le origini di Napoli capitale*, Altavilla Silentina, Edizioni Studi Storici Meridionali, 1984, p. 74.

8   Giovanni Boccaccio, *Filocolo*, Lib. IV, in *Opere volgari di Giovanni Boccaccio*, VIII, Florence, Stamperia Magheri, 1829, p. 32.

9   Giuseppe Pardi, *Napoli attraverso i secoli. Disegno di storia economica e demografica*, Milan-Rome-Naples, Dante Alighieri, 1924, p. 39.

10 See Paola Vitolo, "Immagini religiose e rappresentazione del potere nell'arte napoletana durante il regno di Giovanna I of Anjou (1342–1382)," in *Annali di storia moderna e contemporanea*, 16 (2010), pp. 249–70.

11 On the topic of public intervention concerning environmental matters, see Amedeo Feniello, *Gli interventi sanitari dei secoli XIV e XV* in *Napoli nel Medioevo. Segni culturali di una città*, edited by Alfonso Leone, Galatina, Congedo, 2007, pp. 123–36. Concerning the last episodes mentioned, see Michelangelo Schipa, *Contese sociali napoletane nel Medio Evo*, Naples, Pierro, 1906, p. 106.

12 Alfonso Leone, "Il convento di S. Chiara e le trasformazioni urbanistiche di Napoli nel secolo XIV," in *Ricerche sul Medioevo napoletano*, pp. 166–70.

13 Carlo Pecchia, *Storia civile e politica del Regno di Napoli*, Naples, Stamperia Raimondiana, 1783, III, p. 270.

14 Leone, "Il convento di S. Chiara," p. 167.

15 Monica Santangelo, "Preminenza aristocratica a Napoli nel tardo medioevo: i tocchi e il problema dell'origine dei sedili," in *Archivio Storico Italiano*, 171 (2013), pp. 317–18: "Un processo graduale di ridefinizione della antica e nuova preminenza cittadina e dei suoi ambiti spaziali e politici di egemonia, sotto una maggiore vigilanza della corona."

16 Summonte, *Dell'historia della città e Regno di Napoli*, pp. 209–10.

17 Matteo Camera, *Annali delle Due Sicilie dall'origine e fondazione della monarchia fino a tutto il Regno dell'augusto sovrano Carlo III di Borbone*, Naples, Fibreno, 1860, II, p. 52.

18 See Norbert Kamp, "Vom Kämmerer zum Sekreten: Wirtschaftsreformen und Finanzverwaltung im staufischen Königreich Sizilien," in *Problemeum Friedrich II*, edited by Josef Von Fleckenstein, Thorbecke, Sigmaringen, 1974, pp. 43–92.

19 See the examples in Romolo Caggese, *Roberto d'Angiò e i suoi tempi*, Florence, Bemporad, 1922, I, pp. 81–82.

20 Gian Luca Borghese, *Carlo I d'Angiò e il Mediterraneo. Politica, diplomazia e commercio internazionale prima dei Vespri*, Rome, École Française de Rome, 2008, p. 137.

21 Giuliana Vitale, *Élite burocratica e famiglia. Dinamiche nobiliari e processi di costruzione statale nella Napoli angioino-aragonese*, Naples, Liguori, 2003, p. 39. For the Di Costanzo reference, see p. 184.

22 Alfonso Leone and Filena Patroni Griffi, *Le origini di Napoli capitale*, Altavilla Silentina, Edizioni Studi Storici Meridionali, 1984, p. 88.

23 Leone and Patroni Griffi, *Le origini di Napoli capitale*, p. 92. The reference to King Robert is in Caggese, *Roberto d'Angiò*, I, p. 345.

24 Camera, *Annali*, II, pp. 15–16.

25 Mentioned by Giuseppe Galasso, "Il Regno di Napoli. I. Il Mezzogiorno angioino e aragonese (1266–1494)," in *Storia d'Italia*, edited by Giuseppe Galasso, 15/1, Turin, UTET, 1992, p. 81.

26 Schipa, *Contese sociali*, pp. 99–101.

27 Galasso, "Il Regno di Napoli," I, p. 107.

28 Francesco Petrarch, *Le Familiari*, edited by Vittorio Rossi, facsimile reprint, Florence, Le Lettere, 1997, V, 3.

29 Camera, *Annali*, II, pp. 411–12. And De Blasiis, *Le case dei principi angioini*, pp. 84–86. The anonymous author of the *Vita di Cola di Rienzo* described for Rome a comparable phenomenon and laments the fact that in his day, "cominciò la gente smisuratamente a mutar abiti e a portare barbe grandi e folte" (people began to greatly change their attire and to wear large, bushy beards).

30 Petrarch, *Le Familiari*, V, 6.

31 Camera, *Annali*, II, pp. 424–25.

32 In Carlo De Frede, "Da Carlo I d'Angiò a Giovanna I (1263–1382)," in *Storia di Napoli*, III, Naples, Società Editrice Storia di Naples, 1969, p. 195.

33 Camera, *Annali*, II, p. 413.

34 Vitale, *Élite burocratica*, p. 136.

35 Vitale, *Élite burocratica*, p. 212.

36 Leone and Patroni Griffi, *Le origini di Napoli capitale*, pp. 55–56.

37 Schipa, *Contese sociali*, pp. 120–21.

38 Amedeo Feniello, "Contributo alla storia della 'Iunctura civitatis' di Napoli (secc. X–XIII)," in *Ricerche sul Medioevo napoletano*, edited by Alfonso Leone, Naples, Athena, 1996, p. 153.

39 Camera, *Annali*, II, p. 211.

40 Leone and Patroni Griffi, *Le origini di Napoli capitale*, pp. 49–60. And Camera, *Annali*, II, pp. 368–69.

41 Schipa, *Contese sociali*, pp. 162–66.

42 Petrarch, *Familiari*, V, 4.

43 For these episodes, see Caggese, *Roberto d'Angiò*, I, pp. 333–38 and 343.

44 Camera, *Annali*, II, p. 414.

45 Caggese, *Roberto d'Angiò*, I, p. 341.

46 Caggese, *Roberto d'Angiò*, I, p. 344.

47 Caggese, *Roberto d'Angiò*, I, p. 605.

48 Caggese, *Roberto d'Angiò*, I, p. 349.

V. Victims (and Executioners)

1 Andrea de Jorio, *La mimica degli antichi investigata nel gestire napoletano*, reprint Sala Bolognese, Forni, 1979.

2 Roberto Sabatino Lopez, "Le marchand génois. Un profil collectif," in Lopez, *Su e giù per la storia di Genova*, Genoa, University of di Genoa, Istituto di Paleografia e Storia Medievale, 1975, pp. 17–33. See now also the fine book by Gabriella Airaldi, *Andrea Doria*, Rome, Salerno Editrice, 2015.

3 Giovanni Boccaccio, *Decameron*, Day I, Novella VIII.

4 See Airaldi, *Andrea Doria*, p. 42.

5 Lopez, "Le marchand génois," p. 20.

6 Amedeo Feniello, *Napoli. Società ed economia (902–1137)*, Rome, Istituto Storico Italiano per il Medioevo, 2011, p. 169.

7 See also Giuseppe Galasso, *Le città campane nell'alto medioevo*, Naples, Società Napoletana di Storia Patria, 1960, p. 56; and Mario Rotili, *L'arte a Napoli dal VI al XIII secolo*, Naples, Società Editrice Napoletana, 1978, p. 94.

8 See David Jacoby, "Amalfi nell'XI secolo: commercio e navigazione nei documenti della Ghenizà del Cairo," in *Rassegna del Centro di Cultura e Storia Amalfitana*, 28 (2008), pp. 86–87.

9 Gabriele Capone and Alfonso Leone, "La colonia scalese dal XIII al XV secolo," in *Ricerche sul Medioevo napoletano*, edited by Leone, Naples, Athena, 1996, pp. 173–86.

10 See Giovanni Vitolo, "'Virgiliana Urbs.' Progettualità e territorio nel Regno svevo di Sicilia," in Vitolo, *Tra Napoli e Salerno. La costruzione dell'identità cittadina nel Mezzogiorno medievale*, Salerno, Carlone Editore, 2001, p. 135.

11 See David Abulafia, *Le two Italie. Relazioni economiche fra il Regno normanno di Sicilia e i comuni settentrionali*, Naples, Guida, 1991, pp. 11 and 19 (*The Two Italies: Economic Relations Between the Norman Kingdom of Sicily and the Northern Communes*, Cambridge, Cambridge University Press 2010); and Giuseppe Galasso, *Economia e finanze nel Mezzogiorno tra XVI e XVII secolo*, in *Finanze e ragion di Stato in Italia e in Germania nella prima età moderna*, Atti della Settimana di Studio (Trent, December 6–10, 1982), edited by Aldo De Maddalena and Hermann Kellenbenz, Bologna, Il Mulino, 1984, p. 48.

12 Vitolo, "'Virgiliana Urbs,'" p. 136.

13 Robert Davidsohn, *Forschungen zur Geschichte von Florenz. III. Teil: XIII. und IV. Jahrhundert. I. Regesten unedirter Urkunden zur Geschichte von Handel, Gewerbe und Zunftwesen; II. Die Schwarzen und die Weissen*, Berlin, Mittler und Sohn, 1908, p. 58, Reg. 251.

14 Roberto Sabatino Lopez, "Risse tra Pisani e Genovesi nella Napoli di Federico II," in Lopez, *Su e giù per la storia di Genova*, pp. 217–29, in particular p. 226.

15   See Amedeo Feniello, *Tracce dell'economia catalano-aragonese a Napoli*, in "Bullettino dell'istituto storico italiano per il Medio evo," CXIV (2012), pp. 216–31, p. 183.

16   David Abulafia, "Southern Italy and the Florentine Economy, 1265–1370," in *The Economic History Review*, n.s., 34/3 (Aug. 1981), p. 379.

17   For a more detailed description of the dynamic between the House of Anjou and the Florentine merchant-bankers, see Amedeo Feniello, *Dalle lacrime di Sybille. Storia degli uomini che inventarono la banca*, Rome-Bari, Laterza 2013, pp. 149–56.

18   Georges Yver, *Le commerce et les marchands dans l'Italie méridionale au XIIIe et au XIVe siècle*, Paris, A. Fontemoing, 1903, pp. 228–32.

19   Giovanni Boccaccio, *Decameron*, Day II, Novella IV.

20   Giovanni Villani, *Nuova cronica*, edited by Giuseppe Porta, Parma, Fondazione Pietro Bembo/Guanda, 1991, vol. III, Lib. XII, Par. 24.

21   Matteo Camera, *Annali delle Due Sicilie dall'origine e fondazione della monarchia fino a tutto il Regno dell'augusto sovrano Carlo III di Borbone*, Naples, Fibreno, 1860, II, pp. 133–34; and Yver, *Le commerce*, p. 236.

22   Amedeo Feniello, "Il 'porto Pisano' di Napoli e le trasformazioni in età angioina," in *Bollettino Storico Pisano*, 64 (1995), pp. 225–32.

23   Camera, *Annali*, II, p. 229.

24   The first quotation is taken from a chapter from 1505, which reviews norms established *ab antiquo*: in Camera, *Annali* II, p. 229. For the other quotation, see Benedetto Croce, "Le tre avventure di Andreuccio," in *Storie e leggende napoletane*, Milan, Adelphi, 1990, p. 72.

25   Concerning which, see Paola Vitolo, "Boccaccio nella Napoli angioina: luoghi, personaggi e vicende tra arte, realtà e finzione letteraria," in *Boccaccio e Napoli. Nuovi materiali per la storia culturale di Napoli nel Trecento*, Atti del Convegno *Boccaccio angioino. Per il VII centenario della nascita di Giovanni Boccaccio (Naples-Salerno, 23–25 October 2013)*, edited by Giancarlo Alfano, Emma Grimaldi, Sebastiano Martelli, Andrea Mazzucchi, Matteo Palumbo, Alessandra Perriccioli Saggese, and Carlo Vecce, Florence, Cesati, 2014, especially pp. 107–10.

26   See Boccaccio, *Decameron*, Day II, Novella V; Croce, "Le tre avventure," pp. 53–88.

27   Croce, "Le tre avventure," p. 74.

28   Camera, *Annali*, II, p. 426.

29   Croce, "Le tre avventure," p. 79.

30   Bruno Figliuolo, "Andreuccio da Perugia e (è?) Cenni di Bardella," in *Boccaccio e Napoli*, p. 232.

31 Romolo Caggese, *Roberto d'Angiò e i suoi tempi*, Florence, Bemporad, 1922, I, p. 590.

32 See the fine biography by Francesco Paolo Tocco, *Niccolò Acciaiuoli. Vita e politica in Italia alla metà del XIV secolo*, Rome, Istituto Storico Italiano per il Medioevo, 2001.

33 Yver, *Le commerce*, pp. 353–54.

34 Villani, *Nuova Cronica*, Vol. III, Lib. XII, Par. 138.

35 Villani, *Nuova Cronica*, Vol. III, Lib. XII, Par. 138. For the Peruzzi bankruptcy, see Edwin S. Hunt, *The Medieval Super-Companies. A Study of the Peruzzi Company of Florence*, Cambridge, Cambridge University Press, 1994, pp. 212–29.

36 Caggese, *Roberto d'Angiò*, I, p. 598.

37 Matteo Camera, *Elucubrazioni storico-diplomatiche su Giovanna I regina di Napoli e Carlo III di Durazzo*, Salerno, Tip. Nazionale, 1889, p. 259.

VI. Beyond the Night

1 Matteo Camera, *Elucubrazioni storico-diplomatiche su Giovanna I regina di Napoli e Carlo III di Durazzo*, Salerno, Tip. Nazionale, 1889, p. 14.

2 Camera, *Elucubrazioni storico-diplomatiche*, p. 30.

3 Michelangelo Schipa, *Contese sociali napoletane nel Medio Evo*, Naples, Pierro, 1906, pp. 191–92.

4 Concerning the wars in Italy and the south of Italy during the time of Joanna I, see Christophe Masson, *Des guerres en Italie avant les guerres d'Italie. Les entreprises militaires françaises dans la péninsule à l'époque du Grand Schisme d'Occident*, Rome, École Française de Rome, 2014.

5 See Amedeo Feniello, *Les campagnes napolitaines à la fin du Moyen Âge. Mutations d'un paysage rural* Rome, École Française de Rome, 2005, pp. 30–31.

6 *La correspondance de Pierre Ameilh, archevêque de Napoli puis d'Embrun (1363–1369)*, edited by Henri Bresc, Paris, Centre National de la Recherche Scientifique, 1972, Doc. 228.

7 *Chronicon Siculum incerti authoris ab anno 340 ad annum 1396 in forma Diary ex inedito Codice Ottoboniano Vaticano*, edited by Giuseppe De Blasiis, Naples, ex Regio typographaeo equ. Francisci Giannini, 1887, p. 27.

8 Camera, *Elucubrazioni*, pp. 290–91.

9 Schipa, *Contese*, pp. 179–81.

10 Concerning Sergianni and Ottino, see the entries by Franca Petrucci, in *Dizionario biografico degli italiani*, vol. 19, Rome, Istituto della Enciclopedia Italiana, 1976, respectively on pp. 370–75 and 437–40.

11 Nunzio Federigo Faraglia, *Storia della lotta tra Alfonso V d'Aragona e Renato d'Angiò*, Lanciano, R. Carabba, 1908, p. 406, Doc. 39. And for the other

extraordinary entities, see Giovanni Vitolo and Rosalba Di Meglio, *Napoli angioino-aragonese. Confraternite, ospedali, dinamiche politico-sociali*, Salerno, Carlone, 2003, p. 105.

12   Faraglia, *Storia della lotta*, Doc. 40.

13   Faraglia, *Storia della lotta*, pp. 46 ff.; and Albert Lecoy de la Marche, *Le roi René. Sa vie, son administration, ses travaux artistiques et littéraires d'après les documents inédits des archives de France et d'Italie*, I, Paris, Librairie de Firmin-Didot, 1875, p. 145.

BIBLIOGRAPHY

Primary Sources

Annales Placentini gibelini auctore Muctio de Modoetia, Monumenta Germaniae Historica, Scriptores, 18, edited by Georg Heinrich Pertz, Hannover, 1863.

Annali delle Due Sicilie dall'origine e fondazione della monarchia fino a tutto il Regno dell'augusto sovrano Carlo III di Borbone, II, Naples, Fibreno, 1860.

Boccaccio, Giovanni. *Decameron*.

———. *Filocolo*, Lib. IV, in *Opere volgari di Giovanni Boccaccio*, VIII, Florence, Stamperia Magheri, 1829.

Camera, Matteo. *Annali delle Due Sicilie dall'origine e fondazione della monarchia fino a tutto il Regno dell'augusto sovrano Carlo III di Borbone*, Naples, Fibreno, 1860.

———. *Elucubrazioni storico-diplomatiche su Giovanna I regina di Napoli e Carlo III di Durazzo*, Salerno, Tip. Nazionale, 1889.

Catalogo ragionato dei libri registri e scritture esistenti nella sezione antica o prima serie dell'Archivio Municipale di Napoli (1387–1806), III, edited by Raffaele Parisi, Naples, 1916.

Codice diplomatico dei Saraceni di Lucera, edited by Pietro Egidi, Naples, Pierro, 1917.

Chronicon Siculum incerti authoris ab anno 340 ad annum 1396 in forma Diary ex inedito Codice Ottoboniano Vaticano, edited by Giuseppe De Blasiis, Naples, ex Regio Typographaeo Equ. Francisci Giannini, 1887.

Davidsohn, Robert. *Forschungen zur Geschichte von Florenz. III. Teil: XIII. und IV.Jahrhundert. I. Regesten unedirter Urkunden zur Geschichte von Handel, Gewerbe und Zunftwesen; II. Die Schwarzen und die Weissen*, Berlin, Mittler und Sohn, 1908.

de Lellis, Carlo. *Discorsi delle famiglie nobili del Regno di Napoli*, Naples, Gio. Francesco Paci, 1663.

Excerpta e compendio chronicorum omnium sec. XIV quod Italice concinnavit Angelus Marius Edoardi Da Erba, in *Chronica Parmensia a sec. XI ad exitum sec. XIV,* edited by Luigi Barbieri, Parma, Fiaccadori, 1858 (*Monumenta historica ad provincias Parmensem et Placentinam pertinentiam,* 10).

Il "Codice Perris." Cartulario amalfitano, edited by Jole Mazzoleni e Renata Orefice, I/1, Amalfi, Centro di Cultura e Storia Amalfitana, 1985.

La correspondance de Pierre Ameilh, archevêque de Napoli puis d'Embrun (1363–1369), edited by Henri Bresc, Paris, Centre National de la Recherche Scientifique, 1972.

Minieri Riccio, Camillo. *Studi storici fatti sopra 84 registri angioini dell'Archivio di Stato di Napoli,* Naples, Rinaldi & Sellitto, 1876.

Monumenta ad Neapolitani ducatus historiam pertinentia, edited by Bartolommeo Capasso, Naples, ex Regio Typographaeo Equ. Francisci Giannini, 1881–1892, II/1.

Petrarch, Francesco. *Le Familiari,* edited by Vittorio Rossi, facsimile reprint, Florence, Le Lettere, 1997.

Pietro da Eboli. *Liber ad honorem Augusti,* edited by Giovanni Battista Siragusa, Rome, Tip. Forzani & C., 1906.

Pietro da Ripalta. *Chronica Placentina nella trascrizione di Iacopo Mori* (Ms. Pallastrelli, 6), edited by M. Fillia & C. Binello, Piacenza, Tip.Le.Co.,1995.

Stellae, Georgi et Iohannis. *Annales Genuenses,* edited by Giovanna Petti Balbi, in *Rerum Italicarum Scriptores,* Bologna, Zanichelli, 1975, p. 138.

Summonte, Giovan Antonio. *Dell'historia della città e Regno di Napoli,* Naples, at the expense of Giacomo Raillard, 1693.

Tutini, Camillo. *Dell'origine e fundazion de' seggi di Napoli,* Naples, at the expense of Raffaele Gessari, 1754.

Villani, Giovanni. *Nuova cronica,* edited by Giuseppe Porta, Parma, Fondazione Pietro Bembo/Guanda, 1991.

Secondary Sources

Abulafia, David. *Le due Italie. Relazioni economiche fra il regno normanno di Sicilia e i comuni settentrionali,* trans. Cosima Campognolo, Naples, Guida, 1991 (*The Two Italies: Economic Relations Between the Norman Kingdom of Sicily and the Northern Communes,* Cambridge, Cambridge University Press 2010).

———. "Southern Italy and the Florentine Economy, 1265–1370," in *The Economic History Review,* n.s., 34/3 (Aug. 1981), pp. 377–88.

Airaldi, Gabriella. *Andrea Doria,* Rome, Salerno Editrice, 2015.

Arnoux, Mathieu. *Le temps des laboureurs,* Paris, Albin Michel, 2012.

Benito i Monclús, Pere. "Famines sans frontières en Occident avant la Conjoncture de 1300," in *Les disettes dans la conjoncture de 1300 en Méditerranée occidentale,* edited by Monique Bourin, John Drendel, and François Menant, Rome, École Française de Rome, 2011.

Behringer, Wolfgang. *Storia culturale del clima. Dall'era glaciale al riscaldamento globale*, Turin, Bollati Boringhieri, 2013.

Boccaccio e Napoli. Nuovi materiali per la storia culturale di Napoli nel Trecento, Atti del Convegno Boccaccio angioino. *Per il VII centenario della nascita di Giovanni Boccaccio (Naples-Salerno, 23–25 October 2013)*, edited by Giancarlo Alfano, Emma Grimaldi, Sebastiano Martelli, Andrea Mazzucchi, Matteo Palumbo, Alessandra Perriccioli Saggese, and Carlo Vecce, Florence, Cesati, 2014.

Borghese, Gian Luca. *Carlo I d'Angiò e il Mediterraneo. Politica, diplomazia e commercio internazionale prima dei Vespri*, Rome, École Française de Rome, 2008.

Caggese, Romolo. *Roberto d'Angiò e i suoi tempi*, Florence, Bemporad, 1922.

Capasso, Bartolommeo. *Topografia della città di Napoli nell'XI secolo*, reprint, Sala Bolognese, Forni, 1984.

Capone, Gabriele, and Alfonso Leone. "La colonia scalese dal XIII al XV secolo," in *Ricerche sul Medioevo napoletano*, edited by Leone, Naples, Athena, 1996, pp. 173–86.

Cohen, Daniel. *The Prosperity of Vice: A Worried View of Economics*, trans. Susan Emanuel, Cambridge, MA, The MIT Press, 2012 (*La prosperità del vizio. Una breve history dell'economia*, translated by Giuseppe Maugeri, Milan, Garzanti, 2011).

Croce, Benedetto. *I seggi di Napoli*, in *Aneddoti di varia letteratura*, I, Bari, Laterza, 1953.

———. "Le tre avventure di Andreuccio," in *Storie e leggende napoletane*, Milan, Adelphi, 1990.

Curschmann, Fritz, *Hungersnöte im Mittelalter. Ein beitrag zur deutschen Wirtschaftsgeschichte des 8. Bis 13. Jahrhunderts*, Leipziger Studien aus dem Gebiet des Geschichte, VI, 1, Leipzig, Teubner, 1990.

De Blasiis, Giuseppe. "La chiesa e la badia di S. Piero ad Aram," in *Archivio Storico per le Province Napoletane*, 23 (1898).

———. *Le case dei principi angioini nella piazza di Castelnuovo*, reprint Sala Bolognese, Forni, 1974.

De Frede, Carlo. "Da Carlo I d'Angiò a Giovanna I (1263–1382)," in *Storia di Napoli*, III, Naples, Società Editrice Storia di Napoli, 1969.

de Jorio, Andrea. *La mimica degli antichi investigata nel gestire napoletano*, reprint Sala Bolognese, Forni, 1979.

de la Roncière, Charles. *Prix et salaires à Florence au XIVe siècle (1280–1380)*, Rome, École Française de Rome, 1982.

Les disettes dans la conjoncture de 1300 en Méditerranée occidentale, edited by Monique Bourin, John Drendel, and François Menant, Rome, École Française de Rome, 2011.

Drèze, Jean, and Amartya Sen. *Hunger and Public Action*, Oxford, Clarendon Press, 1989.

Egidi, Pietro. *La colonia saracena di Lucera e la sua distruzione*, Naples, Pierro, 1912.

Faraglia, Nunzio Federigo. *Storia della lotta tra Alfonso V d'Aragona e Renato d'Angiò*, Lanciano, R. Carabba, 1908.

Feniello, Amedeo. "Contributo alla storia della 'Iunctura civitatis' di Napoli (secc. X–XIII)," in *Ricerche sul Medioevo napoletano*, edited by Alfonso Leone, Naples, Athena, 1996.

———. "Il 'porto Pisano' di Napoli e le trasformazioni in età angioina," in *Bollettino Storico Pisano*, 64 (1995), pp. 225–32.

———. *Les campagnes napolitaines à la fin du Moyen Âge. Mutations d'un paysage rural*, Rome, École Française de Rome, 2005.

———. *Gli interventi sanitari dei secoli XIV e XV* in *Napoli nel Medioevo. Segni culturali di una città*, edited by Alfonso Leone, Galatina, Congedo, 2007, pp. 123–36.

———. *Napoli. Società ed economia (902–1137)*, Rome, Istituto Storico Italiano per il Medioevo, 2011.

———. "Federico II di Svevia. Stereotipi intorno ad un mito," in *Mundus*, IV/78 (2011), pp. 17–21.

———. *Tracce dell'economia catalano-aragonese a Napoli*, in "Bullettino dell'Istituto Storico Italiano per il Medio evo," CXIV (2012), pp. 216–31.

———. *Dalle lacrime di Sybille. Storia degli uomini che inventarono la banca*, Rome-Bari, Laterza, 2013.

———. "Entre la terra i el mercat. Les estructures fundacionals de la capital de Nàpols (segles X-XIII)," in *AFERS*, 80–81 (2015), pp. 2–26.

Figliuolo, Bruno. "Andreuccio da Perugia e (è?) Cenni di Bardella," in *Boccaccio e Napoli. Nuovi materiali per la storia culturale di Napoli nel Trecento, Atti del Convegno Boccaccio angioino. Per il VII centenario della nascita di Giovanni Boccaccio (Naples-Salerno, 23–25 October 2013)*, edited by Giancarlo Alfano, Emma Grimaldi, Sebastiano Martelli, Andrea Mazzucchi, Matteo Palumbo, Alessandra Perriccioli Saggese, and Carlo Vecce, Florence, Cesati, 2014.

Fuiano, Michele. *Napoli nel Medioevo (secc. XI–XIII)*, Naples, Libreria Scientifica Editrice, 1972.

Furió, Antoni. "Disettes et famines en temps de croissance. Une revision de la 'crise de 1300': le royaume de Valence dans la première moitié du XIVème siècle," in *Les disettes dans la conjoncture de 1300 en Méditerranée occidentale*, edited by Monique Bourin, John Drendel, and François Menant, Rome, École Française de Rome, 2011, pp. 349 ff.

Galasso, Giuseppe. *Le città campane nell'alto medioevo*, Naples, Società Napoletana di Storia Patria, 1960.

———. "Il Regno di Napoli. Il Mezzogiorno angioino e aragonese (1266–1494)," in *Storia d'Italia*, edited by Giuseppe Galasso, 15/1, Turin, UTET, 1992.

————. *Economia e finanze nel Mezzogiorno tra XVI e XVII secolo*, in *Finanze e ragion di Stato in Italia e in Germania nella prima età moderna*, Atti della Settimana di Studio (Trent, 6–10 December 1982), edited by Aldo De Maddalena and Hermann Kellenbenz, Bologna, Il Mulino, 1984.

Grove, Jean M. *The Little Ice Age*, London–New York, Methuen, 1988.

Guérin, Marie. Forthcoming. *Textiles et parures d'une princesse de Morée à la cour de Napoli au XIII siècle*.

Hunt, Edwin S. *The Medieval Super-Companies. A Study of the Peruzzi Company of Florence*, Cambridge, Cambridge University Press, 1994.

Jacoby, David. "Amalfi nell'XI secolo: commercio e navigazione nei documenti della Ghenizà del Cairo," in *Rassegna del Centro di Cultura e Storia Amalfitana*, 28, (2008), pp. 86–87.

Kamp, Norbert. "Vom Kämmerer zum Sekreten: Wirtschaftsreformen und Finanzverwaltung im staufischen Königreich Sizilien," in *Problemeum Friedrich II*, edited by Josef Von Fleckenstein, Thorbecke, Sigmaringen, 1974.

Lecoy de la Marche, Albert. *Le roi René. Sa vie, son administration ses travaux artistiques et littéraires d'après les documents inédits des archives de France et d'Italie*, I, Paris, Librairie de Firmin-Didot, 1875.

Leone, Alfonso. "Il convento di S. Chiara e le trasformazioni urbanistiche di Napoli nel secolo XIV," in *Ricerche sul Medioevo napoletano*, edited by Alfonso Leone, Naples, Athena, 1996.

Leone, Alfonso, and Filena Patroni Griffi. *Le origini di Napoli capitale*, Altavilla Silentina, Edizioni Studi Storici Meridionali, 1984.

Leone, Alfonso, ed. *Napoli nel Medioevo. Segni culturali di una città*, Galatina, Congedo, 2007.

Lopez, Roberto Sabatino. *Su e giù per la storia di Genova*, Genoa, University of Genoa, Istituto di Paleografia e Storia Medievale, 1975.

Masson, Christophe. *Des guerres en Italie avant les guerres d'Italie. Les entreprises militaires françaises dans la péninsule à l'époque du Grand Schisme d'Occident*, Rome, École Française de Rome, 2014.

Monti, Gennaro Maria. *Il patto dotale napoletano di Capuana e Nido*, in *Dal Duecento al Settecento. Studi storici-giuridici*, Naples, I.T.E.A. Edit. Tip., 1925.

————. "Riferimenti a S. Gennaro di un napoletano del Milletrecento," in *Nuovi studi angioini*, Trani, Vecchi & C., 1937.

Palermo, Luciano. "Il principio dell'entitlement approach di Sen e l'analisi delle carestie medievali," in *"Moia la carestia." La scarsità alimentare in età preindustriale*, edited by Maria Luisa Ferrari and Manuel Vaquero Piñeiro, Bologna, Il Mulino, 2015, pp. 23–38.

————. "Di fronte alla crisi: l'economia e il linguaggio della carestia nelle fonti medievali," in *Crisis alimentarias en la Edad Media. Modelos, explicaciones y representaciones*, edited by Pere Benito i Monclús, Lleida, Editorial Milenio, 2013, pp. 47–67.

Pardi, Giuseppe. *Napoli attraverso i secoli. Disegno di storia economica e demografica*, Milan-Rome-Naples, Dante Alighieri, 1924.

Pecchia, Carlo. *Storia civile e politica del Regno di Napoli*, III, Naples, Stamperia Raimondiana, 1783.

Petrucci, Armando, and Carlo Romeo. *"Scriptores in urbibus." Alfabetismo e cultura scritta nell'Italia altomedievale*, Bologna, Il Mulino, 1992.

Pinto, Giuliano. *Il libro del Biadaiolo. Carestie e annona a Firenze dalla metà del '200 al 1348*, Florence, L.S. Olschki, 1978.

———. "Domenico Lenzi o Benzi? A proposito dell'autore del *Libro del Biadaiolo*," in *Studi sulle società e le culture del Medioevo per Girolamo Arnaldi*, edited by Ludovico Gatto and Paola Supino Martini, Florence, All'Insegna del Giglio, 2002.

Rotili, Mario. *L'arte a Napoli dal VI al XIII secolo*, Naples, Società Editrice Napoletana, 1978.

Santangelo, Monica. "Preminenza aristocratica a Napoli nel tardo medioevo: i tocchi e il problema dell'origine dei sedili," in *Archivio Storico Italiano*, 171 (2013), pp. 273–318.

Schipa, Michelangelo. *Contese sociali napoletano nel Medio Evo*, Naples, Pierro, 1906.

Sen, Amartya. *Poverty and Famines: An Essay on Entitlement and Deprivation*, Oxford, Clarendon Press, 1981.

Sigismondo, Giuseppe. *Descrizione della città di Napoli e suoi borghi*, Naples, Presso i Fratelli Terres, 1788.

Tancredi, conte di Lecce, re di Sicilia, Atti del Convegno Internazionale di Studio (Lecce, 19–21 February 1998), edited by Hubert Houben and Benedetto Vetere, Galatina, Congedo, 2004.

Tocco, Francesco Paolo. *Niccolò Acciaiuoli. Vita e politica in Italia alla metà del XIV secolo*, Rome, Istituto Storico Italiano per il Medioevo, 2001.

Todeschini, Giacomo. *Visibilmente crudeli*, Bologna, Il Mulino, 2007.

Travaini, Lucia. "I tarì di Salerno ed Amalfi," in *Rassegna del Centro di Cultura e Storia Amalfitana*, 10 (1990), pp. 7–72.

Trifone, Romualdo. "La famiglia napoletana al tempo del Ducato," in *Archivio Storico per le Province Napoletane*, 34 (1909).

Verzellino, Giovanni Vincenzo. *Delle memorie particolari e specialmente degli uomini illustri della città di Savona*, Savona, Bertolotto & Isotta, 1885.

Vitale, Giuliana. *Nobiltà napoletana della prima età angioina:* élite *burocratica e famiglia*, in *Ricerche sul Medioevo napoletano*, edited by Alfonso Leone, Naples, Athena, 1996, pp. 187–223.

————. *Élite burocratica e famiglia. Dinamiche nobiliari e processi di costruzione statale nella Napoli angioino-aragonese*, Naples, Liguori, 2003.

Vitolo, Giovanni. *Tra Napoli e Salerno. La costruzione dell'identità cittadina nel Mezzogiorno medievale*, Salerno, Carlone Editore, 2001.

Vitolo, Giovanni, and Rosalba Di Meglio. *Napoli angioino-aragonese. Confraternite, ospedali, dinamiche politico-sociali*, Salerno, Carlone Editore, 2003.

Vitolo, Giovanni, and Aurelio Musi. *Il Mezzogiorno prima della questione meridionale*, Florence, le Monnier, 2004.

Vitolo, Paola. "Boccaccio nella Napoli angioina: luoghi, personaggi e vicende tra arte, realtà e finzione letteraria," in *Boccaccio e Napoli. Nuovi materiali per la storia culturale di Napoli nel Trecento*, Atti del Convegno *Boccaccio angioino. Per il VII centenario della nascita di Giovanni Boccaccio (Naples-Salerno, 23–25 October 2013)*, edited by Giancarlo Alfano, Emma Grimaldi, Sebastiano Martelli, Andrea Mazzucchi, Matteo Palumbo, Alessandra Perriccioli Saggese, and Carlo Vecce, Florence, Cesati, 2014.

————. "Immagini religiose e rappresentazione del potere nell'arte napoletana durante il regno di Giovanna I of Anjou (1342–1382)," in *Annali di Storia Moderna e Contemporanea*, 16 (2010), pp. 249–70.

Vuolo, Antonio. "I Santi Massimo e Giuliana a Cuma e la loro translatio a Napoli," *Hagiographica*, 17 (2010), pp. 173–85.

Weber, Max. *Economia e società*, Italian translation, Milan, Edizioni di Comunità, 1968. (English edition, *Economy and Society: An Outline of Interpretive Sociology*, Berkeley, University of California Press, 1978; German edition: *Wirtschaft und Gesellschaft. Grundriß der verstehenden Soziologie*, 1922).

Yver, Georges. *Le commerce et les marchands dans l'Italie méridionale au XIIIe et au XIVe siècle*, Paris, A. Fontemoing, 1903.

ABOUT THE AUTHOR

Amedeo Feniello teaches Medieval History in the Department of Social Science at the University of L'Aquila in Italy. He has taught and conducted research at the EHESS in Paris and at Northwestern University in Evanston, Illinois. *Naples 1343* is his first book to appear in English.

ABOUT THE TRANSLATOR

Antony Shugaar is the author of a number of books and has translated hundreds of others, including *Tasmania* by Paolo Giordano, *My Shadow Is Yours* by Edoardo Nesi, and *The Piranhas* and *Savage Kiss* by Roberto Saviano. His translation of Gianni Rodari's *Telephone Tales* received the American Library Association's 2021 Batchelder Award. He is the editor-in-chief of Redcar Press.